WAR

the behavioral origins

of

WAR

d. scott bennett
&
allan c. stam

THE UNIVERSITY OF MICHIGAN PRESS
Ann Arbor

Copyright © by the University of Michigan 2004
All rights reserved
Published in the United States of America by
The University of Michigan Press
Manufactured in the United States of America
⊗ Printed on acid-free paper

2007   2006   2005   2004   4   3   2   1

*A CIP catalog record for this book
is available from the British Library.*

Library of Congress Cataloging-in-Publication Data

Bennett, D. Scott.
The behavioral origins of war / D. Scott Bennett and Allan C. Stam.
p.   cm.
Includes bibliographical references and index.
ISBN 0-472-09844-6 (Cloth : alk. paper) —
ISBN 0-472-06844-X (Paper : alk. paper)
1. War.   2. International relations.   I. Stam, Allan C.   II. Title.

U21.2 .B3973   2003
355.02—dc21   2003012933

this book is dedicated
to suzy, kelly, and JDC

CONTENTS

PREFACE & ACKNOWLEDGMENTS

The study of international conflict suffers from an oversupply of theories and a shortage of comprehensive comparative empirical tests. Theories in international relations are typically tested a few at a time, resulting in serious misspecification in analysis, a lack of comparable data sets and findings, and a lack of cumulation in our understanding of international relations. With a plethora of theories, conjectures, and hypotheses of international conflict in hand, we believe that it is appropriate and necessary to conduct a thorough empirical appraisal of those arguments. It is also important and necessary to devote significant attention to several important theories of international relations that have been especially poorly tested, in particular the so-called expected utility theory of war. Empirical tests of variants of expected utility theory have been executed in very limited settings, despite expansive claims about the theory's power and scope. Given the limited tests of most theories in international relations, claims about the power of this and other theories are often overstated.

Different theories, hypotheses, and conjectures about the sources of international conflict are typically seen as competing explanations for observed behavior. Our advocacy of comparative testing emerges from a different view. We conceive of international political actions as emerging from a variety of causes. Most theories focus on one or a limited set of these causes, ignoring the others. Theories focusing on multiple sources of behavior need not be contradictory; rather, they may be either complementary or competing. Following this logic, many theories or hypotheses may simultaneously be correct. We argue that traditional conceptions of and debates over competing approaches to international relations theory that suggest that one theory is necessarily right and another necessarily wrong are dated and not helpful in understanding actual behavior. Instead, while some theories are independent, others are overlapping. Multiple theories purporting to explain a single phenomenon (such as war) may be valid. If this perspective is correct, then cumulative scientific progress in international relations will be made more rapidly if we shift to analyses that focus both on what *set* of theories is valid and on the *relative explanatory power* of those theories. While multiple theories may each explain part of reality, not all theories are created equal, and some theories have more empirical relevance than others. But we cannot tell this without engaging in broad comparative empirical testing.

Unfortunately, typical research designs complicate attempts to evaluate claims about the validity of a broad set of theories of international conflict or the relative power of competing or complementary theories. We develop an appropriate research design for such analysis. We use a methodology based on block maximum-likelihood tests and relative risk analysis that allows us to assess what theories contribute additional explanatory power to our understanding of international conflict, even after taking into account the effects associated with the empirical measures associated with a large number of other theories. We also develop software to allow the creation of the type of data necessary for the analysis we advocate, to allow precise replication, and to encourage further comparative theory testing. This same software allows us to conduct a more thorough empirical test of the expected utility theory of war than has been executed before.

In particular, we evaluate the relative strength of sixteen different explanations for international conflict drawn from the system, dyadic, and monadic levels of analysis, ranging from hegemonic stability theory to expected utility theory to the democratic peace proposition. We include key variables from these popular theories of conflict in a multinomial logit analyses of dispute and war behavior. We find that many theories suggest factors that contribute in important ways to both the initiation and the escalation of militarized disputes. However, while many theories do contribute to the overall prediction of international conflict, most theories are quite weak individually and are generally comparable in terms of predictive effect. We demonstrate that in terms of empirical explanatory power there is no existing single dominant theory of international conflict in the international relations literature. Rather, we must take into account variables from several different theories to explain international conflict more accurately. This is the first empirical test to include key variables from so many theories of international conflict in a single analysis.

As is the case with most large research projects, we owe an enormous debt to a wide range of friends and scholars. This project began with an idea for a paper suggested by the late Ken Organski in 1992. But what started out as an apparently straightforward replication project morphed along the way into something quite different. The end result is part data management venture, part software development project, and part gigantic hypothesis testing effort. Most important, perhaps, we have both undergone a tremendous evolution in our thinking about the way that the intellectual energies of competing research programs fit together in both complementary and antagonistic ways. As you will find as you work through the book, we gore a lot of oxen along the way. While we bear full responsibility for any errors or unfair accusations, we owe a great deal to the people who helped sharpen our spears.

We received assistance and advice from a wide range of people and institutions. At the outset, Ken Organski goaded us into taking on the project. His exhortations helped us through a couple of the points where authors all too frequently throw in the towel. We dearly miss his energy, spirit, and friendship. Without Bruce Bueno de Mesquita's long discussions and assistance to Bennett, the project would never have gotten off the ground. Joshua Goldstein's advice about the importance of careful replication was both wise and heeded to the best of our abilities. Alex Wendt read several chapters and gave us insightful suggestions for ways to knit together parts of the literature that are often seen as mutually exclusive. Bruce Russett read multiple drafts and tolerated numerous long-winded and one-sided discussions about the deeper meaning of our results. Stam remains gratefully indebted to Russett for his constant support in this and many other endeavors. Rogers Smith, Dan Reiter, Bill Wohlforth, Steve Brooks, Errol Henderson, and Daryl Press at numerous times all served as welcome sounding boards and provided insightful criticism when it was much needed. David Yoon, Alastair Smith, Ken Schultz, Jeff Lewis, Don Green, Ken Clarke, Bear Braumoeller, Neal Beck, and Chris Achen read and commented on several of the chapters and provided invaluable methodological advice.

We presented various sections of the book at political science departments around the country, where numerous critical (and even some constructive) comments improved the final product. These talks include seminars held at the government and political science departments at Dartmouth College, Pennsylvania State University, Harvard University, Yale University, Cornell University, the University of Washington, the University of Michigan, the University of Dublin, and Ohio State University. The version you hold in your hands is vastly improved over the talks inflicted on often very patient and helpful colleagues.

Thanks also go to the editors of the *Journal of Conflict Resolution,* the *British Journal of Political Science,* and *International Studies Quarterly* for publishing our initial papers evaluating some expected utility theory models and exploring the importance of fundamental research design decisions. The advice from numerous anonymous reviewers at these journals and at the University of Michigan Press was enormously helpful. While critical reviews are not always pleasant to read, they make for a much better final product. Jeremy Shine at the University of Michigan Press deserves much credit for his support for the project, even as its completion dragged out past our early and overly optimistic expectations. Thanks also go to J. David Singer for his contributions to the discipline and also for his patient reading and careful comments on a late draft of the manuscript.

Yale University and Dartmouth College's Rockefeller Center provided material support for Stam; Pennsylvania State University did the same for Bennett. Last, thanks go to all of you readers. Your tax dollars, administered through the National Science Foundation, generously supported our research, writing, and software development with a series of grants. This material is based upon work supported by the National Science Foundation under Grants No. 9601151, 9975115, and 0079120. Any opinions, findings, conclusions, or recommendations expressed in this material are those of the authors and do not necessarily reflect the views of the National Science Foundation.

1 TOWARD A BETTER UNDERSTANDING OF THEORIES OF INTERNATIONAL CONFLICT

i pass with relief from the tossing sea of cause and
theory to the firm ground of result and fact.
—winston churchill, 1898

Social science, like any science, achieves progress through the accumulation of systematic knowledge. To improve our collective understanding of international politics we need to regularly assess both the empirical regularities observed in the world around us and the theories that profess to explain these facts as we have come to know them. Political science in general and the study of international politics in particular suffer from having numerous competing theories, assertions, and conjectures describing the same phenomena. Although new explanations and descriptions of interstate war appear almost as frequently as the events themselves, new ideas rarely supersede those previously developed. Instead, they simply accumulate with little regard paid to the explanatory power of new accounts versus those previously advanced. This has resulted in the multitude of models, untested hypotheses, conjectures, and normatively grounded assertions that constitute the discipline.

The study of international conflict exemplifies these problems. Over the last forty years, the development of models and conjectures purporting to explain the incidence and escalation of international conflict has proceeded at a rapid pace. In their 1990 survey, for instance, Dougherty and Pfaltzgraff identified over thirty examples of what they characterize as theories of international relations. If we counted variations on familiar themes and arguments developed since, the number would be much higher. Having an array of theoretical approaches and empirical conjectures is not a problem if scholars have a well-founded sense of which explanations or descriptions account for the greatest proportion of events or facts or, more colloquially, which theories or hypotheses work best. While political scientists have been very successful in developing numerous interesting stories about the nature of international conflict, we have been much less successful at conducting the type of rigorous analysis that would allow us to (1) evaluate the relative explanatory power of these various descriptions and (2) reach some sense of consensus about which stories are the most useful or valuable in understanding international political processes. The abandonment of "failed" theories or presumed empirical regularities is rare in political science—and particularly so in the study of international politics.

Apologists for the current state of affairs might claim that, compared to other disciplines, cumulative progress in political science may be particularly difficult to achieve for at least two principle reasons. One has to do with the limited availability of some critical data. For some problems in political science, there simply is insufficient data for researchers to test their hypotheses or arguments. For example, the complete absence of wars between modern liberal democracies after World War II makes it difficult to sort out the competing and often collinear explanations for this important fact. Similarly, tests of explanations focusing on human misperception or the role of private information require data that are notoriously difficult to assemble. Another problem we face, and one that is potentially damning, lies in the possibility that in the realm of politics there may be no fundamental regularities, or equilibria, to predict. William Riker (1980, 443) suggests that the prospects for theoretical advancement in political science are quite bleak by concluding that "politics is *the* dismal science because we have learned from it that there are no fundamental equilibria to predict." From this hypothesized lack of formal equilibria, Riker then concludes that "In the absence of such equilibria we cannot know much about the future at all, whether it is likely to be palatable or unpalatable, and in that sense our future is subject to the tricks and accidents of the way in which questions are posed and alternatives are offered and eliminated."[1] Of course, Riker's gloomy conclusion has not prevented others from (1) vigorously disagreeing with him, (2) continuing to develop new explanations of the political world, and (3) claiming the discovery of new empirical regularities of normative or substantive significance.

These protestations notwithstanding, it is probably premature to conclude that there are no predictable international political events or that there are insufficient data to assess the validity of carefully specified arguments. Nevertheless, we believe that there is a third critical problem hindering scientific advancement in the study of international conflict behavior, namely, the paucity of systematic comparative testing that would allow us to examine, judge, and occasionally abandon explanations and descriptions of the origins of international disputes and wars. Without testing multiple explanations of organized international violence in a simultaneous framework, we cannot judge the relative power of competing explanations or predictions. We believe this lack of comparative testing to be a main culprit for our current state of affairs. In this volume, we turn to developing such comparative tests.

STANDARDS FOR COMPARATIVE HYPOTHESIS TESTING

When testing an empirical conjecture or the observable implications of one theory versus another (that is, conducting comparative hypothesis testing), one of the first tasks is to choose from the variety of standards one could use when deciding that one model of the world supersedes or replaces another. For example, one method we might apply is Popper's (1968) "method of elimination." Using his approach, we end up with relatively more powerful theories, as stronger theories replace weaker ones through a process of "dualistic elimination." An example of dualistic elimination—the process of pitting one "theory" against another—appears in the simulation used by Robert Axelrod in *The Evolution of Cooperation* (1984). There, in round-robin fashion, Axelrod pitted one computer simulation strategy after another against the competition until an overall winner emerged after thousands of iterations. In this case, Popper's method provided a suitable approach because each strategy was an exclusive set of rules to play the game of interest (Prisoners' Dilemma), with each strategy having a clear and unique payoff.

Although simple, Popper's method is not appropriate for testing most theoretical explanations or empirical conjectures in international politics. He notes an important caveat to applying his method of elimination, arguing that it is appropriate only if a theory may be demonstrably falsifiable, that is, if the theory is "sufficiently *precise* to be capable of clashing with observational experience" (Popper 1968, 131; italics in original). The use of such rigid tests is only appropriate when the theories themselves and the data used to test them are well specified and precise. In his work, Popper presents an example of disproving Kepler's description of circular, rather than elliptical, planetary motion. Unfortunately, the level of precision found in most theories and empirical conjectures of international politics is not nearly as high as in the planetary sciences, and the nature of the objects under study is rather different. In fact, most so-called theories of international politics are not really theories at all.

3

Here, by "theory" we mean a logically consistent and empirically falsifiable causal explanation of why some event or set of events occurred in the past and, given similar conditions, will occur in the future. Most international relations "theories" simply describe conditions where some factor supposedly influenced the likelihood or nature of some past international conflict. In other cases, we see arguments about some factor (such as economic interdependence) that supposedly affects the likelihood of conflict without defining precisely what sort of conflict is in question (e.g., small disputes, crises, or large-scale wars). Other "theories" such as balance of power theory suffer from logical inconsistencies when moving from cause to effect. Moreover, since many of these causal factors that are linked to increased risk of disputes or war are not mutually exclusive—that is, multiple factors associated with various theoretical perspectives may simultaneously influence the conflicts we are trying to understand—dualistic elimination is inappropriate.

In addition, because we view human behavior as probabilistic rather than deterministic, we often will not be able to conclude that one explanation is clearly superior in all circumstances, as no single observation is sufficient to falsify a theory in a probabilistic world. By "probabilistic" we mean that there is a stochastic component to human behavior, that under apparently identical conditions, state leaders might choose to do one thing at one time and something quite different at another, but with some predictable probability of doing each. By contrast, a deterministic relationship would be one such as Newton's theory of force, mass, and acceleration, $F = MA$. In the context of classical mechanics it would be nonsensical to assert that a given force would accelerate a known mass with some acceleration 70 percent of the time. Theories of political behavior are more akin to meteorology, where forecasters hope to predict the probabilities of various weather outcomes occurring, given a set of observed meteorological conditions.

In the political world there may be many factors leading to the probabilistic nature of political behavior, ranging from the tiny influences of unmeasured or immeasurable factors to conscious or unconscious strategies of randomized behavior, irrational or impulsive behavior, strategic decision making, and, finally, to the effects of actors making their decisions based on rational expectations in the setting of strategic choice. From this perspective, where chance plays a powerful role in determining the events we ultimately study, we become engaged in the task of forecasting tendencies and influences of a set of observable conditions on the relative likelihood that a decision maker will behave in a particular way. In this book, we focus solely on assessing the empirical content of various arguments purporting to predict or to explain the relative likelihood of war.

Taking a slightly different approach to the problem of falsification and theory rejection than Popper, we generally follow Lakatos's (1978, 32) standard that we should reject an explanation of past events or a prediction of future events if and only if another explanation predicts everything and more that the first one does and that this new empirical content is verifiable. We implement what we see as a statistical version of Lakatos's perspective. By adopting the maximum likelihood logic of inference (King 1989) we are able to make two sets of judgments. First, we can assess whether a set of indicator variables derived from an argument about the relative likelihood of war makes novel contributions to the fit of our statistical models. Second, we can evaluate the relative predictive power associated with each of these variables. This approach allows us to demonstrate that multiple factors simultaneously influence conflict. It also allows us to judge whether or not some conjecture is consistent with more than one unique event when controlling for other explanations, thereby suggesting elimination of this factor as a systematic predictor of war.

Following this perspective, with our analyses we do not attempt to eliminate conjectures based on ontological rigor or the internal logical consistency of the arguments. Rather, we focus solely on their empirical content. A quite different form of comparative analysis might carefully examine the internal logic and assumptions of multiple theories of international conflict and reject those that are logically contradictory or inconsistent (e.g., Zinnes 1967; Niou, Ordeshook, and Rose 1989). While there is much to be said for that approach, all too frequently inductively driven or normatively motivated stories remain at the center of academic and policy debate even after compelling demonstrations of the deductive flaws in the "theory's" logic. For example, consider balance of power theory. Niou, Ordeshook, and Rose (1989) conducted an excruciatingly careful and nuanced evaluation of the logical underpinnings of classical balance of power arguments and found them sorely lacking. However, their formal mathematical analysis did little to change the beliefs of those supporting the view that an equitable balance of power or capabilities will keep the peace between potentially warring nations. Balance of power and other realpolitik arguments appear before students in much the same way as they have for decades, unaffected in many classrooms by careful logical analysis demonstrating the logical flaws of the "theory." With the hope that unimpeachable empirical regularities may be persuasive where elegant logic has not always been, we focus on the empirical content of our models, hypotheses, and conjectures, represented by their associated variables and operational indicators.

SCIENCE AND CUMULATIVE PROGRESS IN INTERNATIONAL POLITICS

Clearly, evaluating the relative explanatory power of different empirical assertions and dropping or modifying those that receive little or no empirical support is an important part of the scientific enterprise. Our beliefs about the power of various empirical conjectures drive our collective research agendas and often mark the starting point for policy prescriptions. To date, however, only limited efforts exist to compare systematically the predictive power of the myriad different explanations of international conflict—or, more precisely, the explanatory power of the independent variables expected to correlate with conflict behavior. While many researchers pay lip service to Lakatos and his principles of progressive scientific research based on careful theory development and testing, in practice most studies of international politics have failed to follow this model. Most so-called theories of international politics are simply broad-brush descriptions based on the observation of small numbers of events rather than carefully deduced explanations of political behavior.

Many of the existing empirical studies fall short in another dimension as well. Studies seeking to compare or cross-validate existing empirical claims all too often use different subsets of data, data cast at different units of analysis, and data sets with different dependent variables. Rather than conducting broad tests of multiple theories, most existing tests of various explanations of international politics assess new explanations against a null model or a small and carefully selected set of competing claims. Typically, an author presents a contrasting set of explanations where one argument is of primary interest with competing explanations presented as control variables. We find, for example, rational deterrence hypotheses compared to variables drawn from psychological approaches (Huth and Russett 1993) or a selected set of international system structure variables compared to a set of variables drawn from a dyadic perspective (Bueno de Mesquita and Lalman 1988). Maoz and Russett launched a veritable cottage industry based on pitting the democratic peace proposition against a variety of control variables (Maoz and Russett 1993; Russett and Oneal 2001). Bueno de Mesquita and Lalman (1992) tested their expected utility predictions along with other predictions drawn from power-based stories but failed to include other non-power-based stories. A few broader studies move beyond a set of closely related alternative explanations to examine several "likely suspects" in the hunt for the correlates of international conflict behavior (Bremer 1992; Huth, Bennett, and Gelpi 1992; Oneal and Russett 1999a). In none of these cases, however, do the authors attempt a comprehensive examination of competing explanations, nor do they systematically assess the strength of the various arguments' predictive power.

   In the domain of formal rational choice theory, the lack of comparative testing is particularly noticeable and unfortunate. While the expected utility approach has been the target of both theoretical and empirical criticism, using both normative arguments and empirical case studies (e.g., Jervis, Lebow, and Stein 1985), formal models of international conflict have received remarkably little empirical evaluation with large-n statistical tests, particularly against a wide range of alternative explanations or predictors. This dearth of empirical testing led, in part, to Green and Shapiro's blistering critique of rational choice models and their advocates in *Pathologies of Rational Choice Theory* (1994, 7). There they find weak empirical support for rational choice theory generally and suggest that, "Despite its enormous and growing prestige in the discipline, rational choice theory has yet to deliver on its promise to advance the empirical study of politics. . . . we believe that this claim can be defended across the board."

   While formal rational choice models are not the only arguments that suffer from a lack of systematic empirical testing, advocates of the rational choice approach make particularly strong claims about the power of expected utility theory. Green and Shapiro also make sweeping and speculative claims about the (lack of) explanatory or predictive power of rational choice theories in all fields of political science. Ironically, they offer no compelling evidence that alternative approaches might perform any better. Their study also suffers from a notable omission—they do not address the rational choice literature on international politics at all, where there have been a few serious efforts to conduct some rigorous tests (Bueno de Mesquita 1980; Bueno de Mesquita and Lalman 1992; Smith 1996a, 1999; Signorino 2000; Filson and Werner 2001).

   There are a few noteworthy attempts to execute a comparative analysis of the empirical literature on international conflict. For example, in Gurr's *Handbook of Political Conflict* (1980) Bueno de Mesquita presents a review of the theoretical and empirical claims of balance of power arguments, power transition models, system structure conjectures, status inconsistency, arms race models, deterrence, and the externalization of domestic conflict. He rejects some approaches (such as balance of power) because of contradictions in their internal logic. His review, while helpful for understanding the reasoning underlying a variety of common explanations for conflict, does not provide any systematic empirical evidence directly comparing the various arguments' relative explanatory or predictive power. More recently, John Vasquez's *The War Puzzle* (1994) provides a self-described meta-analysis of the literature on interstate war. Vasquez similarly makes no overall empirical comparison of the various theories or conjectures that he identifies. Numerous other edited volumes on international conflict exist as well that take a generally similar approach, where each chapter in a volume takes a different tack on the problem of international conflict by focusing on a single argument or approach (e.g., Midlarsky 1992, 2000). While these works help us understand the logic and possible strengths of the various arguments in isolation, they do not provide empirically based comparative hypothesis testing.

Since no project can hope to specify all of the possible variables expected to correlate with the onset of violent conflict, and since few research designs can handle propositions drawn from different levels of analysis, these commonly found testing practices and collective assessments might appear quite sensible. However, the lack of broader comparative testing has had several unintended consequences. Because of ad hoc variations in sets of control variables and the populations of cases across studies, we continue to be uncertain about what explanations or descriptions of the precursors of international conflict are most likely valid. For example, the basic question of whether a relatively equal balance of military and industrial capabilities between two nation-states increases the likelihood of peace or war remains in dispute, even though many policymakers assume that an equal balance of capabilities makes international stability more likely. In the absence of such testing and rejection of unsupported arguments, advocates of various models or empirical conjectures make claims about the power of their explanations and descriptions of historical events that are, in reality, unsustainable.

These authors argue that the regularity they identify (such as the so-called democratic peace) is useful and can stand on its own. This is because they claim that the supposition can be used to make unique predictions about future events (based implicitly on the assumption that the past is a good predictor of the future, something our stockbrokers assure us is a misguided way to pick stocks) or can provide improved understandings of past happenings.[2] Some claim that their "theory" is the best at explaining the events in question and that competing explanations make at best marginal contributions to our understanding of politics. Readers should examine closely claims by those who have apparently identified novel explanations of international politics, as these claims frequently have minimal empirical (and sometimes logical) referent (e.g., Van Evera 1999). When a study presents the apparent effects of different explanations in carefully constructed settings, we must recognize that other excluded factors might be more important than the factors included in the analysis and that the subsequent inclusion of the potentially confounding explanations could even reverse the direction of the previous findings (Gowa 1999; Mansfield and Snyder 1995).

Finally, the lack of large-scale comparative testing has led to recurring and fruitless arguments over what approach to understanding international politics is "best." Scholars often assert the superiority of one perspective or paradigm over another. We see this with "realists," or those advocating the realpolitik approach often associated with Morgenthau, Lippman, Kissinger, and others, arguing that domestic political processes are important only at the margins. In like fashion, rational choice proponents argue that expected utility maximizing behavior explains the critical part of international conflict behavior, with formal theorists claiming that mathematically deduced theory is superior to more informal natural language approaches (Walt 2000). Absent broad comparative tests and rigorous evidence, claims that the realist approach is better than approaches based in domestic politics are certainly premature, despite prominent scholars' assertions to the contrary.[3]

TOWARD A METHOD OF COMPARATIVE HYPOTHESIS TESTING

In dealing with the problems discussed previously, we start with three priors about comparative hypothesis testing and the evaluation of the relative predictive power of international politics explanations. First, we believe (and demonstrate later) that no single current theory, conjecture, assertion, or description stands alone as a dominant predictor of international conflict. In subsequent chapters we will show that there is no single indicator for the onset of international conflict with predictive power approaching a level that we would consider high. None of the variables associated with the arguments we investigate accounts for 75 percent, 25 percent, or even 5 percent of previous conflicts. Instead, we will show that a combination of several factors is necessary to understand the initiation and escalation of international conflict. As we subsequently demonstrate, many different conjectures about international conflict are simultaneously valid, as each operational indicator for a given explanation or description accounts for unique aspects of the conflict initiation and escalation process. From this perspective, international conflicts arise through the confluence of multiple weak factors. This suggests that debates such as whether realist or domestic politics approaches are "best" simply miss the point. A more fruitful question to ask is how much, or when, or under what conditions does each conjecture appear most consistent with some aspect of international conflict behavior.

Our second prior is that, while no single factor is adequate to explain international conflict, we believe that with careful empirical tests we can show that some variables have substantially larger predictive power associated with them than others do. While we conclude that there is no single dominant explanation of international politics, we do not suggest that every model or argument is valid or equally useful. Even if there is, as yet, no governing theory of international politics, we need not descend into some postmodern, antipositivist intellectual anarchy, where all arguments are of equal relative value. Rather, our findings point to the need for more, and more careful, theory development in order to accommodate the insights gained from various lines of research drawing from multiple levels of analysis.

This leads to our final prior. We believe that it is appropriate, necessary, and possible to include factors from multiple levels of analysis in comparative hypothesis testing, as we described previously and execute subsequently. If variables from any level of analysis are to influence international affairs, they must ultimately do so by affecting the decisions of individual actors in the system. Even system-level factors must ultimately influence the outcomes we observe by affecting the decisions of states' leaders since the system is not an autonomous actor, somehow acting on its own to directly influence states' behavior. Rather, identifiable characteristics of the system provide incentives or conditions to which actors may or may not respond.

Given these priors and our Lakatosian approach, we argue that the best way to draw conclusions about the relative power associated with various factors assumed to predict conflict is to estimate a single statistical model incorporating as many of these factors as possible. We do this through a process that we refer to as comparative hypothesis testing. Every testable model or empirical conjecture explicitly or implicitly argues that some measurable variable should correlate with some observable behavior, in our case international conflict. In this book, we focus on a simultaneous analysis of a large set of these variables, which we draw from a variety of arguments, conjectures, and empirical suppositions, cast at multiple levels of analysis. It is possible to include a wide range of key variables drawn from multiple levels of analysis because we use the directed dyad-year as the unit of analysis in our model (more on this later). Since it is possible for multiple explanations to predict the same events, to sort out the competing arguments, it is critical to evaluate them simultaneously, as we cannot have confidence that any particular story actually explains novel events until we control for a range of other competing explanations. Without controlling for a range of other hypotheses, we also cannot assess a conjecture's relative predictive power. Of course, there may be limits to what we can learn with this approach. For example, the variables suggested by the competing explanations may be so collinear that we cannot tell which factors are systematically related to conflict and which are not.

For brevity's sake we might be tempted to lump together under the single and parsimonious moniker "theory" various rigorously specified deductive theories, empirical conjectures, carefully stated hypotheses, and the occasional hunch. While this would spare the eye, it does considerable injury to the word "theory," and so we refrain from the standard practice of referring to all predictive or explanatory arguments about the nature of international politics as "international relations theory." Few so-called theories of international politics contain deductively formal logic or even careful attention to internal consistency and instead pose loosely specified relationships among typically vague concepts along the lines of "more of X will probably lead to more of Y." The lack of internal logic and conceptual clarity is particularly troubling to scholars who argue that most models of international politics are actually, or should be, theories of strategic interaction (e.g., Signorino 1999; Lake 1992). If Lake is correct, then testing causal arguments about relationships between variables and international conflict across levels of conflict will prove particularly challenging and may require statistical estimators whose design matches the strategic causal logic of a particular argument. Under some circumstances of strategic choice, particularly in situations where the logic behind signaling games is particularly important, the unobserved effects of variables such as balance of forces may be more powerful than, and in the opposite direction of, the observed effects, thereby leading to results opposite of what we might expect otherwise (Fearon 1994a; Smith 1996a; Ritter 2001).

In our analysis, we do not redevelop the strategic logic of the typically casually stated arguments we test. Rather, we take the arguments as given by the original authors and test the hypothesized relationships and measures and include them "as is" in our statistical models, even if it means that many of the hypotheses we test are not drawn from carefully specified theories but instead represent an empirical hunch or conjecture. As such, many of the tests here are not really tests of theories or even of careful causal logic. Rather, in the chapters that follow we present careful tests of numerous empirical propositions about the onset of war; a few of these arguments have been deduced from carefully laid out theory, but most of them have not. In the latter case, we are establishing sets of "facts" that need explaining rather than providing tests of a causal explanation of conflict.

If the conjectures we include in our tests suffer from flaws in their internal logic, or if the operational variables do not accurately measure the purported causal influences, our empirical findings will likely be inconsistent with the original authors' predictions. As we reach the end of this book, we will revisit this theme and address in detail the somewhat startling paucity of rigorous theory in international politics. We end with the conclusion that the field of international politics is undertheorized, particularly in terms of the dynamic linkages between existing models and arguments.

In the remainder of this book, we will test the relationships of key variables that emerge from sixteen important explanations and descriptions of international conflict at multiple levels of analysis. We seek to discover which of these variables—and in turn what underlying explanations—are consistent with the largest number of empirical facts about the onset and escalation of interstate conflict while we simultaneously control for several alternative and frequently competing predictors of violent interstate conflict. They include the following:

State Level of Analysis
  1. Democratization
  2. Polity Change and Externalization of Violence

Dyadic Level of Analysis
  3. Alliance and Defense Pact Membership
  4. Arms Races
  5. Balance of Power
  6. Democratic Peace
  7. Expected Utility
  8. Geographic Contiguity
  9. Nuclear Deterrence
  10. Power Transition
  11. Rational Deterrence
  12. Trade Interdependence

International System Level of Analysis
13. Economic Cycles/Kondratieff Waves
14. Hegemonic Stability
15. International System Polarity
16. Systemic Power Concentration and Movement

For some of these explanations, and in particular the expected utility variant we will test, the theoretical logic underlying the relationship between the explanatory variables and the onset of war is quite explicit. In other cases, we have largely ad hoc explanations for why some particular factors appear related to conflict. For instance, "democratic peace theory" is not one clear theory. Rather, the so-called democratic peace is a relatively strong empirical regularity in search of a theory, or explanation, with scholars pursuing multiple arguments about the causes of that regularity (e.g., Maoz and Russett 1993; Gartzke 1998; Gowa 1999; Schultz 1999; Bueno de Mesquita et al. 1999, 2001; Reiter and Stam 2002). The purpose of this book is not so much to test the theoretical explanations for the facts as we know them but rather to more carefully establish the facts for which we need to develop theoretical explanations. Typically, the explanations of conflict that fall short of the bar that constitutes true theory emerge inductively from one or two observations and as such are actually better understood as descriptions of events rather than theories of political behavior. We include several of these important conjectures in our analyses even if there is no deductive or rigorously specified theory behind them. For instance, most scholars reasonably include geographic contiguity in empirical models of conflict because they understand that many states cannot fight across long distances, although they do not have an explicit theory of force projection on which to build this expectation.

In the chapters that follow, our analysis proceeds in a series of careful steps. First, we evaluate whether the empirical predictions associated with each description or explanation stand up in the presence of other explanations. Given that most tests include only a few control variables, this first step is important for those seeking to establish the power and reliability of current predictors of international conflict. The crux of our analysis is to find out whether the empirical predictions drawn from the basic international politics literature continue to find empirical support after we include many other competing explanations in the analysis.

Following our basic hypothesis testing (whether an operational indicator makes a statistically significant contribution to explaining the outbreak of conflict), we evaluate the conjecture's associated relative predictive power. Here our aim is to ascertain whether there are certain dominant variables that are associated with more of the observed conflict than others are. In our analysis, we actually find the opposite. Rather than there being a small number of factors consistent with a majority of the conflict behavior variance, we find that literally dozens of variables have statistically significant but substantively weak associations with international conflict. There is no clearly dominant factor (or even a small set of factors) systematically associated with international conflict behavior. This finding has important implications both for how we study theories of international politics and for the formulation of public policy. It suggests that the search for, or emphasis on, single factors or paradigms is misguided. It also leads us to conclude that we should turn our attention to searching for more interactive and dynamic explanations of interstate conflict that can take into account a multitude of factors from multiple levels of analysis. We conclude with observations about the nature of research across multiple levels of analysis and a demonstration that we can integrate information across multiple levels to make successful predictions about the relative likelihood of interstate conflict at both the dyadic and system levels.

2 COMPARATIVE HYPOTHESIS TESTING AND SOME LIMITS TO KNOWLEDGE

> it is a test of true theories not only to
> account for but to predict phenomena.
> —william whewell, 1840

To model the changes in the risk of war associated with the various models and arguments in our analysis we employ a variant of the maximum likelihood model of inference described by King (1989). Following this approach, and using a series of nested statistical models, we can assess whether the independent variables in our models improve our ability to predict systematically relative change in the risk of conflict between nation-states. For each argument or conjecture we test, we derive one or more independent variables predicted by the original author to correlate with the dependent variable (international conflict and escalation thereof). We then assess (1) whether the independent variable(s) associated with each explanation makes a statistically significant contribution to the overall likelihood of the wars that occur in our data and (2) the relative explanatory power of each variable on a comparable scale. If a variable marking a prediction derived from some "theory" does not contribute to the overall likelihood of the statistical model, or makes little substantive difference in the relative risk of conflict onset, we must question whether that particular argument helps us to understand international conflict in a systematic way compared to being a description of an idiosyncratic event.

We are able to examine and evaluate indicators drawn from multiple levels of analysis by focusing on the directed dyad-year as our unit of analysis. A directed dyad-year is a pair of states in a given year, observed from the perspective of one of the two states. This distinguishes the identity of a potential conflict's initiator and target. For example,

China-Japan in 1990 is one observation, while Japan-China in 1990 is another. In either observation, a conflict could occur. Because each dyad-year contains two states, this choice allows us to incorporate variables such as those from balance of power approaches that require information on two states. It allows us to include unit-level information arguably associated with conflict initiation, such as a potential initiator's regime type or rate of democratization. Finally, we can also examine the power of system-level arguments using this unit of analysis. If the international system in one period is more conflict prone than in another, this will be reflected in a higher probability of multiple states choosing to initiate conflict.[1]

This process of comparative hypothesis testing helps to address several important problems with existing tests of empirical international politics propositions. The first is the problem of overlapping predictions and controls. It is important to include multiple explanatory factors in a single model even if those different explanations appear to be independent. Commonly, the independent variables marking separate arguments correlate to some degree, particularly since many of the variables constructed by theorists draw their inspiration from the same underlying sets of cases. If this is the case, then controlling for the presence of the other variables is critical to minimize the possibility of omitted variable bias, claims of theoretical independence notwithstanding. For example, Bueno de Mesquita and Lalman (1992) present their International Interaction Game (IIG) as an essentially complete data-generating process, but this is so only in the context of the assumptions they need to develop their theory. Even if two competing explanations are mutually exclusive in that they begin with different assumptions (and few theories of international politics are truly so exclusionary or well developed), we must include appropriate predictive variables from both in the same model to properly assess which empirical conjecture better fits the data while controlling for the predictions of the other.

If we only analyze variables or explanations in isolation, we also tend to overlook the epistemological limitations that multicollinearity can pose. For example, NATO emerges as an effective security organization at about the same time that the United States and the USSR both develop secure second-strike nuclear capabilities, the conditions needed to follow the doctrine of Mutually Assured Destruction (MAD). While it is true that no large-scale open war occurred between the United States and the USSR, it is impossible for us to tell whether NATO or MAD (or some other collinear explanation) is responsible for the absence of war using this type of statistical analysis. If we find that the empirical predictions of an argument do not allow us to predict unique events due to severe multicollinearity, we then have a fundamental problem, an inherent limit to knowledge associated with the method used here.

The second inferential problem that comparative hypothesis testing can help address is the possibility that multiple factors might simultaneously affect the likelihood of states initiating an international conflict. States may be inclined to choose war over peace at different times due to the confluence of multiple "weak factors" rather than as a result of a single provocation or set of incentives. Alternatively, it may be that one set of factors drives international conflict at one time or location and that a different set of factors may be more relevant at some other place or point in time. This would imply that there are regionally or temporally distinct paths to war. While some scholars have long argued that multiple factors affect international politics (Waltz 1959), debate continues over what level of analysis, approach, or theory provides the "best" depiction of international politics. A more fruitful question to ask is when, where, and how much each source of conflict influences international conflict behavior. It may be that international power concerns generally dominate domestic political issues, or that international system characteristics trump dyadic factors, or that both play an important role, perhaps under different circumstances that can be specified ex ante. However, we cannot judge the relative risks associated with each of these perspectives by focusing on one explanation at a time. Our method of combining multiple variables in a single equation may also help us understand the relatively weak fit of existing models of international conflict cast at the dyad-year level. If each of the many causal descriptions of international conflict explains separately but simultaneously a piece of the empirical world, then it is only by combining the key predictor variables from those arguments into a single statistical model that we can maximize our predictive power.

LIMITS TO KNOWLEDGE: EPISTEMOLOGICAL PERSPECTIVES

Our perspective here is generally a behavioral one, following in the tradition of those for whom observable behavior is the ultimate outcome begging explanation. From the perspective of the traditional behaviorists, we would hope to be able to explain 100 percent of the observed variation in our dependent variable. While we draw from this behaviorist well, we nevertheless believe that there are several reasons why any statistical model will not come close to approaching perfect predictive accuracy. In this section, we discuss some recent arguments that suggest limits on our ability to predict systematically international conflict.

Typical behavioral research seeking to develop a general explanation for some phenomenon (that is, accounting for variance in the dependent variable) implicitly starts with the ubiquitous regression equation

$$Y = \alpha + \beta X + e, \tag{2.1}$$

where Y is the dependent variable, α is a fixed intercept, β represents a set of parameters applied to a vector of explanatory variables X, and e represents errors assumed to be stochastic.[2] The X vector includes the set of variables whose associated effects analysts are interested in studying. In the context of international politics, these might include state power, domestic political institutions, international trade, or several other measurable variables. More precisely, if we are working with a cross-sectional time-series dyadic data set (data that tracks dyads across both space and time) where i and j represent different states (and so ij represents a particular directed dyad) and t represents time (ijt is the dyad ij at time t), our regression equation becomes

$$Y_{ijt} = \alpha + \beta X_{ijt} + e. \tag{2.2}$$

The standard analytic approach focuses attention on the signs and parameter estimates or coefficients of β, seeking to minimize e by including the "right" set of independent variables in X. We must correctly specify this set of independent variables in order to operationalize the critical aspects of a given theory or conjecture in order to measure the concept(s) in question with as little error as possible and to account for the interactive effects present in strategic situations (Signorino 1999, 2000; Lewis and Schultz 2001). Much of the statistical work on international politics essentially ignores the single fixed intercept α, assuming it theoretically uninteresting. Nor do scholars typically explore variations in β or e over either time (t) or location (ij) (see Green, Kim, and Yoon 2001; Cederman 2001 is a notable exception). Fortunately, however, econometricians have generalized this equation and developed classes of models appropriate for data that consist of a pool of cross-unit, cross-time data. A general form of equation (2.2) is the following:

$$Y_{ijt} = \alpha_{ijt} + \beta_{ijt}X_{ijt} + e_{ijt}. \tag{2.3}$$

Equation (2.3) shows both α and β potentially varying by unit and across time. Econometricians have developed models specifically designed to deal with variations in the intercept (α) across units and variations in coefficients (β) across units and time. Recently, scholars in international politics have also focused attention on the error term e_{ijt} and suggested that due to the strategic nature of political decision making there may be an upper limit to how much we can explain using measurable variables included in either α or β (Gartzke 1999). Next, we explore each of these modeling perspectives and approaches before turning to the arguments and hypotheses we examine for possible inclusion in our vector of variables, X.

Intercept Variation:
The Changing Nature of Politics over Time and Region

Statistical studies of international conflict typically assume that a single intercept (α) is adequate. The estimate of α reflects the baseline probability, frequency, or rate of conflict. However, if α varies so that different regions, countries, or dyads have different baseline risks of conflict not accounted for in the vector of variables X, then estimating a single α is inappropriate and may bias our estimate of β. Similarly, if α varies over time, as would be the case if a dyad's baseline or underlying level of conflict varied from one period to another, so that the intercept in one year differs from that in another, then a single α is again inappropriate. The intercept α may even vary by both time and space, so that the baseline level of conflict differs by dyad (or region) and time period. We take up this problem in detail in chapter 6.

The idea that a dyad's intrinsic level of conflict might change or evolve over time is particularly attractive to constructivists. Wendt (1999) argues, for example, that a dyad's underlying tendency to resort to war is a function, in part anyway, of some mutual socially constructed identity that is subject to change over time. In the language of our statistical model, if α (the baseline level of conflict) in our model is not fixed but instead is specific to some aggregation unit (e.g., region, dyad, or year), then a model with a single intercept risks omitted variable bias. If this unaccounted variance in α is correlated with some of the variables in X, the vector of parameters β_{ijt}, then the parameters we estimate (the effects on the rate of conflict associated with the independent variables of interest) will likely be biased as well. In essence, if different countries or dyads have different baseline conflict propensities not accounted for in the vector of variables X, the covariance that should be associated solely with unit differences may then be attributed to (some of) the coefficients in β. The econometric solution is to provide for the estimation of an intercept for each of the dyads in the study. The class of fixed-effects estimators was developed to deal efficiently with this problem; if α varies by unit in ways that cannot be accounted for by the vector of variables X, then a fixed-effects model may be appropriate (Green, Kim, and Yoon 2001; Bennett and Stam 2000a).

In practice, only a few studies in international politics have used fixed-effects models. The most prominent recent application is by Green, Kim, and Yoon (2001), who argue that the problem of overaggregated intercepts is common in dyad-year studies of international conflict. The authors find important differences in their results when they retest existing models of conflict using a fixed-effects estimator. However, this approach is not a cure-all. Beck and Katz (2001) and King and Zeng (2001) point out some significant problems with fixed-effects estimators. They argue that the solution may be worse than the problem. For instance, if we specify a different intercept for each dyad we cannot estimate the effect of independent variables that do not vary over time even though the cross-sectional variation associated with them may be of interest (such as geographic contiguity, which varies spatially but is time invariant for most dyads). Perhaps, more importantly, with fixed-effects models we cannot use information gleaned from those dyads where there is no variation on the dependent variable. This implies we can learn nothing about what leads to peace by studying the dyads that have never gone to war. In a fixed-effects model, independent variables that do not change over time add nothing to the model's overall fit to the data, since they correlate perfectly with the unit intercept and drop out of the estimation. Dyads for which the dependent variable is constant (e.g., those that never have conflicts) similarly contribute nothing to the likelihood function, and they too drop from the analysis. Importantly, the statistical necessity of dropping these variables and observations from fixed-effects analyses has nothing to do with whether they actually influence the onset of war (Beck and Katz 2001).

If we truly believe that variables such as contiguity that change only across space and not over time are irrelevant (and that they are not correlated with other variables of more theoretical interest) and that dyads without conflict really provide us with no information about the process that leads to conflict in those dyads that suffer from it, then a fixed-effects estimation might be appropriate. However, we do not believe that such variables and dyads are without information and thus agree with those who believe that fixed-effects estimation may be overkill. The problem with mistakenly assuming a single fixed intercept α is again that the relevant and omitted cross-unit effect, α_{ijt}, becomes associated with the other variables in β. We can solve the problem without resorting to the fixed-effects model by properly specifying the causal factors that lead α_{ijt} to vary for some different dyads or groups of dyads. That is, by specifying the factors that cause different dyads to have a different baseline level of conflict. The solution to this thorny empirical problem is more and better theory development rather than brute force statistical fixes. We believe that the better alternative to fixed-effects modeling is to consider carefully whether we should expect different units to have different intercepts for theoretical reasons.[3] By properly specifying variables to be included in X that capture this unit variation, we will essentially move conflict covariance from α to an individual parameter β.

The key element of this process is then to specify properly at what levels of aggregation we expect to find the sources of international conflict. Several possibilities suggest themselves as units to investigate. We might speculate that there are effects that differ by particular years (if some year is more or less dangerous for all states than another year, for instance, in the year after the conclusion of a large war) (Smith and Stam 2002; Werner 1999). Alternatively, groupings of years into eras might make sense if, for instance, we believed the cold war era to be more or less dangerous than the interwar period. Spatially, groupings by state or state type may be called for (for instance, if individual states are more dangerous by virtue of regime type or economic growth). Finally, grouping by region may be reasonable if we believe that states in particular regions engage in different patterns of international behavior by virtue of culture, shared colonial experience, learned interaction patterns, or peculiar regional politics. If these factors (spatial or temporal specific effects) are substantively important, but omitted from the analysis, the ignored differences could bias our parameter estimates. Regardless of the nature of this type of bias, the solution, in the end, is again more and better theory than exists today.

In chapter 6, we will explore whether regional and temporal variations in the fit of rational choice models of international conflict are significant. As we show there, variation in β over space and time proves important. An interesting implication of this is that the distinction between international politics and comparative politics—two traditionally separate subfields in political science—blurs tremendously; the remaining distinctions between the subfields essentially lie in one's normative choice of interesting or important dependent variables.

Coefficient Variation: Different Theories
for Different Regions and Periods

A second type of misspecification suggested in equation (2.3) occurs if the coefficients in β vary over units and time. If a conjecture "works" or a hypothesis holds up for only some dyads, or for only some time periods, and not for others, then assuming that a single β is appropriate for all members of X is again a potential source of bias, inefficiency, or both. If we believe that some hypothesis should hold only in a subset of cases, or at some particular time, then we can easily modify the variables, thereby controlling for this source of bias. For instance, we could account for an argument linking the effects of bipolar international systems to the behavior of just the great powers by including an interaction term of the dummy variable "bipolarity" with "major power." This would produce a third variable capturing the effects associated just with major powers in a period of bipolarity. Situations where the effects of variables change smoothly over time are more difficult but possible to deal with. This might be the case, for instance, if we believed that the balance of capabilities effectively mattered less than institutional democracy as time passes (Wendt 1999; Cederman 2001).

If we have specific theoretical arguments specifying how coefficients should change over time, then one relatively efficient solution is to include particular interactive variables to estimate the expected effect, for instance "time since last dispute" × "balance of forces." If we believe that coefficients vary in relation to continuous time, then time-varying-parameter models are another way to address this problem (Cederman 2001). We investigate this problem in chapter 6, where we use time-interactive dummies to model how the effects of various expected utility equilibria conditions evolve over time.

Uncertainty, Rational Expectations, and the
Limits to Knowledge

Recent work by Fearon and others suggests that there may be an upper bound to the predictability of conflict due to the strategic nature of the decisions leading to international war. The argument is perhaps made most clearly by Fearon (1995; see also Blainey 1988), who argues that it is critical for rationalist theories of international politics to consider why wars ever occur, given that fighting is an inefficient conflict resolution or bargaining mechanism. In any situation where two (or more) sides disagree over the distribution of some stake, rational parties should seek the most efficient (least costly) solution to the disagreement. However, violent and expensive contests such as wars impose large costs on the participants in the process of achieving some settlement. If rational, and assuming the two sides gain no utility from expressive behavior, both parties to such an expensive contest should prefer ex ante to settle the disagreement at the final terms without suffering the costs of the contest.

This poses a puzzle for theorizing about war: since states expect war to be costly, why do they fight before reaching a mutually agreeable settlement? Fearon argues that uncertainty about the war's likely outcome is perhaps the most general explanation of why conflict occurs in the international system. If the parties to a disagreement shared accurate predictions about the costs and outcome of a contest, they would likely settle before the contest occurred. According to this logic, without uncertainty, we would have no costly contests (Fearon also points to potential problems of commitment and divisibility but focuses on the role of private information). Seeing such costly contests, uncertainty is likely a critical factor leading to an increased likelihood of war. Uncertainty in this perspective occurs in the form of private information held by actors and beliefs about factors such as military capabilities and resolve. As long as we cannot measure private information, we cannot directly test the theory, nor can we hope to be able to accurately predict with certainty which situations will lead to war and which will not.

One implication of this argument is that uncertainty is an important variable that should be included in our empirical models of conflict if we can measure its nature or magnitude. We could rewrite our statistical equation again, splitting our error term into two parts, one being uncertainty as discussed previously and one being the more conventional stochastic error with a mean of zero:

$$Y_{ijt} = \alpha_{ijt} + \beta_{ijt}X_{ijt} + U_{ijt} + \varepsilon_{ijt}. \tag{2.4}$$

In equation (2.4), U_{ijt} represents rationalist arguments about the systematic role of uncertainty as it affects our dependent variable, while ε_{ijt} includes truly stochastic or random unobservable effects, assumed to have a mean of zero. Uncertainty may have some distribution different from the distribution of the ε_{ijt} error term. Models that focus on information and signaling are really focusing on the U term as distinct from ε.

Gartzke (2000) develops in detail the logical implications of this representation for what we can and cannot know about the initiation of interstate conflict. If we are unable to eliminate U (which by definition we cannot), then there is an upper bound to the predictability of conflict. Gartzke argues persuasively that we may never be able to predict international conflicts with high levels of certainty. If Fearon and others are on the right track by emphasizing strategic uncertainty as the source of most conflict, the best we may be able to do is to identity situations where the likelihood of conflict occurring is a fifty-fifty proposition. Scholars face a theoretically imposed limit to how much we can understand about international conflict. As Gartzke (2000) provocatively puts it, the wars that actually occur do so only "in the error term"—not in the parameters we estimate because of the immeasurable influence of uncertainty. Again, this theoretical limit occurs because the private information that drives uncertainty is by definition immeasurable. In turn, if a critical factor in a model is immeasurable, it will necessarily cause the systematic variance in our model to fit at less than 100 percent. We might be able to predict at a higher than fifty-fifty rate either if we as analysts know what the leaders themselves do not (but this strikes us as implausible) or if leaders behave irrationally in systematic ways.

It is important to note that this necessity of imperfect fit does not emerge from the more conventional sources of error in the term e in our initial model. In the naive behavioral approach using statistical analysis, the assumption is that if we could properly specify our theoretical model (that is, include all relevant theoretically specified variables), and if we could measure our concepts without error, then we should be able to achieve a 100 percent success rate in prediction (reflected in, for instance, an R^2 of 1.0). Gartzke's argument suggests that, given rational decision makers, even if scholars specify everything in their model exactly right, their rate of correct predictions could not exceed 50 percent. It also leads to a slightly different interpretation of the effects associated with the other conjectures and their indicators found in β. Following Fearon and Gartzke's logic, the other variables in our model then correlate with the situations where informational uncertainty is most relevant, and hence the situations where conflict is most likely to reach the upper bound of predictability.

We may well be able to identify dyads, time periods, countries, or other spatial and temporal aggregations of actors that are prone to conflict with some frequency. That is, we may be able to identify the times and places where the risk of conflict is roughly fifty-fifty compared to the international system's overall risk of war of approximately 1/400 dyad-years. But because the outbreak of any individual war or conflict is driven by uncertainty, and consistent with Riker's (1980) gloomy expectations noted in chapter 1, we will never be able to make an accurate point prediction about the outbreak of any single war or crisis.

The nature of this theorized upper limit to prediction remains to be more completely developed. This limit frames the expectations we should have for any successful theory development and testing efforts in at least two important ways. First, it further strengthens our earlier argument about the probabilistic nature of theories and conjectures in international politics, although for a different reason (the nature of uncertainty and information rather than human "randomness" or misspecification). Second, it suggests that being able to identify situations where conflict is a fifty-fifty proposition may be the best we can do using observable ex ante data. As a result, we should temper our expectations for the performance of all statistical models of strategic behavior. While at times it may appear that empirical predictions are weak in highly strategic settings such as those leading to international conflict, in fact, the measures developed over the past forty years may be performing extraordinarily well once we understand the upper bounds to what these models can explain and what they cannot. Of course, the existence of this predictive limit hinges on the rationalist assumptions that international actors are engaged in bargaining and are concerned with avoiding ex post inefficiency.

It is important to note that this limit to knowledge in predicting conflict is not a problem associated solely with statistical (or, more generally, large-n) approaches. Rather, these limits exist for all approaches to understanding conflict where the aim is prediction rather than retrospective understanding. Since the source of the problem lies in uncertainty and private information, no methodology that relies on evidence can solve it. In fact, of the available testing approaches, statistical tools provide the most leverage on the problem. Over several iterations, we can understand tendencies and probabilities that allow us to approach the limit of predictive understanding. Assuming we are only able to predict wars with probabilistic accuracy, these predictions are reliable only in samples large enough to reduce random error to acceptable levels. While archival methods will continue to reveal ex post private information that decision makers held when they made the decisions leading to war (something the approach here cannot capture), they cannot predict future conflicts beyond the limits we have discussed, which affect all research.

COMMON QUESTIONS ABOUT COMPARATIVE HYPOTHESIS TESTING

Throughout this chapter, we have given our perspective on comparative hypothesis testing. Along the way, we have also addressed several possible problems with this approach. Here, we bring together some additional possible concerns and attempt to address them more comprehensively.

Can You Test an Explanation of War with Just a Single Dependent Variable?

We test the arguments and conjectures presented later by comparing their predictions to the evidence. Our research design focuses on predictions and evidence in only one area of state behavior, international war. Some might argue that conflict theories might have important implications for a variety of areas other than or in addition to conflict initiation. For instance, balance of power advocates have used the concept of power balances to make predictions about alliance formation (Walt 1987), behavior under different system structures (Waltz 1979), the national imperative for expansion (Schweller 1996), and how violent conflict correlates with situations of power balance or imbalance (Mearsheimer 2001). These authors correctly point out that a theory is more than a prediction of a single empirical relationship. Rather, a theory is a set of closely related set of assumptions and logical arguments designed to illuminate a causal process. To test a theory we must assess its predictions across a number of events; for instance, if we see states' actions following the patterns predicted by the theory and we observe relationships that the theory predicts in multiple areas, then we should be relatively more likely to accept the veracity of the theory.

Our concern here, however, starts from the opposite direction, namely, the puzzle of explaining violent international conflict and assessing the value of the arguments and conjectures that purport to be able to predict the relative risk of international conflict. From the behaviorist perspective, we do not want theories for the sake of having theory per se. Rather, we want theories that help us to understand and to predict future empirical patterns of behavior. In our case, we have narrowed our focus to the empirics of international war. If the evidence about when conflict is more or less likely does not support the key hypothesis from some theory, or if we do not find consistent support for some empirical conjecture about the relative likelihood of war, this raises important questions about the value of "international relations theory." If an explanation of international conflict cannot predict conflict, either its likelihood or severity, then what good is it? Our concern is with the scientific nuances of prediction, not the aesthetics of retrospection. Some argue that balance of power models do not explain much of the observable interstate violence and instead only suggest what kinds of coalitions will emerge (Schweller 1996; Levi 2002). This take on balance of power theory is not of interest to us here, as it does not predict the behavior we are seeking to explain and only explains possible prior steps in the conflict process.

What about Relationships between Theories?

Because theories are more than single predictions of behavior but instead posit a set of underlying linkages, some theories are logically compatible while others are not. For instance, balance of power and power transition arguments make opposite predictions about whether conditions of power equality increase or decrease the chances of conflict. Power transition theorists add further that it is not just equality, but equality plus the presence of a dynamic transition and dissatisfaction, that drives conflict (Lemke 2002). If we include variables from each argument in an additive statistical model, the contradictory causal logic of these two explanations makes it impossible for both sets of variables simultaneously to affect conflict behavior in the direction adherents expect. Whether it is due to weak operationalization or possible logical flaws in a theory, if our results suggest that two logically opposed arguments or propositions both work, it would be an indication that we must carefully examine the models, their assumptions, and the nature of the operational measures.

What Does Using an Additive Statistical Model Imply?

Our tests in chapter 4 primarily exploit an additive specification in a multinomial logit model. In practice, few if any theories of international conflict are comprehensive enough to provide a description of a complete data-generating process, which logically would exclude the possible validity of other arguments. As we noted earlier, most "theories" of conflict are actually not really theories at all but rather empirically based descriptions of some factor believed to influence the likelihood of interstate conflict. These so-called theories typically do not provide any explicit consideration regarding which other factors might also warrant simultaneous consideration or exclusion.[4] By focusing on individual factors, authors implicitly assert that "this single causal factor matters and others do not," or else they unwittingly assume away the problem of omitted variable bias in the tests at hand.

The story we try to convey throughout this book is that most theories or conjectures on the initiation and escalation of conflict simply are capturing isolated examples of the multiple factors that influence policymakers' decision making. We know that many factors influence decision making in the real world; leaders are constantly subject to the push and pull of competing interest groups often with mutually exclusive preferences. Taken as a group, our models of international conflict reflect this understanding of the real world. However, individual tests of a single or a few factors in isolation do not. As Clarke (2001, 730–31) points out, we are testing a "supermodel" of international conflict that he also refers to as "artificial" and atheoretic. We believe that the models need not be, however, given the plausible assumption that many forces simultaneously influence leaders' decisions and therefore the risk of conflict.

Can We Test a Theory with a Single Independent Variable?

Previously we discussed testing theories, hunches, and conjectures using a single dependent variable (the level of militarized conflict). It is equally important to consider whether we can test a "theory" using a single independent variable. Many models of international conflict specify simple and direct relationships between a single variable and conflict and as such are not really theories but rather hypotheses or conjectures that we can test in straightforward fashion. For instance, some long-cycle explanations of conflict suggest that particular global economic conditions are favorable to conflict. There is a single variable, "global economic prosperity," that Goldstein (1988) argues should influence the dependent variable "international war." In these cases, obviously, we need to only include a measure of the single relevant concept to be able to assess the empirical validity of the argument. Other models posit more complicated, interdependent relationships between any numbers of concepts that do not readily lend themselves to simplistic testing schemes. For instance, realists commonly argue that the anarchic character of the international system affects the nature and behavior of interstate alliances. The number and scale of alliances in some conceptions define polarity, which in turn affects the relatively likelihood of conflict. Given our concern here—predicting conflict—it is appropriate to focus on the final relationship in this process—the relationship between polarity and conflict. If there is no empirically verifiable relationship between polarity and conflict, then the concept of "polarity" does not help us to predict the onset of war and we must question whether and how neorealism *theory* is useful to us (from the perspective of trying to understand better the onset of interstate disputes and war). In this example, if we find that alliances do affect conflict but polarity does not, then it would suggest that some parts of the realist causal argument are flawed.

What about Conditionality?

Some models or approaches predict that several variables should affect conflict, in some instances conditionally. By "conditionally," we simply mean that the argument in question suggests that variables will have particular effects only in the presence of other conditions. For instance, power transition models predict that equal power between states contributes to an increased risk of conflict. But conflict should emerge only when a rough bilateral equality of power combines with a shift in the two states' relative power, marking a transition from one state being in the lead to its suddenly being behind, simultaneously combined with the overtaking state being dissatisfied with the nature of the rules that constitute the international system. We can easily test propositions that specify such conditionality simply by building and including appropriate interactive variables. For the case of power transition models, such an interaction term could simply be "equal power" times "rapid power movement" times "satisfaction." If there is either unequal power or no movement, the variable will have a value near zero, whereas only if power is equal and there is a transition will the variable have a value of one. Of course, if we only included the variables for "power" and "movement" separately, we would not properly capture the conditionality aspect of the power transition logic. As a result, the inclusion of appropriate interactions is critical for proper testing of many arguments and hypotheses.

A similar approach can account for arguments that focus on "context." Signorino's (1999) point that the inclusion of "component" utility variables may be inappropriate in the presence of strategic interaction is correct but easily remedied by the inclusion of terms that do capture strategic interactions such as point predictions of various equilibria.

Finally, for some arguments or conjectures, single variables quite accurately represent or capture the intuition of the argument. For instance, if we expect a curvilinear relationship between the independent variable and conflict behavior, as Mansfield (1994) argues regarding the relationship between system power concentration and the onset of war, we must include a polynomial term to capture the effect. Alternatively, a "theory" might predict that one variable should be positive but another negative, as Snyder (2000) speculates regarding the relationship between democracy, democratization, and war. In this case, our test of Snyder's argument consists of evaluating several variables simultaneously. This involves assessing the substantive effects of the block of two or more variables together, as well as the statistical significance of the individual variables. For instance, to test the dyadic variant of the democratic peace conjecture we estimate a model with the democracy level of a conflict initiator, the democracy level of the target, and the interaction of those levels. We examine the explanatory power of the variables by varying both the individual democracy scores as well as the interaction term.

What about the Possibility of Varying Effects across Different Levels of Conflict?

Commonly, theories built around rational expectations, selection effects, or signaling mechanisms contain careful deductive language, with assumptions and causal logic explicitly stated. Sometimes empirical tests of the causal mechanism do not lead to clear-cut results as we might expect to see in more simplistic conjectures. For example, when leaders strategically select their actions, we commonly see positive effects on the likelihood of conflict at one level of escalation and opposite or null effects at other levels. For example, Fearon (1994b) used this line of argument to explain why alliances appeared to have little effect on extended deterrence in Huth's work (1988). Fearon argues that, when leaders considering an attack observed an alliance between a protégé and a defender but chose to challenge the status quo anyway, they must be particularly resolved, and so we would expect an insignificant relationship between the presence of the alliance and the success and failure of the extended deterrence attempt. In the context of theories built around signaling games, leaders facing severe domestic constraints or audience costs (e.g., democracies) may be quite willing to engage in conflict at low levels and simultaneously quite averse to participating in large-scale wars (cf. Senese 1997; Gartzke 1998).

To allow our analysis to be sensitive to these types of problems, we construct our dependent variable with multiple unordered categories that reflect various levels of conflict. As a result, with tests like the ones employed here, we can examine the effects of key variables representing theories across multiple levels of conflict.

Signorino (1999) points out another way in which imprecise or poorly specified theories and tests of them create implicit limits to knowledge. Signorino argues that most theories of international relations are actually theories of strategic interaction. That is, leaders make decisions about war while taking into account the likely reactions and responses of their opponents, either domestic political ones or international military ones. If this is the case, then simple decision-theoretic arguments about the presumed relationships between variables and international conflict are likely to be wrong and, even worse, may suggest including variables in a form that will lead to incorrect inferences about the variables' effects. Two implications of this argument then follow. First, when testing these theories based on the logic of strategic choice, we must be very careful to include variables in a form that matches the theory's internal logic (such as including game theoretic equilibria and not the expected utility components that factor into the equilibria). Second, our "theories" must be specified clearly enough to allow us to determine this form. Unfortunately, most so-called theories of international politics do not do this. Instead, they pose far looser or poorly specified relationships among vague concepts. In our analysis, we are unable to take each of the theories we include and redevelop their arguments in keeping with strict deductive logic. Rather, we take their hypothesized relationships and measures and include them "as is" for testing. If these "theories" suffer from flaws in their internal logic, or the operational variables do not accurately measure the causal influences, this may result in empirical findings that are inconsistent with the theories' predictions.

How Meaningful Is It to Talk about "Relative Predictive Power"?

We have repeatedly discussed the relative power of different models, and comparing theoretical arguments based on their relative explanatory or predictive power. Some may wonder how this is possible. We discuss the details of our methodology for predicting the probability of conflict from our comparative model in the next chapter, but we provide a preview here to demonstrate that relative comparisons among competing explanations and conjectures are feasible and can be quite useful. As we have discussed, one or more variables represent each argument or conjecture in the models we estimate. We assess the effects of individual variables by focusing on the relative risk of conflict initiation and escalation, that is, the increase in the risk of conflict caused when an independent variable changes by some known amount. For instance, if the probability of conflict in a dyad went from 1 percent to 3 percent when the democracy scores of the potential initiator went from highly democratic to highly autocratic, we would assess the increase in risk at "3x," a threefold increase in the odds of conflict. For any variable in our model, we can estimate the increase in the relative risk of conflict in this manner. We can then make meaningful comparisons because the effects are in the same units (multiples of conflict risk); if changing one variable increases the risk of conflict three times and changing another increases the risk four times, then we will say that the second factor or argument has a relatively stronger effect.

The key to comparing the effects associated with the various propositions is to ensure that we are changing the values of the independent variables by a "comparable" amount (if we change one variable across its full range and another by a fraction of how it could change, then the comparison would be meaningless). This appears at first glance to be difficult, as there is no common metric for a wide set of independent variables measured using different scales. Democracy scores, for instance, are measured on a 20-point scale developed by the Polity project, while arms races are simply either present or absent, and the power concentration of the international system is measured on a scale potentially ranging from 0 to 1 (and in our data set between about 0.2 and 0.3). Nevertheless, even though the scales are different, we can still speak of "typical" changes in these variables based on the observed patterns found in the real world. For theories marked with dummy variables, this is relatively easy, as we can simply identify the no (0) versus yes (1) condition. With continuous variables, we use the mean as a typical value and use standard deviations to identify a range of real-world values that occur with some known probability.[5] Given normally distributed variables, we would expect that, given a large enough sample, 95 percent of the cases in a set of data will fall within plus or minus two standard deviations of the mean. Most of our variables do not follow the normal distribution, so therefore the standard deviation does not capture precisely this number of cases for all variables. Nevertheless, it does give us some indication of the range of values we see in the real world. We can then use the standard deviation to suggest specific cut points in the data set where we will assess the estimated probability of war. In most cases we choose to change the values of the independent variables by two standard deviations, moving from one standard deviation below the variable's mean to one standard deviation above the mean, a range that approximates a common set of occurrences. Note, however, that we are not using the once-common approach of presenting standardized regression coefficients. We focus on real-world changes in each variable to project outcome probabilities, but our unit of change is simply standard deviations for convenience as a measure of typical values. The fact that the variables use different scales is not a problem. By focusing on the range of data one standard deviation above or below the mean, our results remain general, so that we can look across theories and variables at the explanatory power in terms of relative risk. If one chooses the values for the simulation unwisely, of course, then the comparison may simply not be a very useful one. We agree with Clarke (2001) that we do not want to use this information to select the model with the greatest number of important variables and then present this set of independent variables as a better model of politics than another. We take exception, however, to Clarke's (2001, 730) assertion that we cannot meaningfully compare the effects of several variables, given changes in independent variable values and outcome probabilities.

Comparisons of other variable shifts could be useful in other settings, particularly for policymakers choosing what actions to undertake in the context of a budget constraint. Many of the independent variables in the model are manipulable to greater or lesser degree. Some of the indicators do not vary in a manipulable sense at all—for example, polarity and geographic contiguity are simply descriptive facts, although in the long run polarity could perhaps be altered by conscious actions, such as European unification. Other variables are more directly manipulable by policymakers. For instance, leaders might be able to influence a country's level of democracy (Przeworski et al. 2000) or take steps to expand trade with it. Changing a country's level of democracy or trade might not be easy, or even certain, but an investment of a given size correlates with some probability of future regime change or increase in future trade flows. If we were to develop expected value estimates for each variable in our model, we could compare their relative effects based on the cost-effectiveness at reducing the risk of conflict.

Finally, we consider an analogy to our arguments concerning relative explanatory power, namely, the question of which is a more important influence on a child's development, its environment or its heredity. If genetics were the determining factor in development, then we might logically resign ourselves to never improving our fate (future advances in gene therapy notwithstanding). Of course, in reality we expect that both environment and genetics play an interactive role in influencing the growth and achievement of children. Children who are brought up in loving homes, with adequate food and education, are likely to do better than those raised in less advantageous environments. Simultaneously, children with certain genetic traits are likely to grow faster or suffer fewer ailments compared to those with a different genetic makeup.

When cast in such general terms as "environment" and "heredity," the question of relative importance has no meaningful answer. Within the category of environment, however, specific and carefully measured environmental factors may have more or less powerful effects. If these factors, such as head start programs versus prenatal care, have comparable costs but differ greatly in their ultimate outcome, then assessing relative risks associated with the variance in manipulable factors such as a state's level of democratization is a prudent strategy. Similarly, if genetic precursors of disease are associated with varying degrees of risk, and if we possessed a limited budget for genetic screening, we would want to focus on those factors associated with the highest risks where the hope of gene therapy was greatest. In the context of international relations, given that the actors are strategic, simply knowing that a given situation is potentially dangerous may lead decision makers to be more risk averse than they would be otherwise, thereby potentially averting conflicts we would otherwise expect to see. Absent this sort of comparative explanatory knowledge, advocating policy on efficiency grounds becomes next to impossible. In the next chapter, we turn to a fuller discussion of our selection of the theories, hypotheses, and conjectures we investigate, as well as our research methodology. In chapter 4, we will examine each of the arguments and the key variables that we derive from them. We then turn to our actual tests and to a comparison of the various arguments' explanatory power.

3 CHOOSING AND TESTING THE ARGUMENTS: THE PRACTICE AND PITFALLS OF COMPARATIVE HYPOTHESIS TESTING

dear friend, all theory is gray, and green the golden tree of life.
—johann goethe, 1832

To test the validity and explanatory power of our hypotheses on conflict initiation and escalation we must complete two basic tasks. First, we must choose the hypotheses we wish to test. While there are many models of international conflict, as well as innumerable arguments and asserted empirical regularities, not all hypotheses are suitable for comparative testing using statistical tools. Second, we must design and construct a suitable data set. Assembling the data needed to test a large number of competing arguments drawn from multiple levels of analysis is not a trivial undertaking. We turn to these tasks later.

To be included in our analysis, a model or empirical assertion must make empirical claims that are falsifiable, are testable quantitatively, and can be specified using ex ante information. First, by "falsifiable," we mean that there must be conditions or facts we can observe that would be inconsistent with the predictions of the argument. We cannot test, for example, the neorealist assertion that anarchy contributes to the repeated formation and collapse of balances of power and therefore international war. "Realists" assume that anarchy is an ever-present condition—a constant. Measurement concerns aside, being an invariant condition, systemic anarchy is not amenable to the type of analysis we employ here.

Second, the arguments' hypotheses must be testable using quantitative evidence. We know of no other epistemological approach that would allow us to evaluate a large number of hypotheses, while simultaneously letting us control for dozens of alternative explanations as well as

35

allowing us to generate comparable predictions of associated explanatory power. Importantly, however, our method excludes several theoretical approaches, perhaps most notably arguments based on models of human cognition, which we cannot test or compare using our research design and data. This is particularly unfortunate because psychologically based theories are the natural alternative to rational choice arguments about politics. The most efficient way to test cognitive or psychological theories is to use an experimental design (McDermott 1999).

Finally, to be included in our tests, the conditions that purportedly influence the initiation or escalation of conflict must be measurable ex ante. That is, the condition must be identifiable in advance of the events in question. For example, using ex ante information, we cannot test offense-defense balance arguments (e.g., Van Evera 1999; Biddle 1998). Van Evera argues that if the offense enjoys an intrinsic advantage over the defense, states will be more willing to initiate war. Unfortunately, the true offense-defense balance is a systemic characteristic revealed during an actual war. Leaders' beliefs about the balance (the factor that actually influences the likelihood of war) are private information, and, hence, we cannot measure them in a systematic and wide-ranging fashion.

Partly for this reason, we exclude some variables such as "major power" status from our analysis. Although the "major power" variable is commonly found in many quantitative studies of international politics (e.g., Bremer 1992), usually its inclusion is not well justified on theoretical grounds. Typically, its operationalization and relation to conflict behavior is tautological. The large states that are most active in international politics become, by definition, major or great powers. For example, in many data sets, the United States suddenly morphs into a "great power" in 1917 by virtue of its entry into World War I. By focusing on a state's frequency of interaction, this inductive definition automatically includes states that engage in frequent conflict. It should not surprise us when we then find a strong association with major power status and the probability of a state engaging in international conflict. Alternatively, we could develop a definition of "great power" based on objective measures of some industrial or military capability—not behavior that is essentially a restatement of our dependent variable of interest. However, the development of such a measure and the logic behind it is beyond the scope of the somewhat narrower goals of this project. Regardless, collapsing a continuous variable or set of variables into a single categorical one such as great power simply throws away information.

Even with these criteria limiting our selection there are still hundreds of hypotheses we could test with a large statistical model. As an additional guide to winnow the field, we conducted a count of citations in the Social Science Citation Index (SSCI) from 1990 through 1999. In our final analysis, we include a subset of arguments that the recent literature on international conflict cites widely. While a large number of citations does not demonstrate the veracity of an argument or the validity of a conjecture, it does indicate that the academic community believes the argument deserves attention, for better or worse. The models and conjectures we include are among the most frequently cited in the SSCI, although there is substantial variation in citation frequency.[1] Table 3.1 presents the citation counts for the theories and arguments we test later.

Figures 3.1 through 3.3 present the graphical results of our investigation. For each theory, argument, or conjecture, we identified one or more books and articles. For some we identified several works, while for others there were only a few seminal pieces.[2] Figure 3.1 shows an absolute count of the total number of citations for all of the pieces associated with each theory since 1991. This initial count underrepresents the importance of models whose key works appeared after 1991, since they have not had time to become "classics." Figure 3.2 normalizes the citation count by the number of years in our time period for which we have citation counts, that is, years after the work first appears.

While corrected for time, figure 3.2 still advantages those arguments for which we were able to identify many associated and widely cited works. Attracting significant follow-on work is a mark of influence or importance, but such work may be either supportive or unsupportive of a core hypothesis. As a result, figure 3.3 further normalizes the citation count both by year and by number of pieces for which we counted citations, leading to a measure of citations per year per work.

Balance of power approaches, neorealism (polarity), psychological approaches, the democratic peace proposition, and expected utility theory appear near the top of each list. Citations of the balance of power literature (through discussions of realism and citations of Morgenthau 1956 and Waltz 1979) top all of our charts. In our analysis, we are able to include variables derived from four out of these top five, the exception being psychologically based theories, along with many of the other models and arguments on the list. Citations to articles addressing arms races and systemic hegemony are also frequent. Our statistical models will include variables emerging from the following models, conjectures, or research approaches: expected utility theory, the democratic peace proposition, balance of power, power transition, externalization/diversionary war, neorealism, system structure (power concentration and movement), hegemonic stability, arms races, democratization, alliances, nuclear and conventional deterrence, trade dependence, and economic cycle hypotheses. We also include geographic contiguity, which, while

37

TABLE 3.1.   Citation Counts for Representative Publications, 1990–99

Theory	1990	1991	1992	1993	1994	1995	1996	1997	1998	1999	Total Citations per Piece	Citations per Year per Piece, since Year of Publication	Total Citations for Theory	Citations per Year per Theory, since Year of Publication	Citations per Year per Piece
Expected Utility	20	35	39	33	49	59	59	75	47	52			468	51.6	17.2
Bueno de Mesquita (1981)	16	26	25	13	20	21	25	31	22	26	225	22.5			
Bueno de Mesquita (1985a)	4	9	7	6	6	4	2	4	1	8	51	5.1			
Bueno de Mesquita and Lalman (1992)			7	14	23	34	32	40	24	18	192	24.0			
Democratic Peace	14	40	78	92	79	120	125	172	108	130			958	127.2	15.9
Small and Singer (1976)	3	6	10	13	14	12	12	17	7	7	101	10.1			
Doyle (1983)	5	9	32	25	25	39	25	32	15	16	223	22.3			
Doyle (1986)	5	15	22	31	21	21	30	34	15	15	209	20.9			
Russett (1990)	1	10	14	23	12	20	16	16	15	12	139	13.9			
Maoz and Russett (1993)					7	22	28	39	17	31	144	24.0			
Ray (1995)						6	14	28	21	16	85	17.0			
Oneal and Russett (1997)								3	15	26	44	14.7			
Senese (1997)								3	3	7	13	4.3			
Balance of Power	70	107	113	128	123	140	126	186	141	140			1,274	127.4	42.5
Morgenthau (1956)	30	39	42	49	50	46	50	68	52	48	474	47.4			
Waltz (1979)	37	58	68	72	68	92	74	115	87	86	757	75.7			
Niou, Ordeshook, and Rose (1989)	3	10	3	7	5	2	2	3	2	6	43	4.3			

	1	2	3	4	5	6	7	8	9	10	N	%	
Power Transition	10	23	30	20	30	28	38	44	46	66	335	40.4	4.0
Organski (1958)	2	7	9	5	8	8	10	14	13	14	90	9.0	
Organski and Kugler (1980)	8	16	18	10	16	14	15	17	19	21	154	15.4	
Huth, Bennett, and Gelpi (1992)			1	3	4	5	4	4	2	1	24	3.0	
Kim (1992)			1	1	1	1	2	2	1	1	10	1.3	
Kim and Morrow (1992)			1	1	1	0	3	3	4	4	17	2.1	
Lemke (1993)							1	1	1	0	3	0.4	
Lemke and Kugler (1996)							1	1	3	7	12	2.4	
Lemke and Werner (1996)							1	1	1	4	7	1.8	
Lemke and Reed (1996)							1	1	2	12	16	4.0	
Oneal, De Soysa, and Park (1998)										2	2	1.0	
Alliances	14	10	12	20	17	21	24	27	14	20	179	17.9	2.2
Holsti, Hopman, and Sullivan (1973)	4	5	3	1	4	3	3	5	1	3	32	3.2	
Wallace (1973)	1	1	2	4	1	3	0	1	1	3	17	1.7	
Ostrom and Hoole (1978)	1	0	0	1	2	2	2	2	1	4	15	1.5	
Siverson and King (1980)	4	1	0	0	2	2	2	2	2	3	18	1.8	
Siverson and Tennefoss (1984)	1	0	2	1	3	3	5	3	1	2	21	2.1	
Snyder (1984)	3	3	4	9	3	6	6	10	7	2	53	5.3	
Oren (1990)	0	0	1	4	2	2	6	4	1	3	23	2.3	
Contiguity/Territory	3	2	1	1	12	16	18	31	15	21	120	16.4	8.2
Diehl and Goertz (1988)	3	2	1	0	3	1	0	3	2	3	18	1.8	
Vasquez (1996)				1	9	15	18	28	13	18	102	14.6	
Arms Races	36	47	69	41	69	69	37	56	60	50	534	53.4	8.9
Richardson (1960a)	9	12	10	6	9	19	11	8	8	5	97	9.7	
Jervis (1976)	25	29	51	29	42	41	22	39	42	39	359	35.9	
Wallace (1982)	0	3	1	2	6	2	1	0	2	1	18	1.8	
Diehl (1983)	1	0	1	0	4	1	1	2	5	0	15	1.5	
Diehl (1985)	1	0	1	2	5	5	1	6	1	5	27	2.7	
Morrow (1989)	0	3	5	2	3	1	1	1	2	0	18	1.8	

(continues)

TABLE 3.1.—Continued

Theory	Citation Year										Total Citations per Piece	Citations per Year per Piece, since Year of Publication	Total Citations for Theory	Citations per Year per Theory, since Year of Publication	Citations per Year per Piece
	1990	1991	1992	1993	1994	1995	1996	1997	1998	1999					
Democratization						1	14	38	28	33			114	31.0	7.8
Mansfield and Snyder (1995)						1	13	29	15	22	80	16.0			
Enterline (1996)							1	7	6	2	16	4.0			
Thompson and Tucker (1997)								2	7	9	18	6.0			
Ward and Gleditsch (1998)									3	7	10	5.0			
Hegemony	29	48	48	50	43	45	35	70	55	60			483	51.3	12.8
Krasner (1976)	7	13	15	14	6	6	6	13	13	10	103	10.3			
Gilpin (1981)	22	35	33	36	36	30	18	48	37	40	335	33.5			
Kindleberger (1981)	0	0	0	0	0	0	0	0	0	0	0	0.0			
Mansfield (1994)					1	9	11	9	5	10	45	7.5			
Polarity	45	64	82	95	80	106	91	130	99	93			885	88.5	17.7
Deutsch and Singer (1964)	3	2	6	7	5	4	7	4	2	2	42	4.2			
Bueno de Mesquita (1978)	2	1	3	5	3	3	2	1	2	2	24	2.4			
Waltz (1979)	37	58	68	72	68	92	74	115	87	86	757	75.7			
Snyder (1984)	3	3	4	9	3	6	6	10	7	2	53	5.3			
Wayman (1984)	0	0	1	2	1	1	2	0	1	1	9	0.9			
Long Cycles/Kondratieff Waves	35	36	42	37	31	30	22	27	13	30			303	30.7	5.1
Kondratieff (1935)	11	4	7	5	4	3	5	7	3	5	54	5.4			
Doran and Parsons (1980)	3	1	6	2	7	2	3	2	0	4	30	3.0			
Modelski (1987)	9	10	8	8	10	9	5	10	1	4	74	7.4			
Goldstein (1988)	12	19	18	15	9	8	5	5	7	15	113	11.3			
Beck (1991)		1	0	3	0	2	1	0	0	0	7	0.8			
Goldstein (1991)		1	3	4	1	6	3	3	2	2	25	2.8			

	1	2	3	4	5	6	7	8	9	10	Total	Mean	SD
System Structure	6	8	8	8	13	12	21	23	9	17	125	12.5	7.8
Singer, Bremer, and Stuckey (1972)	6	8	8	8	12	3	10	14	4	7	80	8.0	
Mansfield (1994)					1	9	11	9	5	10	45	4.5	
Psychological Models	56	50	81	31	61	69	38	62	60	60	568	56.8	18.9
Jervis (1976)	25	29	51	19	42	41	22	39	42	39	349	34.9	
Lebow (1981)	15	13	14	9	12	19	10	14	11	14	131	13.1	
Jervis, Lebow, and Stein (1985)	16	8	16	3	7	9	6	9	7	7	88	8.8	
Diversionary Conflict/Polity Change	8	27	23	24	30	26	30	41	41	53	303	30.3	7.1
Blainey (1988)	5	11	13	9	18	9	12	14	14	21	126	12.6	
Gelpi (1997)								1	3	4	8	0.8	
Levy (1988)	2	8	3	7	5	8	8	10	8	6	65	6.5	
Levy (1989)	1	8	7	8	7	9	9	11	9	12	81	8.1	
Smith (1996a)							1	5	7	10	23	2.3	
Conventional Deterrence	12	9	13	8	17	11	9	17	24	16	136	13.6	6.8
Huth (1988)	4	4	5	5	11	5	4	10	9	5	62	6.2	
Mearsheimer (1983)	8	5	8	3	6	6	5	7	15	11	74	7.4	
Nuclear Deterrence	92	88	81	126	102	115	109	105	106	99	1,023	102.3	20.5
Betts (1987)	9	6	6	5	6	3	3	6	6	3	53	5.3	
Huth (1990)	0	0	3	1	2	2	1	0	2	1	12	1.2	
Powell (1989)	1	4	3	4	0	3	3	0	2	2	22	2.2	
Sagan (1985)	8	2	2	3	1	1	2	2	2	2	25	2.5	
Schelling (various)	74	76	67	113	93	106	100	97	94	91	911	91.1	

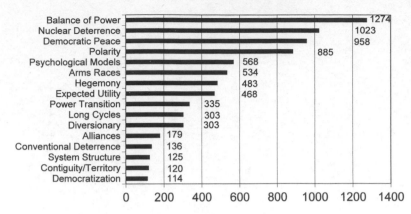

Fig. 3.1. Total citations, Social Science Citation Index (1990–99)

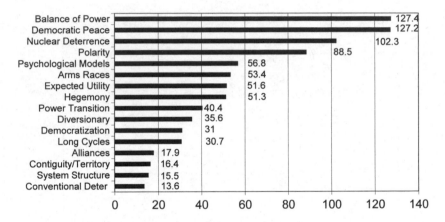

Fig. 3.2. Total citations per year, Social Science Citation Index (1990–99)

not a theory by any stretch of the imagination, has been perhaps the most consistent and substantively powerful control factor included in analyses of international politics. Because many of the factors of theoretical interest such as democracy and democratization cluster geographically, controlling for contiguity will help minimize any bias we might suffer otherwise.

The hotly contested trend in current research toward the rational choice approach in general, and game theory in particular, might suggest that the formal model of strategic decision making tested here will

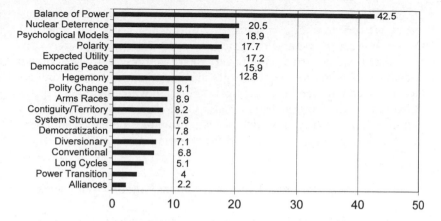

Fig. 3.3.   Citations per year per work, Social Science Citation Index
(1990–99)

prove to be more powerful than other international systemic factors. Aside from hypotheses deduced from Bueno de Mesquita and Lalman's (1992) IIG, which we carefully test, many of the other models are also rationalist in nature. Nevertheless, they are not formally stated deductive theories that follow standard rational choice axioms such as transitivity of preferences. The results we present in the chapters that follow suggest that political scientists' newfound faith in formal models of social choice theory is potentially misplaced, as our results indicate, at best, modest effects associated with variables representing this approach. Of course, proponents of expected utility theory may argue that measurement error is severely attenuating our results. Regardless, without operational measures we cannot test hypotheses, and so measurement issues go hand in hand with theory development in this analysis. Other competing dyadic approaches (e.g., arms races, joint democracy), while also posing thorny measurement challenges, will prove to be more strongly associated with the relative risk of international conflict than will our game theory equilibria predictions, even after controlling for numerous other factors.

THE DATA

Our second task is to assemble an appropriate data set covering a temporal range of over 175 years. To control for the effects of the dozens of variables needed to operationalize our sixteen models and arguments, we turn to a large-n statistical approach. As with any quantitative analysis, it is essential that the tests exploit an appropriately conceptualized and constructed data set. Next, we present a wide-ranging discussion of some of the trade-offs and alternatives that researchers face in research design and statistical estimation when planning a quantitative analysis in international politics. We then present an overview of our overall research approach or plan, providing a detailed summary of our research design choices and the resulting data set.

Data Construction and Evaluation: Some Fundamental Issues

Three fundamental sets of questions arise when setting out to execute a quantitative analysis of some puzzle in international politics. The first set of questions involves research design. These issues include the population of cases one should analyze, the type of sample drawn from that population, and critical decisions about the unit of analysis and various exclusions from the data set. A second important question is what particular statistical estimator to use. We discuss three important alternative methods that have been used recently for the analysis of international conflict, namely, multinomial logit with a "peace-years" spline (the estimator we use for most of our analysis), GEE panel estimation, and a fixed-effects logit model. The third question addresses the set of competing explanations. With a sample of cases in hand, and an appropriate estimator selected, the intrepid researcher also needs to choose a suitable set of control variables. In the remainder of this chapter, we address the first two issues; the third we tackle in the next chapter.

The choices we make in addressing these questions sometimes have important effects on our results, while at other times the relationships between our independent and dependent variables are relatively robust in the face of different research designs and estimators. Not knowing beforehand which situation one is in, it is important to think through and explicitly justify one's choices a priori rather than after the fact.

RESEARCH DESIGN ISSUES

The Starting Point: Dyadic Analysis

We start our discussion of an appropriate research design from the perspective that dyadic analysis offers the best way to test comparatively hypotheses drawn from multiple levels of analysis. The directed dyad-year is increasingly the favored unit of analysis for quantitative studies of international conflict (Green, Kim, and Yoon 2001). One reason for this is that dyadic interaction lies at the heart of strategic behavior. A second reason is that using the dyad-year makes it possible to examine explanations from multiple levels of analysis. In particular, directed dyad-year studies can easily include variables from the individual state level (e.g., polity type), dyadic level (e.g., balance of power, distance), and system level (e.g., polarity, system uncertainty) in studies of conflict initiation as follows. (1) Because each dyad-year contains two states, we can test hypotheses such as those developed from balance of power theory that demand information on two states. Since each dyad has a direction, with one state identified as a potential dispute initiator and the other the potential target, we can test hypotheses drawn from theories of deliberate dispute initiation by one party against another. (2) We can also test hypotheses about the general likelihood of conflict as compared to the deliberate choice of war, because hypotheses about the likelihood of conflict imply that at least one state *must* have a higher probability of initiating a conflict (conflict cannot occur without an initiation by one state). (3) Directed dyads let us include unit-level information that may affect the likelihood of conflict, such as the initiator's regime type or the target's level of democratization. (4) Finally, we can also test system-level arguments. If the nature of the international system plays an important role in the onset of international conflict, then system-level effects must ultimately influence the decisions of individual states. If the international system in one period is more conflict prone than in another, this will appear in a higher probability of multiple states initiating conflict.

Directed dyad analysis offers the most straightforward way to examine hypotheses at multiple levels of analysis. Studies built around higher levels of aggregation (e.g., the system-year) must omit dyadic and unit-level features of states as variables influencing conflict or else must aggregate from such lower-level attributes to some system-level characteristic (such as the percentage of states with some characteristic), thereby risking problems with ecological inference. Studies at this higher level of aggregation also must combine information on the dependent variable into aggregated summary characteristics, such as a count of conflicts. Such aggregation throws away important information, such as who is fighting with whom.

Studies cast at lower levels of analysis, that is, the monadic or country-year level, also lose information to aggregation. Country-year analyses can include information about systemic characteristics (e.g., polarity in some year). However, the dependent variable must still be some characteristic of the country in a year (e.g., number of disputes a state was involved in), again losing information on who fought with whom. If dyadic information is to be included, it again must be included through some aggregation mechanism, such as taking information on the largest dyadic threat or the average polity score of surrounding states.

The widely accepted unit of time common to nearly all quantitative analyses of international politics is the year. In pragmatic terms, annual data for the key variables of interest are widely available, while data from shorter periods (e.g., the quarter, month, or week) are available only for limited numbers of states and, generally, more recent time periods. There is also a theoretical rationale for focusing on annual data. The year represents a natural political break due to budget cycles, electoral cycles, and the presence of winter or a rainy season in most of the world that hampers military action and makes military decisions a somewhat time-dependent process. If leaders make their decision to use force while considering annual or seasonal timing (evidence that they do so includes Blainey's [1988, 98] finding that war initiation is highly seasonal), then this unit of time is reasonable.

Directed versus Nondirected Analyses: Unit of Analysis and Variables

The terms "directed" and "nondirected" provide further specification to the dyad as a unit of analysis. Taking a given dyad-year, such as the United States and the USSR in 1953, a nondirected dyadic analysis has one case:

1. U.S.   USSR   1953

A directed analysis would have two possible cases:

1. U.S.   USSR   1953
2. USSR   U.S.   1953

With the dyad-year, already the typical unit of analysis in international politics, the switch to the directed dyad-year is of relatively small consequence from a statistical perspective. Moving from (for example) three hundred thousand observations in a nondirected analysis to six hundred thousand has only a minor effect on standard errors because the *n* is already quite large (Beck 1998).

The second important implication of separating the dyad into separate directions is that a directed dyad study easily allows for choices and outcomes to be different in the two directions. If the dependent variable was whether some demand occurred between states A and B, for instance, a demand could occur in either individual direction, in both directions, or in neither. With a nondirected analysis, the analyst must aggregate the outcome, typically using an ordinal variable that neither, only one, or both states made demands. For the analysis that follows, we use the Militarized Interstate Dispute (MID) data set (version 2.1, Correlates of War 1999). Where there are multiple MIDs within a dyad in a single year, we measure the characteristics of the first MID. We code our dependent variable based on the initiation of a militarized dispute by one state against another. We focus only on the first day of conflict and exclude "joiners" into a conflict (discussed later). The decision to drop joiners means we will not overcount large conflicts. For example, our World War dyads do not code as separate disputes every state on the allied side versus every state on the axis side (or every state in the triple alliance versus every state in the triple entente).

Our use of directed dyads leads to an important difference in how we can formulate the dependent variable versus what we would necessarily do if we used a nondirected analysis. In a directed analysis using MID data, the dependent variable can take the form of "state A initiated a dispute against state B." In a nondirected analysis, though, the dependent variable must take the form of "a MID occurred between states A and B." There is a subtle but important theoretical distinction between these two-dependent variables. Nondirected analyses allow us to study the onset of conflict but less elegantly the deliberate initiation of force by one state against another. An important consequence when using nondirected dyads is that it is more difficult to test rational choice models and other similar hypotheses that specify the targeted decisions and actions of individual states. If the theory under consideration specifies that a particular state is more likely to initiate conflict, then a directed design is appropriate. On the other hand, if a theory specifies only that some situation is "prone" to conflict, then a nondirected design will suffice.

Third, the independent variables that can be (and usually are) included in directed dyad-year analysis are rather different from those we might include in a nondirected analysis. For instance, directional variables tied to the state-level identity of the potential initiator and potential target can be easily included in a directed analysis, with a clear distinction between the two states in a dyad. If we believe that individual states' characteristics affect the initiator's behavior differently than they do the target's—for example, by making the initiator more likely to act if it alone has characteristic X—then these variables can easily be included in directed dyads. Similarly, particular characteristics of the target that might cause the initiator to act (for example, brutal political repression within the potential target state) can also be included. Dyadic variables that are directional, such as the initiator's probability of winning a war against a specific target, can also be included in a directed dyadic analysis.

In contrast, in a typical nondirected data set where the dependent variable is the onset of conflict, it is more difficult to include separate and clearly identified state-level variables for the initiator and target. It also requires additional assumptions to convert individual-level variables into a nondirected form. Consider regime type, commonly measured as a state's level of democracy. If we use nondirectional dyads, then the data can contain information only of the form "democracy$_A$" and "democracy$_B$," with A and B being entirely arbitrary. We must then combine or transform these individual variables to eliminate identity and directionality to create a variable that is usable in nondirected analysis. For example, we must compute variables such as the average or minimum value of a variable across A and B, such as "democracy$_{HIGH}$" and "democracy$_{LOW}$," or the ratio of the larger to the smaller. Ideally, theoretical concerns would drive this type of variable construction. In their nondirected analyses of the democratic peace proposition, Oneal and Russett adopt the "weak link" hypothesis initially presented in Dixon (1993, 1994) and use the lower democracy or trade dependence score between two states in a nondirected dyad (Oneal and Russett 1999a; Russett and Oneal 1999). They argue that the state with the lower democracy score drives the observed relationship (and, similarly, the lower trade dependence of the two states, the lower economic growth, and so forth). While this approach seems plausible, it does impose an additional untested assumption, the weak link hypotheses. Unfortunately, we cannot test the assumption in a nondirected framework, because we have already assumed that the hypothesis is true during the process of variable construction. In combination with a dependent variable of "dispute occurrence," the inclusion of a lower score (or any other nonactor specific variable) does not allow us to judge the effect of democracy on the particular actions of the initiator, target, or some other particular actor.

In summary, nondirectional independent variables pose both practical and theoretical problems when testing hypotheses that (1) predict conflict initiation (as opposed to conflict onset), (2) specify particular directed actions, or (3) focus on selection effects. Consider Bueno de

Mesquita and Lalman's (1992) IIG, the only one of our arguments meeting the criteria of true theory. The IIG predicts the equilibrium outcome from directed dyadic interactions. The expected outcome of the game may be different, depending on who moves first. Because the outcome of an A-B interaction may be different from the outcome of B-A, we need to apply the game's predictions to directed dyads, as nondirected analysis cannot differentiate A-B from B-A. If we force variables such as the IIG predictions into a nondirected dyadic analysis, we must make additional theoretical (and largely untestable) assumptions by specifying decision rules to eliminate the directionality.

Similarly, consider the question of whether and how democracies or autocracies target or avoid other regime types because they anticipate the consequences of fighting (e.g., Bueno de Mesquita et al. 1999; Gartner and Siverson 1996; Lake 1992; Ray 1999; Reiter and Stam 1998, 2001, 2002; Stam 1996). If we care to test hypotheses about whether states initiate conflict in accordance with such arguments, or if we wish to focus on selection effects (Fearon 1995; Gartzke 1999; Schultz 2000), it is simplest to use a directed analysis that identifies potential initiators and targets of conflict and not just the fact that some conflict occurred. For these reasons, the directed dyad-year offers the best overall unit of analysis for our project.

POTENTIAL PROBLEMS WITH DIRECTED DYADS

While directed dyadic analysis has useful features, it poses potential problems as well, both theoretical and empirical. At least four important issues need careful consideration when planning to use directed dyadic data. These include (1) what we mean by the concept "initiator," (2) whether the data really reflect that meaning, (3) whether our arguments predict conflict initiation or conflict onset, and (4) assumed independence of observations within a dyad.

What Do We Mean by "Initiator"?

We need to think carefully about what we mean by the "initiator" of an international conflict. One type of initiator is the predatory state, which attacks a state that otherwise prefers peace (Rasler and Thompson 1999). Alternatively, if the initiator is simply the state that acts first in a conflict, a conflict initiator might actually prefer the status quo ante but may believe that they must preempt an opponent assumed to be the true aggressor (Reiter 1995). Reiter points out, however, that preemptive wars are exceedingly rare, Israel's attack in 1967 being the only clear example in the twentieth century. States may also try to manipulate their opponent into making the first move so they can claim that the other state is to blame. This was Bismarck's strategy at the onset of the Franco-Prussian War, for example.

The Correlates of War (COW) project always defines the initiator of a militarized dispute as the "first mover," that is, the state that first crosses the MID threshold by making a threat involving force, moving military forces, mobilizing, or actually using military force against a target state. This initiating state is always side A in the MID data. This increases clarity at the cost of ignoring intentions, which are notoriously difficult to measure. It is rare to find direct evidence of leaders saying openly that they want war. Historical discoveries after World War II of Hitler's statements that he wanted an excuse for war or George Bush's fears in 1991 that Saddam Hussein would back down before the United States was able to initiate Operation Desert Storm are the exception rather than the rule (Reiter and Stam 2002).

The indicator that comes closest to a measure of intent in existing data is the COW's variable marking "revisionist" states, defined as those who want to alter the international status quo. However, it is possible for both states in a dyad to want to change the status quo. Moreover, realists assume that almost every state is somehow dissatisfied with the status quo (Morgenthau 1956; Waltz 1979). This suggests that "revisionist intentions" alone do not match our intuition of what "initiation" means either, since initiation requires some type of action. One possible partial fix to this problem might be to code as "aggressive initiators" those states that both move first and are revisionist, but this operationalization would have its own problems. Nondirected dyads avoid this issue altogether by simply coding the onset of a MID.

Are Initiators Identified Correctly in Current Data?

Some scholars question whether the COW data sets consistently and accurately identify initiators. One problem lies in their coding rule that considers incidents within six months of each other to be part of the same militarized dispute. Because multiple incidents can occur in a single dispute, it is sometimes difficult to identify the specific incidents that led a conflict to escalate to war. For example, at the outset of World War I, which was the more salient event—the assassination of the Austrian archduke or the Russians' decision to mobilize their forces? Critics of the MID initiator coding often point to the beginnings of World War II. Close inspection of the MID data reveals that on March 25, 1939, Poland first crossed the militarized dispute threshold against Germany. This initial March action is coded in the MID (version 2.1) data as marking the beginning of the dispute that eventually escalates to World War II, since the Polish challenge to Germany (which was quickly resolved) occurred within six months of the outbreak of the wider world war. While this is technically correct, it strains our intuitive sense of "initiator" to consider that Poland is responsible for starting World War II. In contrast, the COW "Interstate War" data set lists Germany as the initiator of World War II. Researchers need to carefully consider what "initiation" means in the context of their study and to ensure that their data are consistent with that conception.

What Do Our "Theories" Predict?

Perhaps the most fundamental question about the use of directed dyads is whether our models and arguments predict the deliberate decision to initiate the use of force or just the circumstances under which conflict is somehow more likely. The difference is that in the first perspective, the model must identify those factors that make individual leaders more likely to choose to use force against a particular target. In the second perspective, models could describe "dangerous" situations where wars are more likely to occur than other situations, whether desired or not by the protagonists. Directed explanations of war focus clearly on individual choices and actions, while nondirected arguments take on the character of "wars happen." From the second perspective, events occur that make state interactions more or less dangerous, without predicting that an individual state is more likely in one circumstance or another to take the deliberate step of using force against another state.

This distinction overstates the problem somewhat. Directed analyses can incorporate nondirected dyadic hypotheses. Although nondirected hypotheses about conflict may not specify which state in a dyad will be the initiator, we know that, for conflict to occur, leaders in at least one state must decide to undertake hostile actions toward its opponent. That is, conflicts arise out of the choices one or both states make that ultimately lead to the use or threat of force. As a result, variables expected to map to nondirected dyadic conflict will necessarily have some relationship to directed conflict actions by one or more states.

Directed explanations of conflict initiation also need not identify which of the two states in a dyad is more likely to initiate but only that some factor makes one or both more likely to start a conflict. It could certainly be the case that some factor increases the chances that each of the two states in a dyad will initiate the use of force. For example, some factor at the international system level in a given year could have this character. If a year is a "dangerous" year for the system, due perhaps to increasing system power concentration, then all states might have a higher probability of initiating a conflict against some target. On the other hand, some other factor might increase the chances that one state in a dyad will initiate while lowering the probability that the other will take similar action. The dyadic balance of forces might fit this latter situation: If state A has more capabilities than state B, then it is more likely to win a conflict, and so it should be more willing to fight (and more willing to initiate, since initiation might lead to the use of force) than state B. We then do not need our theory of conflict initiation to say that A or B is the state more likely to initiate.

Are Directed Cases Independent?

A final concern with the use of directed dyads is the statistical assumption that the observations within a dyad are independent, in terms of both their generation and the errors associated with our measures of them. In practice, this assumption is commonly violated in quantitative studies of international conflict (perhaps in most studies of politics), since (1) countries persist over time and have enduring relations with other countries across time and space and (2) comprehensive corrections for serial and spatial autocorrelation and heteroskedasticity have not, until recently, been readily available for limited dependent variable models. Recent work has dealt with some of these problems by incorporating counters for "peace years" and "spline" variables to capture the effects of serial autocorrelation (Beck, Katz, and Tucker 1998) and by using robust standard errors accounting for dyadic clustering. When using directed dyads in which both observations (A versus B and B versus A) are included in the analysis, the two directional dyads are likely to be correlated. Unfortunately, there is no obvious fix for this problem. Our solution is to drop the B versus A dyad from the analysis if there is an initiation in the A versus B dyad (see the section entitled "Including Target versus Initiator Directed Dyads"). Once side A initiates versus side B in a given year, there is clearly less opportunity for B to initiate versus A (and so the cases are closely connected). A different solution would be to include in data sets only one direction of each directed dyad, randomly selected, or more usefully to include all directed dyads A versus B for dyads in which A initiates versus B and randomly select either A versus B or B versus A in other dyads. In other tests, when we kept only one direction of each dyad, the results were not remarkably different from those we report here.

CASE EXCLUSION IN DIRECTED DYADIC ANALYSIS

Beyond choosing what range of dyad-years to study, there are certain observations that one may want to exclude deliberately from the analysis. Such cases include dyad-years in which a dispute or war was ongoing at the start of the year, cases in which a state chooses (or is forced) to join in an ongoing conflict, and the reverse cases in a directed dyad (that is, the dyad B-A when dyad A-B is central to analysis). We discuss these possible exclusions next.

Ongoing Disputes or Wars

While most disputes and wars end relatively quickly (the mean dispute duration is less than six months, the median dispute duration is less than two months, the mean war duration is fifteen months, and the median war duration is four months), many conflicts continue for more than one year. The second and subsequent years of a multiyear dispute or war are problematic cases, given our focus on the decisions leading to disputes or war. Ongoing war dyads do not represent the decision to start a new conflict, nor are they peaceful dyad-years. Two questions come to mind. First, should dyad-years where a dispute (or war) was ongoing at the beginning of the year be included in our data set? Second, should we code such "ongoing conflict" dyad-years as a "1" on the dependent variable (conflict)? In an analysis of conflict initiation and escalation, we should only include cases where all values of the dependent variable could actually occur, and we should exclude any problematic cases. Accordingly, we include in our analysis only cases where no conflict was ongoing at the beginning of the year, and we drop the second and subsequent years of ongoing conflicts altogether, for the reasons detailed subsequently.

Some researchers (e.g., Oneal and Russett 2001) code a "1" on the dependent variable of "conflict occurrence" for every year in which a conflict is occurring between states. Others have argued that the "beginning of wars, the prolonging of wars and the prolonging or shortening of periods of peace all share the same causal framework" (Blainey 1988). However, simple assertion does not make this argument true, and recent empirical research supports the contention that the factors that make conflicts continue or end are quite different from those that lead to war in the first place (Werner 1998, 1999, 2000; Fortna 2003). The incentives for continuing or ending a dispute, given the presence of fighting, may be quite different from the incentives for avoiding conflict before it begins (Regan and Stam 2000). For instance, once a conflict begins, leaders may fear retribution for a war going badly (Goemans 2000). Leaders and the public may vow revenge on an enemy that started, or is perceived to have started, a conflict—hence Bismarck's desire to be a target rather than an initiator. In addition, the assumed independence across observations breaks down dramatically in consecutive years of conflict. This is quite likely as leaders respond rapidly to shocks to the status quo, leading them to undertake actions that may dramatically change the values of key independent variables (as leaders suspend political freedoms, for example, changing our judgment of their polity type). Theoretically, we are focusing here on decisions to initiate a conflict and on the move from a state of peace to a state of conflict. We leave to others further investigation of the decision to continue using force after the initiation of conflict (e.g., Goemans 2000; Bennett and Stam 1996, 1998; Filson and Werner 2001; Smith and Stam 2001).

Years where there was an ongoing conflict at the start of a year are also likely to be years with reduced opportunity for new conflict initiation; in effect, these are cases with censored outcomes. We attempt to include only cases where new conflicts were possible by excluding dyad-years in which there is an ongoing dispute unless there is a new initiation in that year as well. If a new dispute begins, then it is clear that there was in fact an opportunity for a new initiation. Such an opportunity may have been present in other years when a dispute was ongoing but there was no new dispute, but we cannot be certain of this, and so we drop these problematic cases. Of course, we recognize that the absence of an effect (new conflict initiation) is not proof of the absence of the cause (opportunity). Not knowing with any certainty that there was an opportunity, and suspicious that there was not, we drop these cases.

In sum, adding together two different types of cases—namely, adding those where the decision is whether to initiate conflict with those where the decision is between continuing and ending an ongoing conflict— muddles the question and analysis. For our purposes, we code a "1" on the dependent variable of "conflict initiation" only in the first year of a conflict and we drop subsequent years of conflict from the analysis altogether.[3]

Originators versus Joiners

Individual states can become involved in conflict in one of two ways: as either conflict "originators" or "joiners." Originators become involved at the conflict's onset by being either the initiator or the target. Joiners enter a dispute already in progress. The distinction between originators and joiners is an important one. States that join an ongoing war face quite different conditions than did the states that originated it. After a conflict begins, states begin to choose sides or to announce their neutrality; perhaps, most important for theories focused on information asymmetries, capabilities and escalation patterns become clearer. States then may have more or different information than they did before the conflict began. Because states that join an ongoing conflict face different information and structural conditions than the state(s) that originated the dispute, we believe that we should code only the original participants of a conflict as initiators. We drop states that joined a dispute later, because their decision is not directly comparable to that made by the initiators and original targets.

Censoring issues relate to this problem: when a state joins an ongoing conflict, we are not certain whether we have observed an independent and active choice to initiate a dyadic dispute with its opponent. A practical data problem with the COW MID data causes a further complication, as it is not possible to tell in this data set whether joiners initiated their entry into the conflict or became targets for attack subsequent to the initial opening of the dispute. "Joiners" as identified in the MID data really means "latecomers" and does not indicate a voluntary choice to become involved. Including latecomers in analysis, even if they ended up on the side of the initiator, is problematic, as these states may have been the targets of escalation and conflict expansion. As a result, we also reject the possibility of including in the analysis joiners who entered the dispute on the side of the conflict's initiator(s).

Including Target versus Initiator Directed Dyads: "Reverse Dyads"

When using directed dyads, we may include one direction, both directions, or neither direction of any dyad (e.g., for the U.S.-USSR dyad 1953, we could include U.S. versus USSR 1953, USSR versus U.S. 1953, both, or neither). Given that we want to study initiation, the correct population to employ includes cases where there could have been a MID initiation. However, along with the problem of curtailed opportunity given an ongoing dispute, "reverse directed-dyads" may not have an opportunity for initiation. This problem occurs if, when state A initiates a dispute, B does not have an opportunity to initiate its own dispute against A. If neither state in a dyad initiates against the other in a given year, or if the data reveal that both states initiated a dispute, then it is clear that both directed dyad-years should be included in a data set for analysis, because both sides clearly had the opportunity to initiate a dispute, as revealed by their choices. However, if an initiator A starts a dispute against a target B, but we do not observe a new MID by B versus A, it may be problematic to include the reverse dyad B versus A in our analysis. This is a theoretical problem of opportunity separate from the problem of nonindependence across cases, which reverse dyads also have, as previously discussed. If we do not observe B initiating a dispute with A in that dyad-year, there are two possibilities: (1) both A and B had opportunity for dispute initiation, but only A took advantage of it, or (2) A had the opportunity for initiation and took it, leaving B without a similar opportunity. We do not know which of these is true. We deal with this problem by including the reverse dyad B-A only if we also observe a separate initiation by B against A.

ESTIMATOR ISSUES

The estimation of regression-like models in international politics research is particularly complex because of the nature of the data sets we employ. Our typical data design in international politics is a panel design with a limited dependent variable, where we track both cross-sectional variation (n) and cross-temporal variation (t) without the benefit of a continuous dependent variable. Several problems emerge in analyzing such data, and several trade-offs exist when choosing a statistical estimator.

Limited Dependent Variable: Logit

The most obvious feature of the data we employ about international conflict is that we typically end up with a limited dependent variable, most often a binary dependent variable marking dispute versus no dispute or escalation to war versus de-escalation. Typically, analysts use logit or probit to analyze this type of data, although in some cases event history models have been used (e.g., Nordstrom 2000; Werner 1999). While logit is probably the most commonly used estimator, in part because it is simple to employ, interpretation of the results produced with any nonlinear estimator is not straightforward. Logit fits a curvilinear relationship between our independent variables and an unobserved probability of conflict associated with the os and 1s that make up the dependent variable in our data. In our analysis, since at least one of our key theories (the expected utility theory of war as implemented in the IIG) combines conflict initiation and escalation into a discrete and discontinuous set of outcomes, we employ multinomial logit to deal with the dependent variable containing several nonordered categories. We discuss this choice later.

Autocorrelation: Splines and GEE Approaches

A second problem in the typical study of international conflict is temporal autocorrelation. Our observations in n (cross-section) are not independent over t (time), thereby violating a standard statistical assumption of independence of observations. What happens in any given dyad at time t is in part a function of what happened in that dyad at $t - 1$ (and possibly $t - 2, \ldots, t - n$). There are at least two possible problems here, the first being correlation of our dependent variable over time and the second being correlation of our disturbances (supposedly random errors) over time. A limited dependent variable complicates any attempt to address these problems. To deal with the problem of the autocorrelation of the dependent variable, if the variable were continuous, we could begin to control for the temporal correlations among the observations by using a lagged dependent variable as an additional independent variable. Alternatively, we could employ sophisticated procedures to estimate an additional parameter (rho [ρ]). This would serve to capture the autocorrelation in the model. Unfortunately, with limited and possibly unordered dependent variable categories, and with rarely observed 1s on the dependent variable, these solutions are problematic. As an alternative, Beck, Katz, and Tucker (1998) developed a cubic spline procedure that, in effect, creates a set of four lagged time variables whose weights are parameterized to help deal with this problem. We include this correction in our subsequent estimations.[4]

An alternative tactic is to use the general estimating equations approach (GEE). GEE is a general class of regression type models that allows the user to specify the underlying distribution of the data (in our case the logistic) and whether there are expected correlations of various types within the groups over time (Liang and Zeger 1986; Robins and

Greenland 1999). Correlation structures can be included in the GEE models to allow for several possible autocorrelation patterns, although in the published international politics literature only a simple first-order autoregressive structure (AR1) has been used (Oneal and Russett 1999b).

While the GEE approach is very flexible, it does require one to specify ex ante the correlation structure expected in the data (an advantage of the spline approach is that one does not have to specify the temporal correlation structure in advance). It also makes other assumptions that might lead us to conclude that it is not the appropriate estimator. For instance, Robins and Greenland (1999) argue that the GEE approach cannot sort out temporal correlation problems when changes in the independent and dependent variables occur in the same year (assuming annual data), since there is no way to know which event occurred prior to the other, a problem induced by the assumptions of the GEE averaging approach. Our data do not allow us to know precisely when such key changes occur. Another potentially problematic feature of the GEE approach (also a problem with logit and logit with spline) is that it estimates a slightly different parameter than an observation or cluster-specific estimator, such as the fixed-effects estimator. Perhaps, more important, GEE estimations may or may not be appropriate for data sets with rich temporal information (Beck, Katz, and Tucker 1998, 1263).

GEE employs an averaging procedure that fits the average values of the independent variables across a panel to the average value of the dependent variable for a given year. This may lead to a difference between the estimates of β (beta) that we want and the β^* estimated by GEE representing the GEE averaged beta. For example, when considering the use of GEE models (or other population-averaged models), one needs to consider that the odds ratio generated by this approach represents the odds of an average democracy initiating the use of force compared to the odds of an average nondemocracy using force. Under the alternative cluster-specific model (conditional logit, fixed-effects models) the odds ratio represents the odds of a democratic state initiating the use of force compared to the odds of the same state using force if it were not a democracy. If we want to estimate how democracy makes a particular state more pacific, then we should attempt to estimate β. If we want to look at conflict levels for the average democracy compared to the average nondemocracy, then it is appropriate to attempt to estimate β^*.[5] In our case, the relevant question is whether we are interested in how democracy, contiguity, power, and so forth influence the likelihood of conflict within a dyad across time, as opposed to influencing disputes between the average traders (for example) as compared to the average nontrading dyad. As a result, we are after β and not β*. This issue leads us to a final class of estimators, conditional likelihood (fixed-effects) estimators.

Unit Heterogeneity: Fixed-Effects Estimation

A third problem in our data is the possibility of heterogeneity across units that makes the averaging procedures of the standard logit and GEE approaches problematic. Typically, international politics scholars have simply ignored this problem, treating all units as identical (Green, Kim, and Yoon 2001). In some cases, one could justify this based on the belief that domestic or dyad-specific effects are largely irrelevant to the study of international politics (Waltz 1979). Recent research investigating and demonstrating the relationships between domestic political institutions and international outcomes makes this implicit assumption of unit homogeneity seem implausible (e.g., Goemans 2000; Bueno de Mesquita et al. 2001). If our data are heterogeneous, with different dyads in the international system each having unique characteristics correlated with the dyad's propensities to initiate a dispute, then each dyad conceivably could have a unique intercept associated with it.[6] If we ignore this problem, and unit heterogeneity is present, we run the risk of inducing omitted variable bias. In this case, the omitted variables are the unique intercepts for each dyad. It is possible for such bias to be so severe as to reverse the signs of some of the other parameter estimates. The simple fix is to include a dummy variable marking each directed dyad, the approach taken in fixed-effects estimation. The heterogeneity we are concerned about may not appear at the dyad level but instead could occur at the state, regional, or some other level. The Hausman test (see Greene 1993) is an appropriate way to check whether one's assumptions about homogeneity are justifiable. The Hausman test compares the fit of the fixed-effects estimate to the constrained estimate (constrained in that it does not include dummies marking unit intercepts). However, the test does have a significant limitation in that it assumes, aside from potential bias introduced by the dyad-specific intercepts, that the specification of the statistical model is otherwise correct. If the underlying statistical specification is poor, the Hausman test will attribute the estimated bias to the ignored fixed-effects and not to the omitted variable bias due to poor model specification. Given that the overall explanatory power of most dispute-onset models is quite low, we cannot dismiss this criticism, which suggests that estimations showing powerful dyad-specific effects may do so simply because of underspecified theoretical models.

The fixed-effects approach allows us to model and to control for the parametric heterogeneity resulting from each dyad having a unique intercept. It gives us consistency at the cost of efficiency due to the inclusion of potentially thousands of dyad dummies. In data sets with large numbers of units where the t varies from unit to unit, maximum likelihood estimates using dummies may be inconsistent or difficult to obtain. Therefore, most analysis does not actually include and estimate the individual intercept parameters. Instead, analysis may employ a conditional logit estimator where we estimate $y_i = (y_{i1}, \ldots, y_{iTi})$ conditional on $\sum y_{it}$. This conditional probability does not involve the intercepts, and so they drop from the estimation, thereby saving degrees of freedom.

However, fixed-effects estimators have two very important drawbacks. First, with this approach we cannot estimate the effect of independent variables that do not vary over time within a unit on any dependent variable. In fixed-effects estimations, we are estimating the influence on the dependent variable of the change in the independent variables over time (pooled temporal variation) and holding fixed or constant the cross-sectional variation present in the data set. The key reason to control for unit level heterogeneity is to eliminate omitted variable bias generated by the possibility that the heterogeneity in the unit level intercepts may correlate with other variables in the model. Fixed-effects and random-effects models (or any accounting of dyad-level heterogeneity) correct for the omitted variable bias resulting from heterogeneity found in the intercept or error term, respectively. The random-effects estimator is more efficient but relies on the somewhat Herculean assumption that the regressors and the dyad-specific effects are uncorrelated. The Hausman test is again the appropriate test to distinguish between the two estimators. Note, however, that if we use a fixed-effects estimator when the random-effects estimator would suffice, the penalty is loss of efficiency. However, if we use the random-effects estimation when there are dyad-specific effects found in the intercepts, then we risk bias in the parameter estimates of the independent variables of interest.

The models have another, potentially important drawback. Independent variables that do not change over time add nothing to the estimation and drop from the model. This does not mean that these types of variables do not influence the onset of war but rather that we simply cannot estimate their influence using a fixed-effects estimator. If we have theoretical reasons to believe that factors such as contiguity have strong influences on the probability of conflict and believe it is important to control for those as potentially confounding effects, then we should not use the fixed-effects approach.

The second problem with the fixed-effects estimator is that we must also drop dyads where there is no variation on the dependent variable. This means that all truly quiescent dyads drop from the analysis. Statistically this is not a problem for a fixed-effects analysis because these cases are not providing unique information to the overall likelihood. However, using this approach, we cannot understand why some dyads never have disputes, nor can we incorporate information from these dyads in any other way.

POPULATION OF CASES: POLITICAL RELEVANCE

In our analysis, we examine both the set of all directed dyad-years and the subset of politically relevant dyads. Maoz and Russett (1993) define politically relevant dyads (PRDs) as those that include at least one major power or where the states are geographically contiguous. These dyads encompass approximately 75 percent of all militarized interstate dispute initiations. The advantage of analyzing this subset is that we exclude those cases that we believe ex ante to have no chance of conflict. War within dyads such as Brazil-Thailand, Norway-Chile, or Belize-Bhutan is simply unthinkable, so the argument goes, and we should not bother to include information about them in our data sets. More generally, the argument about identifying a set of politically relevant dyads for analysis is that the a priori probability of conflict is much higher in a set of identifiable dyads than between any two randomly selected states and that this probability is higher for some theoretical reason. For example, typically only contiguous states have the military transport capabilities needed to prosecute a war, with the exception of the major powers. According to this logic, including "politically irrelevant" dyads includes irrelevant data in our population of cases, introducing noise that can only interfere with our analysis.

The disadvantages of focusing attention solely on PRDs are that we know we will exclude (miss) approximately 25 percent of all violent interstate disputes before we even begin our analysis and that we know we are introducing selection bias. The bias resulting from focusing on the PRD subpopulation emerges because a variety of the factors theorized to cause conflict (such as capabilities, wealth, and possibly democracy) correlates quite strongly with the selection criteria for political relevance. Major powers by definition have greater capabilities and wealth than the average state, and they tend to be disproportionately democratic. States with many contiguous neighbors may also have higher levels of capabilities than states facing few potential threats, and recent work suggests that regime type tends to cluster geographically (Gleditsch 2002). These are all variables that we want to include in our statistical models. If we want to avoid bias, then rather than exclude cases with configurations of these variables that make them unlikely to fight, we should build a properly specified model that takes into account these factors. Lemke and Reed (2001) demonstrate that focusing solely on the set of politically relevant dyads causes measurable selection bias in analysis, although the size of the bias appears to be small.

OUR RESEARCH PLAN OVERVIEWED

Now that we have considered the range of choices we must make in planning a research design, we turn to our research plan.

Unit of Analysis and Cases

Employing the directed dyad-year as our unit of analysis, there are over one million directed dyad-years from 1816 to 1992. Because of missing data, in particular information on regime type, and after dropping problematic cases as described later, we end up with 753,306 observations in our main analyses. We concentrate on the population of all dyads because few theories specify that they should only apply to a particular subset of cases. However, we also fit our model to the politically relevant subset to allow comparison of our results to other studies and to examine the extent of selection bias that results from examining only a select subset of cases. We analyze 116,057 of the approximately 126,000 politically relevant directed dyad-years from 1816 to 1992. We used the software program EUGene (Bennett and Stam 2000d) to generate our observations.

While we generated the population of all directed dyads-years, we excluded several particular types of problematic cases from our analysis. We drop from our base data set all dyad-years in which there was a dispute (or war) ongoing at the beginning of the year in the dyad, unless there was an additional, new initiation in the directed dyad-year. For similar reasons, we also drop reverse dyads B versus A when A initiates a dispute against B in that year, unless B also initiates another dispute against A (in the latter case, both directed dyad-years are included). If neither A nor B initiates a dispute, both directed dyad-years are included in the population, since both states clearly had the opportunity to initiate but did not. Finally, we drop dyads that involve the choice of joining ongoing militarized disputes, that is, dyads where the states became involved in a dispute or war that was already in progress.

Dependent Variable

Our dependent variable combines the initiation and escalation of MIDs. MIDs include incidents where at least one state used or threatened the use of military force against another (Jones, Bremer, and Singer 1996). We separate the final level of conflict in each directed dyad-year into five levels. At level 0, there is no dispute initiated by state A against B, representing a status quo outcome. At level 1, state A initiates a MID against B, but the dispute never escalates to the use of force. At level 2, state A initiates a MID and only one state (either A or B) ultimately uses force in the dispute. At level 3, both states use force following A's initiation of the dispute but the dispute does not escalate to a full-scale war. Finally, at level 4, A initiates a MID and it escalates to the level of interstate war.

We analyze both conflict initiation and escalation together because one of the key theories we test, Bueno de Mesquita and Lalman's (1992) IIG, predicts simultaneously whether an actor will try to alter the status quo and what level of escalation the resulting confrontation will reach. Most theories of conflict do not distinguish between the conflict initiation and escalation, instead phrasing hypotheses more generally as "factor X leads to more, and more intense, conflict." Our multilevel dependent variable allows us to examine whether these theories' key factors lead to more dispute initiation, to a higher level of escalation, to both, or to neither. Of course, there are trade-offs in settling on any research design. By combining initiation and escalation, we cannot model dispute escalation as a multistage process. We might prefer such an approach if we believed that the start of disputes was largely random or caused by exogenous and unpredictable shocks to dyadic relations. If this is the case, we might expect a poor fit to conflict behavior at the stage of dispute initiation but a better fit at later stages (see Reed 2000 for a discussion of this approach, typically using either the Heckman filter or bivariate probit). An alternative approach would be to model the initiation of disputes along with the costs or durations of the dispute in a second stage or set of stages.

Again, dispute initiators in the COW MID data set (version 2.1) are those states on side A of the dispute on the first day of the dispute (we code all states in this data set as being on the initiating or target side). If there were multiple disputes in a directed dyad-year, we code the escalation level of the first dispute in that year (there are approximately 100 such cases out of 2,200 dispute dyad-years).

Estimation Technique

We analyze conflict initiation and escalation using multinomial logistic regression. Multinomial logit is an appropriate technique when the dependent variable has unordered multiple outcomes or when the independent variables may not relate to the various outcome categories in a monotonic fashion. The outcome categories present in the MID data set are not clearly ordered. The MID data describes the highest level of force reached, and not if (or when) the states passed through prior stages. States, for example, could use force (level 4) without a display of force first (level 2). Moreover, ordered estimators are inappropriate here because they rely on the assumption that variables have consistent (monotonic) effects on the escalation of conflict through multiple levels. For instance, ordered probit (which estimates one set of coefficients and a series of cut points) does not allow a variable to have a positive effect on dispute initiation but a negative effect on escalation (as some hypotheses might specify). More generally, if our set of outcome categories is in fact ordered, multinomial logit will capture everything an ordered procedure would at a cost to efficiency and parsimony, but if the categories are not ordered and we used an ordered procedure, we would end up with biased results. Multinomial logit is the most flexible estimator given our multiple outcome dependent variable, allowing us to assess independently how variables in a model affect the initiation of disputes—by examining whether they predict positively any outcome level other than 0—and to what level they escalate.

Multinomial logit models estimate the probability that the actual outcome Y will take on each of a set of discrete possible outcomes, given a vector of independent variables X.[7] Given $J + 1$ outcomes, the model estimates J equations (sets of coefficients β), which show the effects of the variables on the likelihood of a particular outcome occurring. Estimates are relative to a base category, and the selection of the base category is mathematically unimportant. We obtain the predicted probability that any given case (set of data x_i) will have a particular outcome Y as follows:

$$\text{Probability } (Y = j) = \frac{e^{x_i \beta_j}}{1 + \sum_{k=1}^{J} e^{x_i \beta_k}} \qquad \text{for } j = 1, 2, \ldots, J.$$

$$\text{Probability } (Y = 0) = \frac{1}{1 + \sum_{k=1}^{J} e^{x_i \beta_k}}.$$

We estimate robust standard errors (Beck 1996; Huber 1967) based on clustering by dyad and follow the Beck, Katz, and Tucker (1998) procedure of using three cubic spline variables along with "peace years" to deal with the problem of time dependence in qualitative dependent variable data.[8]

ASSESSING STRENGTH OF ASSOCIATIONS

Because multinomial logit produces multiple coefficients for each independent variable (one for each possible level of escalation beyond the status quo), it is difficult to interpret the variables' statistical significance and substantive effects merely by examining tables of coefficients. In terms of statistical significance, simple *t*-tests on individual coefficients may not be adequate to establish whether some variable had a statistically significant effect on the disputes in our analysis. Coefficients in each equation represent the effect of some variable on the level of escalation reached relative to a base condition (in our analysis, the status quo). Any individual significance test suggests only whether a variable has a statistically significant effect associated with a state moving between the base category and the level of escalation in question. It is possible for a variable to be statistically insignificant in one equation (or more) but still have an important substantive effect in another (for instance, increasing levels of democracy might lead states to initiate greater numbers of low-level disputes but fewer wars). In addition, since coefficients and *t*-tests are relative to a base category, selecting a different base category will appear to make different coefficients more or less significant, although the underlying model's fit to the data is identical.

Since individual *t*-tests are unreliable as a sole means of assessing variable significance across the full model, we employ two related techniques. First, a statistically significant coefficient in any equation suggests that a variable is important in differentiating between the base outcome and the outcome in question. Given any significant coefficient, we conclude that the variable has some systematic effect on outcomes associated with it. By rotating through the possible outcomes as base categories in pair-wise fashion, we can gain a fair understanding of what variables significantly influence the difference between categories. Second, following the logic of Lakatos, we use a series of block likelihood ratio tests to assess the statistical significance of our independent variables in affecting behavior across multiple outcomes. To conduct a block test we drop a variable (or set of theoretically related variables) and reestimate the model, resulting in a second model nested in the first. Given J outcomes on the dependent variable, we can then assess twice the difference in the log likelihood ratios of the two models in a χ^2 test with $J - 1$ degrees of freedom (or, if n variables are dropped in a block, $n*(J - 1)$ degrees of freedom). A statistically significant difference suggests that including the variable(s) improves the model as a whole.

ASSESSING SUBSTANTIVE EXPLANATORY POWER

In terms of substantive effects, direct inspection of the direction or magnitude of (multinomial) logit coefficients is an unreliable way to judge the substantive effect of some variable on the outcomes of interest. With multinomial logit in particular, in order to calculate the marginal effects (both direction and magnitude) of a variable on any outcome, we need to use information from all of the coefficients across all of the possible outcomes as well as information about the actual values on all of the independent variables. The marginal effects associated with each independent variable depend on the initial probability of each outcome and on all the β values (see, for instance, Greene 1993, 666–67, for a detailed discussion of this problem). This is because the marginal effect of any variable for any outcome depends on where the case falls on the outcome probability distribution (e.g., near a 50 percent probability or near a 100 percent probability). The best way to interpret the marginal effects associated with the independent variables is to produce estimated probabilities of each outcome using the complete set of coefficients and various sets of independent variable values. We can then observe which outcome probabilities rise and which fall as we increase the value of a particular independent variable. Since the predicted probabilities for all of the possible outcomes in each case must sum to one, whenever the probability of one outcome rises, the probability of some other outcome(s) must fall. In addition, given the nonlinear relationships that we fit to the logit distribution, it is possible for a probability to rise over some range of variable values and to fall over others.

To examine the marginal effects of the various independent variables, we apply the "method of recycled predictions" to generate sets of predicted values. Generally, this method keeps the actual independent variable values from the data set, setting the value of the variable under investigation to a specific value for all cases while leaving all the other independent variables at the actual values we observe in the data set. The predicted probabilities then take into account the frequency distributions of the other variables across the full data set. After generating predicted probabilities at one value, we change the variable in question to some other value and generate new probabilities.[9] By examining the change in probability (both direction and magnitude) from one value to the other, we can assess the effect of the variable across outcomes.

ASSESSING EXPLANATORY POWER THROUGH A MEASURE OF RELATIVE RISK

International conflict in general and wars in particular are exceedingly rare events. As a result, the probability of conflict for the typical dyad is quite small, as are the changes in probability associated with changing values of the independent variables. We judge the size of a variable's relative effect on the likelihood of war in the context of Gartzke's (1999) conjecture regarding the upper limit of predictability. Even if the upper limit of predictability were 0.50, a case where the probability of war is 0.50 would be a vastly riskier situation than a randomly selected dyad year with the approximately 0.0005 base probability of a war. Such a prediction would still represent three orders of magnitude more predictive power than we would have by making naive predictions based on the relative frequency of war overall.

To assess the marginal effects and relative explanatory power associated with each argument, we focus on the relative risk of conflict at different values of the independent variables in our model as measured by the *risk ratio*. We initially set the value of an independent value to a level that leads to a lower probability of conflict (assuming, for the sake of argument, the veracity of the democratic peace proposition, we set the value of joint democracy to "true") and then estimate the probability of conflict. We then change the value of the variable to a value leading to a higher level of conflict (for example, joint democracy equal to "false") and reassess the probability of conflict. We then focus on the probability of conflict in the second condition *relative* to the first. For example, we might find that changing some independent variable doubled the probability of conflict, or led to a 2x increase in risk, or that it increased the probability of conflict by 30 percent, giving a 1.3x risk ratio. A key advantage of using risk ratios is that the risks computed do not depend on the incidence of events in the data set, while the absolute probability does. In addition, because we know the actual frequency of conflict events in the population of dyads, we can use true risk ratios rather than simply "odds ratios" computed within a sample (see King and Zeng 2002 for a discussion of the incomplete nature of odds ratios; see also Beck 1998). We report both absolute, base probabilities and risk ratios as we change the values of independent variables, providing full information to assess the variables' associated effects.

To assess the relative power of our variables, we will make our risk assessments comparable across variables by changing independent variable values by a comparable amount determined by the distribution of each variable. With these comparable changes, if we find that changing one variable leads to a 3x increase in risk and that changing another variable leads to only a 1.5x increase in risk, we will say that the first variable has a stronger effect. We change each variable by an amount that marks a typical real-world change ("typical" being measured by a two standard deviation change in the independent variable in question).

The use of relative risk analysis is common in fields such as medical research or industrial failure testing, where the absolute probabilities of events are small. For instance, it is common to see statements such as "exposure to environmental [secondhand] tobacco smoke raises the risk of lung cancer by 1.8 times" or "exposure to 60 pack-years of tobacco smoke raises the risk of lung cancer by 22 times" (both amounts are approximately correct given current medical research). In the medical literature, one rule of thumb is that a 2x (or sometimes 4x) relative risk is a useful benchmark of importance; experimental findings demonstrating risk effects of less than this amount are frequently overturned in subsequent studies. As we will see, the variables we employ generate a range of relative risk scores, a few of them well above the 2x or 4x rule of thumb, but the majority of the arguments or conjectures we test have associated risks less than 2x.

Presentations of relative risk are often confusing, as some studies use the term "relative risk" to refer to the odds ratio (used, for instance, in cases where the population frequency of events is not known, such as when studying rare diseases), while others use the term to refer to the risk ratio (which is computed knowing actual population frequencies). Our presentation, which has the advantage of using full retrospective population data, employs risk ratios.

To sum up, our study uses the population of directed dyad-years from 1816 to 1992, minus some problematic cases. We use a multinomial logit model with spline corrections for temporal autocorrelation problems. To test for statistical significance, we use block likelihood ratio tests. To gauge the relative explanatory power of the variables analyzed, we will present our results in the form of risk ratios. In the next chapter, we turn to the specific theories, arguments, conjectures, and hunches that we review and include.

4 ARGUMENTS AND
OPERATIONAL MEASURES

since the measuring device has been constructed by the
observer . . . we have to remember that what we observe is not
nature itself but nature exposed to our method of reasoning.
—werner heisenberg, 1958

In the previous chapter, we laid out the epistemological issues surrounding our research design and many of the choices we made therein.
Next, we discuss in detail the models, arguments, and conjectures that
we will examine with our statistical tools. We group these by level of
analysis, beginning with the individual state level. We then turn to the
dyadic level, or pairs of states, and finally examine the arguments cast
at the international system level. In chapter 6 we look at regional level
variation. For each argument we test, we first lay out the logic or intuition behind it. Then we explain how one might go about testing empirical propositions consistent with the argument's theoretical expectations. To accomplish this, we operationalize the set of key concepts that
each hypothesis implies should be associated with more or less international conflict. In many instances, the logic behind the "theory" is so
vague or poorly specified that it is impossible to test critical underlying
causal steps of the argument. Instead, we set goals that are more modest—we aim to test carefully the empirical claims various authors make
about the relationship between operational measures linked to their stories and the onset and escalation of interstate conflict. Part of the
dilemma is that, in most cases, the various authors do not really have an
explicit theory of the decisions that lead to war. Instead, they make con-
jectural arguments linking some operational measure to some vaguely
specified mechanism that makes the decisions leading to war more or
less likely. Our aim here is to see which of these conjectures finds enough

empirical support to suggest where further theoretical development will be most fruitful.

STATE LEVEL OF ANALYSIS

In this section, we discuss our indicators that purport to measure the effects of state level, or monadic, factors on the relative likelihood of war. The arguments in this section predict the behavior of states in a dyad based solely on a single state's internal characteristics, without reference to the joint characteristics or interactions within the dyad.

1. *Democratization*

While most scholars agree that democracies fight less with one another than with other types of states, Mansfield and Snyder (1995) argue that the transition to democracy is quite dangerous, largely because of institutionally insecure leaders looking for support from an increasingly nationalistic populace. Others disagree with this proposition (Thompson and Tucker 1997; Enterline 1996, 1998; Ward and Gleditsch 1998). Some critics concentrate on Mansfield and Snyder's research design, changes in which seem to yield rather different conclusions about the dangers (or lack thereof) of democratization. Others focus on the relatively simplistic initial conceptualization and measurement of what constitutes democratization. We focus on Ward and Gleditsch's work (1998), which presents one of the more sophisticated analyses of whether and how democratization affects international conflict. Ward and Gleditsch break the concept of democratization into three separate aspects of regime change: direction, intensity, and nature. By "direction," they mean whether the change in a regime is toward or away from democracy. By "intensity," they mean how rapidly change occurs or how much of a shift in the nature of the regime there ultimately is. Last, by the "nature" of regime change, they address whether the shift is smooth and relatively linear or if it is marked by reversals or rapid spurts in regime transformation. It is this third characteristic in particular that is unique to their analysis.

We follow the operational methods detailed in table 2 of Ward and Gleditsch's (1998) work but use updated data and make minor modifications following conversations with Ward and Gleditsch. Using the Polity IV data, we first compute the change in a state's regime type over a ten-year period as ($\text{Democracy}_{i,t} - \text{Democracy}_{i,t-10}$). If the tenth lag is missing, we use the next closest possible lag, a nine-year lag if available, otherwise an eight-year lag, and so forth. We also include the direction of that regime change as a second variable, which takes the value -1 if change was away from democratic regime characteristics, 0 if there was no change, and $+1$ if change was toward democratic regime characteristics. Finally, we include a measure of the variance of change in the state over the ten years. If data were missing during the period, we used the variance of the available data, as long as there were at least three years of data. We include these three variables separately for each state in the directed dyad. We are then able to observe whether democratization in the potential initiator, potential target, or both has an associated effect on conflict behavior.

2. Polity Change and Externalization of Violence

Related to the democratization literature is a set of arguments about regime change in general. Levy (1988) summarizes these arguments and points out that a government's concerns about maintaining internal support may lead to war through any of several mechanisms. Analysts of externalization and diversionary war argue that conflict is more likely when states face significant internal problems. Problems such as economic downturns and a subsequent (or anticipated) drop in internal support may lead national leaders to look for ways to boost their domestic political standing by searching for an explicit "rally round the flag" effect (Russett 1990). Historically, appeals to nationalism have served states well and often serve as sufficient justification to generate internal support for war (Snyder 2000; Reiter and Stam 2002). Following the rally round the flag logic, military confrontation with another state may provide a way to achieve a boost in popular support for a state's leader or support for a larger war that the public would not have otherwise backed. Similarly, when there is a change of government in a state, a new government may look for ways to bolster internal support, as well as to establish an international reputation for toughness, which state leaders sometimes focus on to the detriment of long-term state goals (Mercer 1996). In this latter situation, other states may see an opportunity to press a claim over some disputed issue because they see the government as less in control than an established regime (Blainey 1988). According to the logic of either argument, a state's involvement in international conflict will be more likely when there is substantial change in a state's domestic political institutions.

An alternative chain of logic in the psychological literature focuses on leaders' reactions to crises. These arguments suggest that, in situations of internal political vulnerability, leaders may suffer from motivated bias, leading them to see the enemy as they wish to see them, typically weaker and making an easier target than would be expected given a "rational" evaluation of the situation (Jervis 1976; Lebow 1981). Expectations about the escalation of conflict under these conditions are less than clear, however. Following the diversionary argument from a rationalist unitary actor perspective, states engaged in actions to shore up their domestic political situation may not want to pay the costs of a long-running conflict or war, and so we should see less escalation beyond low-level disputes. However, if challenged by another state, leaders facing intense internal political dissent may be likely to force a confrontation initially in order to gain needed, and expected, domestic political benefits by standing tough against an external foe. Similarly, if such a state faces a challenge over some outstanding issue, there is no guarantee that it will be more willing to give in to the challenger compared to times when the government is in a position of domestic political strength. Following the motivated bias argument, we might expect more or faster conflict escalation as a leader blindly pushes ahead in his or her dispute with an opposing state.

Insufficient systematically collected historical data make it impossible for us to test directly arguments about the effects of internal political conditions using measures of a state's economic situation or the relative number of political protests in a cross-national time-series analysis. However, we can examine the effects of abrupt changes in a regime's political institutional characteristics on international conflict. Based on Polity IV data we include a variable that marks whether the states in a dyad experienced an abrupt polity change. As noted in the democratization section, we use several variables to code general polity changes. We also mark a change corresponding to two additional conditions: (1) when a regime comes to an abrupt end according to the Polity IV "eyear" variable and (2) under conditions marking a polity change coded when the "polity" variable (autocracy-democracy) takes a value of -66, -77, or -88, indicating an interruption, interregnum, or transition period, respectively. All of these are circumstances where the state's political institutions are in significant flux. We lag the regime change variable one-year to avoid the possibility of accidentally picking up conflicts that led to a polity change rather than vice versa. If arguments about domestic instability leading to international conflict initiation or escalation are correct, following a polity change we should find that (1) states initiate disputes more frequently but may escalate those disputes less often and/or (2) states initiate and/or escalate disputes more frequently against other states that have recently experienced a polity change.

DYADIC LEVEL OF ANALYSIS

Next, we turn to arguments cast at the dyadic level of analysis, beginning with alliances and defense pacts.

3. Alliance and Defense Pact Membership

Alliances lie at the core of a vast literature. These foci include the realist balance of power/threat debate (Morgenthau 1956, Walt 1987), empirical work in international relations (Singer and Small 1967), the formal or deductive rational choice literature (Bueno de Mesquita 1981), and the norms or domestic political institution literature (Risse-Kappen 1991; Simon and Gartzke 1996). The best available evidence suggests that military alliances between states serve several functions. Early empirical work demonstrated their role as mechanisms of war diffusion (Siverson and King 1980; Siverson and Tennefoss 1984; Oren 1990) and as capability-aggregation mechanisms (Morgenthau 1956; Liberman 1996; see Brooks 1998 for an alternative view). More recently, others argue that they serve as indicators of bilateral satisfaction (Lemke and Reed 1996) and as a sign of beliefs about the likelihood and nature of future conflict (Walt 1984; Morrow 1999). More generally, alliances may be simple reflections of common interests (Bueno de Mesquita 1981). Longer-term interests and continuing interaction may lead allies to trade more with one another, or they may develop certain shared institutional structures over time that will provide incentives and/or mechanisms to avoid conflict. We do not attempt to sort out the often conflicting logic of the many hypotheses about the effects of alliances on international politics. These include how alliances serve states' interests and how they affect the nature of interstate conflict (for a large set of additional inductive hypotheses see Holsti, Hopmann, and Sullivan 1972).[1] Our tests here simply aim to identify whether and when alliances are associated with the onset and escalation of interstate conflict.

We include two measures of dyadic alliance membership to see whether allied states are better able to avoid conflict than nonallied states. Alliances may take many forms: offensive, defensive, ententes, and formal institutionalized arrangements (such as NATO). We first include a variable marking whether a formal defense pact existed between the members of the dyad in the given year. To capture the basic intuitions of those that argue that alliances simply aggregate capabilities and those that argue that some alliances may evolve into theoretically distinct defense communities, we include a separate measure marking that the two states were jointly members of NATO.[2] This second measure is particularly important to control for a confounding alternative to the democratic peace argument, namely, the possibility that in fact it is NATO rather than democracy that has driven peaceful relations in Europe since World War II and provided evidence for the apparent democracy-peace relationship. The argument points out that the most stable democracies since World War II have also been members of NATO. If NATO is the true motive force behind peace between these countries, then the democratic institutions' contribution is merely an illusion.

4. *Arms Races*

Arms races occur when two states build their military armaments in response to each other's purchases and manpower mobilizations, leading to an action-reaction cycle of rapidly increasing military expenditures and/or forces. Some of the most sophisticated and careful thinking about the nature of arms races harks back to Huntington's (1958) and Richardson's (1951, 1960a, 1960b) work in the 1950s. Huntington observed that an arms race could take place both in terms of the quantity of arms and in terms of technological innovations (see also Evangelista 1988). Richardson developed the first mathematical formalizations of arms races in the 1930s, models that remain the foundation for much current formal work in the area.

The argument that arms races increase the probability of conflict and escalation draws more recently from Jervis's (1976) informal but highly influential spiral model of hostility (see also Herz 1959; Butterfield 1951). According to this model, as each state observes the other building up its weaponry and reacts in-kind, the level of hostility between the states increases, because neither side can know the true intentions of its ever increasingly armed potential opponent. The key factor lies in each side's uncertainty over the private intentions of their opponent (Kydd 1997). It is difficult for a state to claim credibly that their increased arms are strictly for defensive purposes. According to Jervis, arms races create an intensifying cycle of hostile action and reaction, which ultimately may lead either to inadvertent or to deliberate armed conflict. The increase in hostility and the expected subsequent increase in conflict are consistent with both rational and cognitive psychology models. In the rational explanation, the observation of an opponent's buildup is a signal of hostile intent on the part of the other actor.[3] In psychologically based models, arms races produce misperception, which leads to tension, and increase the likelihood of emotionally driven or expressive reactions (as opposed to instrumentally rational choice), which in turn may lead to unintended conflict escalation.[4]

An important debate in the empirical literature broke out in the early 1980s over whether increases in arms did in fact increase the probability of conflict. Wallace (1982) found that arms races had a major substantive effect associated with an increase in likelihood of war, while Diehl (1983) found that arms races had little, if any, impact on the probability of war (see also Intriligator and Brito 1984; Diehl 1985). Subsequent formal analysis by Morrow (1989) suggests that a more sophisticated arms race model based on a rational choice premise can help to explain the difference in findings. The most recent empirical work on this subject suggests that arms races do in fact contribute positively to dispute escalation (Sample 1997). However, Sample's work fails to control for the potentially confounding effects associated with power transition logic, which in many instances should be quite collinear with arms races. While the measures may be quite collinear, the two arguments (arms races and power transitions) rest on quite different theoretical foundations. Arms races focus on military expenditures and joint reactions therein. Power transition logic focuses on the relationship of more aggregate measures of state power, status hierarchies, and relative status or dissatisfaction. One could argue, however, that in both cases the measures marking the presence of an arms race are poor instruments for the underlying theoretical mechanisms, which in fact are tapping into the same dyadic pressures. The aggregate data approach we employ here cannot distinguish between the psychological and signaling variants about how arms races affect interstate conflict. However, we do control for other factors, such as the presence of systemic and dyadic power transitions, and so hope to establish more clearly the empirical relationships between carefully specified operational measures of arms races and conflict.

An empirical criticism of using any objective measure of arms races notes that there may be multiple reasons or motives for what appears to be "arms racing," such as bureaucratic incentives to expand budgets or technological pressures to innovate (see Evangelista 1988 for a discussion of the role of technological innovation compared to quantitative arms racing). However, subjective measures of when leaders perceived themselves to be in arms races do not exist.

For our logit model, we build on Diehl's (1983) measure of arms races and code an arms race as present if the three-year moving average of constant-dollar military expenditure growth is greater than 8 percent for both states. Diehl's measure used current military spending; here we deflate spending to avoid coding as present an arms race simply because one or both states are experiencing a period of high inflation. One could argue from a psychological perspective (Jervis 1976) or a dominant indicator approach (Gartner 1997) that leaders attend to other measures, potentially including actual (current) spending along with stocks of particular weapons or specific technological innovations. As one check, an analysis using Diehl's measure based on current expenditures produces similar results to those we report here. Nevertheless, in keeping with existing arguments and tests, we maintain our focus on military expenditures.

We include only the three years before the occurrence of a militarized dispute and not expenditures for the year of the dispute. If the moving averages show greater than an 8 percent average military expenditure growth for both states, we code a final dummy variable marking arms race as a "1." If this joint condition does not hold, we code a "0."[5]

5. Balance of Power

The notion that an equitable balance in power or capabilities will maintain the peace between nations is one of the oldest and most central notions in world politics. It is also one of the most hotly contested. At the most basic level, balance of power theorists maintain that when a balance of military power, typically a relatively equal one, exists between two or more states, the states in question will be less likely to go to war with one another (Morgenthau 1956; Waltz 1979). Waltz argues explicitly that it is the likelihood of high costs and uncertain outcomes that exist when power is equitably balanced that leads to stability and peace, suggesting that "Where a balance of power does exist, it behooves the state that desires peace as well as safety to become neither too strong nor too weak" (Waltz 1959, 222). In contrast, when one state is more powerful than another, it may go to war against the other to enhance further its power position; in this view, weakness thus encourages aggression.

The balance of power literature is too extensive to allow a detailed review in the space of this entire volume, much less a section of a chapter (see Levy 2002). Realism, the international relations paradigm based on states' pursuit of power or security in an anarchic environment, has the most to say about the role that balances of power should play in interstate relations. Perhaps the earliest recorded balance of power theorist was Thucydides. Laying the foundations for much of the modern study of international politics, Morgenthau (1956) and Kaplan (1957) laid out what were, in essence, inductive arguments linking relative power parity to the likelihood of conflict. One source of confusion regarding balance of power arguments has to do with what precisely authors mean when they refer to the, or a, balance of power. Some refer to balancing behavior in the context of a state's option to join potential alliances (the alternative being bandwagoning), while others such as Waltz argue that the balance of power explanation of war "is a theory about the results produced by the uncoordinated actions of states" (1979, 122). Waltz's characterization is one of the clearest linking the behavior of states to some balance of their capabilities. In an elegant formal model of how power balances might affect the probability of war, Powell (1999) argues that "War is least likely when the existing distribution of benefits reflects the underlying distribution of power" (85). As he points out, this argument is in contrast to the standard supposition of the balance of power school, that power parity between actors should be associated with the lowest probability of war.

Unfortunately, testing balance of power "theory" in its common variants poses several problems. These problems interfere with developing a test of the argument as a whole for two principal reasons. First, several variants have been developed that define the concepts of "balance" and "power" in different ways. For instance, power may flow from capabilities (which are measurable ex ante) or on outcomes (in which case the argument becomes tautological). Some have noted that the "balance of power" may be a description of the status quo, a description of past conflict behavior, or a description of a state's foreign policy. Even once a conflict begins, the "balance of power" may exist at different levels. For example, in a simple model of bargaining and war, Smith and Stam (2001) show that the "balance of power" exists meaningfully in at least three separate ways. They point out the following interpretations of the "balance of power:" (1) the likelihood of one side or the other winning a single battle; (2) the likelihood of one side or the other being able to win a war to the finish; or (3) either side's subjective beliefs about either of the first two.

A second problem is that some variants of "balance of power" logic are inconsistent (see Organski 1958; Zinnes 1967; Bueno de Mesquita 1980; Niou, Ordeshook, and Rose 1989). For example, in contrast to the standard realist notion that an equal balance of power between two states (commonly assumed to mean the bilateral or dyadic military balance of capabilities) will reduce the likelihood of conflict, an equally logical argument has been made that states should in fact be most likely to fight when power is equal. According to the "power preponderance" model of war, when capabilities are roughly equal, the states involved will be less certain of a potential war's outcome than when there is a clear advantage. They may then both "push" in a dispute or low-level conflict, each believing it can prevail. As a result, low-level conflicts will be more likely to escalate into larger ones (Blainey 1988). However, when one side enjoys a preponderance of power, the outcomes of potential conflicts are clear and states will settle disputes before they escalate to war. According to this logic, it is when both states see a reasonable chance of winning—namely, when power is balanced—that disputes will be most likely to break out and to escalate to war.

We do not test various ancillary arguments and extensions to the basic balancing logic. Therefore, we set aside questions about how states react to shifting power balances depending on their risk attitudes or their relative degree of satisfaction (Huth, Bennett, and Gelpi 1992; Lemke 2002).[6] Many critiques of balance of power approaches suggest that it is too simplistic to expect all situations of balance to provide the same incentives for states to react uniformly and suggest interacting power balances with markers for particular situations when an equal power balance should lead to peace. Much of the recent work in this area has focused on how uncertainty about the bilateral balance of power may drive conflict, focusing on incomplete or private information about costs, outcomes, and durations. Most authors cite Blainey (1988) as the progenitor of this literature, primarily focused on bargaining and war (e.g., Fearon 1996; Wagner 2001; Werner 2000; Powell 2002; Reiter 2003; Smith and Stam 2001). While this is one of the most exciting areas of theory development concerning the role of national power to emerge in the past several years, we do not provide direct tests of related hypotheses here. It is not clear yet how to test these theories directly since we, as analysts, are likely to share the same ex ante information asymmetries or deficits as do the decision makers.

While direct tests of models driven by private information are beyond the scope of this project, we do provide some indirect tests of the balance of power approach. Some of the operational indicators claimed by various scholars to be direct measures of the critical variable needed to "test" their "theory" may actually be serving as proxies or indirect measures of incomplete information or uncertainly (for example, system power concentration or arms races may influence, or reflect, the level of uncertainty in the system). It may be this uncertainty that drives the observed probability of mutual armed conflict. Ultimately, the constraint of being unable to measure uncertainty directly may not be a problem if we can develop theoretically sound instruments or proxies. However, the challenge of integrating various interpretations of such measures leads us to the conclusion that we need more and better theory and more thought behind what our various measures actually capture rather than simply more rigorous empirical testing of existing arguments.

In our analysis that follows we ignore the logical flaws in balance of power arguments and instead focus on an empirical proposition drawn from one of the most basic balance of power notions, namely, that the closer the capabilities of two states are to one another, the lower the probability is of conflict initiation or escalation. We measure "power" using the national capability score from the COW project (Singer, Bremer, and Stuckey 1972). We create a ratio of the larger state's capabilities to the total capabilities of the dyad. The final variable ranges from 0.5 (at parity) to 1.0 (when one state possesses 100 percent of the capabilities in the dyad). Balance of power advocates would expect the variable to relate positively to conflict, while power preponderance advocates predict the opposite. Note that while the underlying argument whose hypothesis is being tested here is balance of power "theory," the variable in fact measures the balance of capabilities; we refer to the variable as the "balance of forces" to maintain the operational distinction.

6. Conventional Deterrence

Conventional deterrence models focus on the potential costs, either human or material, faced by or threatened against a potential attacker that may dissuade it from using force against a deterring state or its protégé, logic somewhat similar to balance of power arguments. In a setting of immediate deterrence, a variety of factors may come into play (see Huth 1988; Huth, Gelpi, and Bennett 1993; Huth and Russett 1993; Mearsheimer 1983). Here, in our general deterrence setting, we examine the associations between military superiority and the potential attacker's probability of initiating a conflict as compared to the non-directed hypotheses that emerge from balance of power logic. When considering conventional warfare, some scholars argue that deterrence by denial is likely to be an effective means of deterring a potential attacker. If an attacker's chances of victory decrease, or if the costs of likely victory increase, then a rational attacker is more likely to demure.

Frequently, scholars model the attacker's naive probability of winning simply as the attacker's capabilities divided by the dyad's total capabilities. Such a measure necessarily neglects the possible contributions of allied forces and distances between the attacker and the defender. To incorporate at least some of these contributing factors to likely outcomes of a conflict, we include in our model the initiator's subjective probability of winning a conflict developed as a component of the expected utility measures underlying the IIG predictions. This subjective probability discounts the direct capabilities of the initiator and target in a dyad by distance and adds expected assistance for each side by examining the likely contribution of other states in the international system for each of the dyad members. Using the measure in this way does not run the risk of introducing significant collinearity with the IIG equilibria variables, because the probability measure filters through several additional steps in leading to the dummy IIG predictions. Here, we include our measure of predicted war outcomes (predicted probability of winning from the initiator's point of view) as a continuous measure ranging between zero and one.

It is important to note that the measure is expected to be correlated with the balance of power measure discussed previously. At its heart, our war outcome probability measure remains the (adjusted and supplemented) capabilities of a potential attacker divided by the (adjusted and supplemented) summed capabilities of both states in the dyad. The balance of power measure is the (raw) capabilities of the larger state divided by the (raw) summed capabilities of both states. When the potential initiator is the larger state, these measures should have similar values. The two measures are theoretically distinct, however, and, empirically, differences created by adjusting capabilities in the probability of winning measure and in those dyads where the target is larger lead to sufficient differential variance to compute reliable estimates of their separate effects.

7. Democratic Peace

The large body of literature on the so-called democratic peace derives from the straightforward empirical observation that there has not been a war between modern liberal democracies. Importantly, the democratic peace proposition (DPP) has taken root in U.S. foreign policy circles; President Bill Clinton cited the proposition as partial justification for the U.S. military involvements in Haiti and the Balkans. George Bush noted the potential democratization of Iraq as a motive for a U.S.-led war in 2003. Recent theoretical arguments about the relationship between democracy and war begin with Doyle (1983), who built on Kant's notion of an emergent perpetual peace among liberal states based on shared norms of democratic compromise and the presence of restraining domestic institutions that prevent democracies from fighting one another. Following shortly after Doyle, Russett (1990) and Maoz and Russett (1993) focused on the role of elite level norms, or standards of behavior.[7] More recently, rational choice scholars turned their theoretical lenses on variants of an institutional constraint mechanism (Bueno de Mesquita et al. 2001; Reiter and Stam 2002) and signaling games (Schultz 2000). In the former, democratic leaders choose policies more carefully due to potentially punishing electoral constraints. In the signaling literature, democracies are better able to signal their resolve than other types of states.[8] Empirically, Oneal and Russett (2001b) present some of the most thorough tests of the DPP, although the first observations of the relationship between joint democracy and war appeared earlier (Babst 1964; Small and Singer 1976).

The democratic peace literature contains two dominant strands. The first uses increasingly sophisticated statistical methodologies and controls to increase our certainty regarding the veracity of the empirical claim (e.g., Senese 1997; Beck, Katz, and Tucker 1998; Raknerud and Hegre 1997; Green, Kim, and Yoon 2001). The second begins with the premise that the empirical finding exists and seeks to develop better theoretical explanations of the supposed facts (e.g., Schultz 2000; Fearon 1994; Bueno de Mesquita et al. 1999; Cederman 2001). While most current research continues to suggest that jointly democratic dyads are much less conflict prone than others, arguments persist over alternative explanations of the DPP. The most common counterarguments are that the "democratic peace" is merely a coincidence of alliances, the cold war, or some other factor creating common interests between democracies (e.g., Gowa 1999; Gartzke 1998; Lemke and Reed 1996; Henderson 2002). Other systematic empirical work has found that democracy does not exert the same pacifying effect for lower-scale dispute initiation as for wars (Senese 1997; Reiter and Stam 2003), suggesting a more complex relationship between democracy and conflict than a straightforward extension of the democracy and war findings might suggest. Finally, there is some evidence of an "autocratic peace," and it appears that pairs of similar states (either autocratic or democratic) appear to fight less than mixed pairs (Werner 2000; Raknerud and Hegre 1997). This suggests that political similarity or shared identity (rather than shared democracy) is the key to conflict avoidance.

Unfortunately, most of these studies have not taken a comprehensive approach when controlling for alternative explanations, including those suggested by expected utility models, which explicitly incorporate shared interests. Here we do not examine any particular mechanism through which democracy affects the level of interstate conflict. Instead, we examine whether the democratic peace finding holds up, given the most comprehensive controls to date. Ours tests include variables to examine numerous competing explanations and forms of the relationships between domestic political institutions and the likelihood of disputes and war.

Our specification for testing the effect of joint polity type on conflict is substantially more complex than previous designs, but it allows us to obtain more nuanced findings than existing work. We begin with the now-standard individual measures of regime type for the potential initiator and potential target in each dyad; we then add several interactions and variables measuring political similarity in order to explore a variety of hypotheses about democracy, democratization, and interstate conflict. As a result, we are able to capture the monadic effects of polity type on conflict, a variety of dyadic effects, the possibility of an autocratic peace, and the possibility that it is political similarity rather than shared democracy that drives the democratic peace.

We begin with individual regime-type scores from the Polity IV data set (see Jaggers and Gurr 1995; Marshall and Jaggers 2000). The Polity IV data now include this base regime-type coding as the "polity" variable, while other work has previously called it the "dem" score. The variable consists of the level of democracy in a state ("democ") minus the level of autocracy ("autoc"). This index ranges from -10, indicating states with low democracy and high autocracy, to $+10$, indicating states with the opposite. Following the methods suggested in the Polity IV codebook we interpolate data for years in which there is an interruption or interregnum (polity codes -66, -77, -88), setting those years to the average of the last year before interruption and first year after interruption, as long as that gap was not greater than five years in either direction. This interpolation allows us to measure the "polity" score for almost five hundred more nation-years than we would be able to otherwise (of about twelve thousand) and political similarity in about twenty thousand additional dyad-years. In most cases, the interpolation fills in a gap of one to three years of data; in no case does it fill in more than five years sequentially for a single country. We include separate indicators of initiator and target polity type to pick up linear trends linking regime type and conflict. If democracies initiate or escalate disputes more or less often than do autocracies, the indicator of the initiator's regime type alone will capture this. Similarly, if democracies are targets of conflict more or less often than autocracies, the indicator of the target's regime type will capture this.

We also include indicators of regime similarity to allow for the possibility that there is a lower probability of conflict when both states are highly autocratic. To examine the possibility of either an autocratic or a democratic peace in one step, we compute two interactive variables. We compute an interaction of the initiator's democracy score multiplied by the target's democracy score. In this case, both democracy scores range from -10 to $+10$, their original ranges. This interactive variable will be high (large and positive) for jointly autocratic *and* jointly democratic pairs, in a middle range for pairs of mixed regimes (e.g., democracy scores for either state near 0), and at the lowest value for pairs of dissimilar states (with one large and positive and one large and negative democracy score, for instance). The measure thus captures similarity, and if similar regimes do not fight one another, then this variable will have an effect on the relative risk of conflict while the other democratic peace variables do not. Because we wish to allow for the possibility that there is either only a democratic peace or both a democratic and an autocratic peace, we also include this term squared. This allows for a curvilinear relationship across the range of joint democracy-autocracy (specifically, this allows for an inverted U-shaped relationship, so that jointly democratic and jointly autocratic pairs may have lower conflict probabilities than middle pairs).

Finally, we wish to test whether democracies or autocracies differ in whether they initiate and escalate disputes against similar types of states. We begin by constructing a second measure of regime similarity as $20 - |Dem_{Initiator} - Dem_{Target}|$. This differenced regime score measure will range from 0 for similar regimes to 20 for dissimilar regimes. We subtract this value from 20 so that similar regimes have a score of 20 (indicating similarity) while dissimilar regimes have a score of 0. We then interact the initiator's regime type with our regime similarity measure. For this interaction, we cannot combine the initiator's raw democracy score (which ranges from -10 to $+10$) with similarity (which ranges from 0 to 20). Instead, we add 10 to that score (so that both range from 0 to $+20$) so that the interaction is consistently higher for states that are more similar and more democratic. If we allowed the initiator's democracy score to range from -10 to $+10$, then an autocracy times a similar state would have an X value of -200, while a democracy times a similar state would have an X value of $+200$, and all dissimilar states would have a value of 0 from the interaction. A single coefficient on this interaction would not tell us what we wish to know. However, if we transform the initiator's democracy score to be strictly positive, then the interaction is also always positive and is consistently higher when a more democratic state is the initiator and a more similar state is the target. Autocratic initiators and dissimilar pairs always have a low value on the variable.

While our specification of democracy is more complex than most found in the literature, it has the advantage of allowing us to test a variety of current and overlapping conjectures relating democracy and conflict. Most analyses in the current literature include dummy variables marking "joint democracy" if both states have a regime score over some level and "joint autocracy" if both scores are under some level, where the level varies widely from study to study (see Bennett 2002 for discussion). States not included in either of those two categories clump together into a third group. Our continuous specification allows for nonlinear effects that vary across the range of joint democracy-autocracy without forcing us to prespecify cutoffs for the joint categories. Overall, we expect disputes among more democratic dyads to escalate to war less often than disputes in less democratic dyads, but we also expect the effects of democracy to differ for different levels of dispute escalation following Senese's (1997) findings.

8. Expected Utility

Applications of expected utility theory to war initiation and escalation begin with the assumption that we can best model states' behavior as the result of leaders' conscious, instrumentally rational choices. In this approach, the anticipated costs and benefits of alternative actions guide leaders' choices. When faced with a choice between alternatives, rational choice theorists assume that states' leaders will choose the strategy with the best expected net return—the choice with the highest expected utility. Of the various arguments we investigate, expected utility theories are typically the most carefully developed and come closest to achieving a fully specified theory of war. Based on deductive logic, presentations of expected utility models typically begin with an explicit statement of the model's assumptions, and, typically, the hypotheses deduced from the model are exquisitely clear. Unfortunately, while theoretically precise and mathematically elegant, such models can also be devilishly difficult to test (Smith 1996a; Morton 1999; Signorino 1999; Lewis and Schultz 2002). Expected utility theorists make very strong claims about the theoretical superiority of their approach, and there are numerous examples in the international relations literature (e.g., Fearon 1994; Bueno de Mesquita et al. 2001; Morrow 1989; Werner 1999).

The empirical tests we present make a substantial contribution to the debate on the relative scientific value of expected utility models, in part because most of the standard criticisms of rational choice models have been theoretical. Attacks on rational choice models come from several directions. Some argue that tests of equilibrium-based models are problematic because a model's predictions simply reflect the underlying solution concept the authors employ rather than reflecting any particular truth about the nature of politics (Riker 1982; Signorino 2000; Lewis and Schultz 2002). It is more common that critics question whether we should characterize leaders' decision-making processes as "rational" in the first place (e.g., Lebow 1981; Jervis, Lebow, and Stein 1985; Rosen 2002) or whether the expected utility approach is as comprehensive and encompassing as its proponents claim (Simowitz and Price 1990). Some critics have been willing to make quite strong condemnations of rational choice models. For instance, Green and Shapiro (1994, 6) argue, "The case has yet to be made that these models have advanced our understanding of how politics works in the real world."

Despite vigorous theoretical criticism, there has been limited critique of the various expected utility theories of war based on systematic empirical analysis. We will investigate most closely Bueno de Mesquita and Lalman's 1992 domestic variant of the IIG, the most widely cited of these conflict models. We choose to test this particular model for two reasons. First, the model that Bueno de Mesquita and Lalman develop is very ambitious. While most expected utility models depict a relatively narrow puzzle or specific question (see Fearon 1995; Schultz 1999; Powell 2001), the IIG is a game that can apply to almost any international interaction, in that it incorporates both domestic and international political actors in a wide variety of possible outcomes ranging from the status quo to negotiation to war. Of the extant expected utility models, the IIG comes closest to approximating a complete conflict-data-generating process. Second, Bueno de Mesquita and Lalman go to great lengths to develop observable empirical measures for many of the abstract concepts lying at the heart of their model. Most rational choice theorists treat abstract concepts such as similarity of interests, risk aversion, and the costs of war as implicitly immeasurable (Powell 1999).

The IIG is a stylized series of strategic decisions in extensive form that lead to eight possible outcomes for any dyadic interstate relationship (see fig. 4.1). A very general overview is that the game represents an interaction structure between a potential conflict initiator (state A) and a potential target (state B). The game begins with a choice by state A to issue some type of demand to state B. If A does not make a demand, then B may make a demand. If neither state does, then the out-

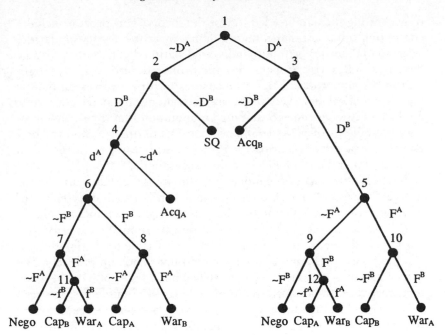

Fig. 4.1.   International Interaction Game.
(Reprinted from Bueno de Mesquita and Lalman 1992, fig. 2.1, with permission.)

come of the interaction is the status quo. If one state initiates a crisis by making a demand, then at subsequent decision nodes in the game, actors A and B alternately choose to make further demands (escalating the conflict) or not (resulting in some type of settlement). Each actor makes the choices it believes will yield the greatest expected utility.

An appropriate test of the IIG examines whether its equilibrium predictions match actual dyadic outcomes, as the game predicts a unique outcome for each directed dyad-year. The independent variables for testing the model are not the utility scores. Oneal and Russett's (1999a) analysis does not represent a thorough test of the model, as the utility scores combine in a nonlinear manner through the structure of the IIG to yield an equilibrium prediction of the game's outcome. In Bueno de Mesquita and Lalman's very limited tests (707 European dyad-years), they claimed to find substantial evidence that the predictions of the IIG fit actual conflict behavior. Tests using a larger set of cases seemed to support this claim (Bennett and Stam 2000b, 2000c) but with only a limited set of control variables. Testing the propositions laid out in the IIG is difficult because of the complexity of generating the data needed to test the theory. This process includes computing utility estimates that combine measures of the similarities of dyadic alliance portfolios, individual national capabilities, dyadic distances, states' risk propensities, and projected third party choices to join in. Computation of risk propensities in turn involves estimating the hypothetical best and worst security situations in which a state might find itself, a time-consuming computation that involves searching over billions of possible alliance patterns in order to find the best and worst security scenarios for each country-year (see Bennett and Stam 2000d and on-line EUGene documentation).

We begin the tests of the model by estimating the states' utilities for different outcomes in each directed dyad-year. For each directed dyad-year, we created a prediction of which of the eight outcomes should result. Because these equilibrium predictions are mutually exclusive, we must exclude one from the logit model, the variable predicting the status quo.[9] The MID data and the game do not match up precisely. The MID codes five outcome categories, the game codes eight. For the game outcomes that do not correspond directly to MID outcomes, we need to match them to the most appropriate MID outcome. Since they represent middle levels of escalatory behavior after a demand is made (and a dispute is initiated), we would expect the acquiescence and negotiation equilibria to bear a positive relationship to dispute initiation and escalation to medium levels, but probably a negative relationship to escalation at very high levels. We would also expect a positive association of the war equilibrium with both the initiation of militarized disputes and escalation through all levels of force.

9. Geographic Contiguity

While there is no "theory of geographic contiguity" per se, some argue that contiguity is a necessary condition for war between most pairs of states (Bueno de Mesquita 1981; Maoz and Russett 1993). Maoz and Russett argue that, for all but the most powerful states, the challenge of projecting military power across long distances presents a hurdle that most states simply cannot clear. The vast majority of states simply cannot fight one another across long distances, as they lack the power projection and logistical capabilities needed to do so. As a result, distant pairs of states that might otherwise consider the mutual use of force remain eternally quiescent. In addition, contiguous states may be more likely to have unresolved disagreements over the settlement of territorial issues between them that noncontiguous states do not, either because noncontiguous states have no point of contact or because the salience of bordering territory is higher than more remote territory (Vasquez 1996). Others have argued that contiguity is merely incidental to conflict. Holsti (1991), for example, argues that in fact only certain strategic borders are friction prone. Empirically, however, studies have continued to find that geographic contiguity has a powerful positive association with violent conflict (Diehl 1991; Bremer 1992; Kocs 1995).[10]

Although contiguity is one of the selection criteria for politically relevant dyads, its inclusion in our analysis of that sample is not a problem, as the variable serves to distinguish between contiguous dyads and those that are noncontiguous but where one state is a major power. We measure contiguity as a dummy variable, with a "1" marking a dyad in which the states are contiguous on land and a "0" otherwise, based on the COW 1993 contiguity data set.

10. Nuclear Deterrence

Many scholars have argued that nuclear deterrence—particularly MAD—between the superpowers was a key factor in avoiding war between the major powers after World War II (Glaser 1992; for a contrary view, see Jervis, Lebow, and Stein 1985). Because each state knew that it faced unavoidable destruction—or, rather more likely, unacceptable damage, in the case of a nuclear exchange—neither side would rationally take the final escalatory step of initiating a nuclear attack. The deterrent effects from a threatened nuclear exchange on lower levels of conflict were less clear, though. Some argued that nuclear armed states would be very careful about taking lower-level aggressive steps that might escalate conflicts to a level at which there was a risk of nuclear exchange. However, others argued that the certainty that neither side would use its nuclear weapons made the world safe for conventional confrontation between the superpowers, leading to a need for large conventional defensive forces as well as massive nuclear arsenals. The evidence cited for the effectiveness of nuclear deterrence appears in the lack of a war between the United States and the Soviet Union during the cold war. However, the nuclear deterrence explanation is almost perfectly collinear with other equally compelling explanations, including post–World War II war weariness, bipolarity, and increasing interdependence (see, e.g., Mueller 1994). The evidence in favor of the pacifying effects of superpower MAD is limited at best (specifically, the single observation of no superpower war).

As nuclear weapons spread beyond the superpowers, more testing of

the behavioral origins of **WAR**

their effects is now possible. Huth and Russett (1984) provide some additional evidence, finding that nuclear weapons appear to have some deterrent effect in crises between the superpowers and other states. The belief in the efficacy of nuclear deterrence has led some to suggest, in fact, that we should actually encourage the spread of nuclear weapons. For instance, Waltz (1995, 4) argues, "the gradual spread of nuclear weapons is better than either no spread or rapid spread. . . . Nuclear weapons make wars hard to start. These statements hold for small as for big nuclear powers. Because they do, the gradual spread of nuclear weapons is more to be welcomed than feared" (see also Bueno de Mesquita and Riker 1982).

The past three decades have seen an increasing number of dyads where one or both states have nuclear capability. On one hand, if nuclear weapons affect states' calculations of the likely costs of conflict, and if nuclear weapons may actually be used, then we should see the deterrent effect of such weapons in any dyad where they are present. On the other hand, if there is a nuclear taboo that prevents states from seriously considering the use of these weapons, then they may have no effect (Tannenwald 2001). Empirically, our investigation seeks to discover whether there is now enough variation in the possession of nuclear weapons across states and time to sort out their effects from other factors.

We include three dummy variables concerning the possession of nuclear weapons. The first marks whether the potential conflict initiator in a dyad has nuclear capability, the second marks whether the potential target has nuclear capability, and the third marks whether both states have nuclear capabilities. The third variable is particularly important to test arguments that nuclear powers are unlikely to use nuclear weapons against nonnuclear states for fear of adversely affecting their reputations. With these variables, we can see whether possessing a nuclear capability affects a state's behavior toward nuclear armed targets or nonnuclear targets. We code the following states as having nuclear capability: the United States from 1945; the USSR from 1949; Britain from 1952; France from 1960; China from 1964; Israel from 1973; India from 1974; Pakistan from 1986; South Africa between 1980 and 1991; and Ukraine, Kazakhstan, and Belarus in 1992.

11. Power Transition

In stark contrast to balance of power advocates, Organski and Kugler (1980) argue that periods of power parity are more likely to lead to war than periods of power preponderance.[11] Unlike simple power preponderance arguments, however, power transition logic suggests that it is power parity plus shifts in power, plus dissatisfaction with the status quo on the part of the overtaking state, that lead to conflict. Power transition theorists maintain that it is when states are passing one another in relative power (with changes driven by domestic political and economic development) that the probability of war and conflict is greatest. Organski (1958) argues that states gain benefits from a higher position in the international hierarchy of states, in part due to subjective notions of status and in part due to greater coercive capacity, and so constantly strive to rise in the system and become the system's leader. However, Organski assumed that the system leader would not willingly concede its leadership role when challenged, particularly if the leader and challenger differ in their preferences for the system's rules and distribution of material resources. The resulting competition for the system's leadership role increases the chances for violent conflict. Power transition arguments specifically focus on the decisions made by state leaders, with Lemke and Kugler (1996, 4) explaining that

> The cornerstone of power transition theory is that *parity* is the necessary condition for major war. However (unlike balance of power theories), power transition theory does not deny the importance of decision-making, nor does it imply that structures determine outcomes. Rather, power transition theory contends that parity sets the stage where decision makers *can, but need not necessarily,* choose major war as a viable alternative. [italics in original][12]

The definition of what constitutes a "major war" is an important distinction. Organski and Kugler focused on what they called "system altering" wars, which tend to be more easily identified than creating distinctions between wars fought on a smaller scale. (For an exception to the claim that system altering or major wars need to be materially large, see Bueno de Mesquita 1990). The problem with following Organski and Kugler's focus on system altering wars is threefold. First, it is unclear what constitutes an alteration of sufficient magnitude for a war to be "major." Second, these wars, as they inductively describe them, are so rare that their claims are untestable with the means employed here. Third, "major wars" can only be identified ex post, creating a set of epistemological problems about studying the origins of conflict.

Power transition theorists initially focused on transitions between the dominant state in the international system and close contenders as those that are most likely to produce conflict. Organski and Kugler, for example, examined relations only between the most powerful state in the system and those that they reasonably expected to challenge it, operationalized as states within 80 percent of the aggregate power of the dominant state. From this original version, power transition theorists have developed the logic in several ways. First, some now include a focus on transitions within regional hierarchies. For example, Lemke (2002) finds that power transitions do occur in this setting. Second, others have focused on transitions within rival dyads. Huth, Bennett, and Gelpi (1992) found that power transitions among all great power rival dyads increased the initiation of militarized disputes. Third, others focus on how satisfaction and power may function in driving conflict within transitions (see Lemke and Werner 1996; Lemke and Reed 1998; Oneal, De Soysa, and Park 1998). Others have examined the precise timing of the parity, power shift, and war relationship to try to determine which moment is the most dangerous. It might be just before parity emerges or the period immediately after the rising state overtakes the declining state.

Lemke (2002), who advocates the expansion of power transition logic beyond its original scope to include a far greater population of dyads, suggests that the narrow initial focus of the approach is inappropriate. While he focuses on regional leaders and regional hierarchies, an extension of his argument suggests that we should examine every dyadic relationship for a dominant state, even if neither state is the top state in the international system. Following this line of argument, we might expect to see power transition dynamics apply in any dyad we select. This more inclusive power transition logic argues that we should expect to observe dyadic parity and power shifts associated with greater incidence of conflict, the direct opposite of balance of power arguments (in its dyadic variant). For dyadic-level power transition logic to make sense, the key distinction comes down to what we believe a system of states to be. It might be the entire system of all states, a regional subsystem, or simply a system of two. Physical geography may outline the boundaries of the various systems we might expect to find. We begin our empirical investigation as the broadest possible notion of systems, at the dyadic level.

Our measures of power transition here include measures to examine the relationship between power parity, dynamic power shifts, satisfaction with the status quo, systemic leadership, and the incidence of war linked together through power transition logic. First, our basic balance of power variable (discussed previously) captures the effects of static parity. The sign for the dyadic power balance parameter should be positive from the perspective of power transition advocates and negative for balance of power advocates. Second, we compute a variable measuring dynamic dyadic transitions in power as an interaction of equal power and differences in growth rates, not taking into account the satisfaction of the actors that may be passing one another. This variable results from the interaction of two variables measuring "equality" and "growth," producing a coding of how intense the power transition is in every dyad in our study. Since power transitions occur only when states are close to each other in power, we begin by measuring how close to power parity the two states are. We start with our continuous balance of forces measure, which ranges from 0.5 when the states are equal in power to 1 when they are unequal. We then transform the variable into the range from 0 when unequal to 1 when equal by computing degree of equality = 2 − (2*balance of forces).

We then compute a five-year moving average of the two states' annual percentage growth, using the COW national capabilities index (CINC). We then difference these two rates and take the absolute value to obtain a measure of how quickly the gap between the two states was either shrinking or growing. For example, if one state had average growth of 2 percent and the other average growth of 6 percent, the difference was 4 percentage points. According to power transition advocates, this situation of rapid transition should be more conflict prone than a situation where the difference was only 1 or 2 percentage points. Here the intuition is that the states should have greater difficulty designing diplomatic solutions, thereby becoming more prone to miscalculations and strategic error during times of rapid change or greater instability. We then create an interaction term with the degree of equality and the difference in growth rates. The value of the variable is high when the two states are close in power and the differences in their rates of growth are large. In contrast, the value of the variable is low when the states are far apart in terms of power or have similar rates of growth. Power transition theorists would expect the variable to correlate positively with conflict behavior.

Third, to capture Organski's (1958) original notion of hierarchy and status, or more recent variants' emphasis on relative satisfaction, we follow Lemke and Reed's (1998) arguments and compute a variable that also incorporates states' satisfaction with each other's international policies. We measure the satisfaction of two states with one another by using the tau_b score of the two states' alliance portfolios. Tau_b is a correlation coefficient representing the similarity of the two states' alliance portfolios. Lemke and Reed argue that states that are dissatisfied with the nature of the dyadic hierarchy will seek different allies, creating a measure of revealed preferences. States satisfied with their status or role in the hierarchy should have relatively similar alliance portfolios. Note that this logic is inconsistent with Walt's (1984) balancing and band-wagoning logic. Walt argues that it is the perception of threat and not satisfaction or dissatisfaction that drives a state's alliance choices.

We then multiply the tau$_b$ measure by -1 so higher values represent disagreement and interact it with our dyadic power transition measure to obtain the final variable.[13] Finally, to contrast Lemke's logic with Organski's original argument, we compare power transitions in all dyads to the effects of power transitions among the most powerful states in the system by creating a final interaction of the dyadic transition measure. Following Organski's argument that Britain was the system leader through World War II and the United States after that, we interact our transition variable (measured with satisfaction) with a dummy variable marking (1) dyads through 1945 where Britain is one dyad member and (2) dyads from 1946 on where the United States is one member. These dyads could be involved in a system leadership transition. The measure will have a value of zero for all dyads not involving the system leader, and so the effect of the variable on conflict will always be zero in these cases. Other values will allow us to estimate whether there is any additional probability of conflict in situations involving the dominant state.

12. Trade Interdependence

The argument that increased international trade lowers conflict between nations dates back centuries. The idea was particularly in vogue in the period before World War I, but the nature and length of that war helped to discredit the liberal idea that interstate trade would make war obsolete (Carr 1946). More recently, the argument that trade should lower the likelihood of armed conflict between states has been revived in arguments about the so-called Kantian peace (Russett and Oneal 2001). In *Triangulating Peace,* Russett and Oneal argue that an interaction of democratic institutions, interstate trade, and international organizations contributes powerfully to international cooperation and the reduction of international conflict. Their straightforward argument is that, when states are interdependent, they have incentives to avoid conflicts that may result in a costly disruption of trade. The more one state depends on another for trade, the greater the likely cost of adjusting to a reduction or cutoff of trade flows. Trading countries may also learn about one another, lowering conflicts of interest and misconceptions about one another. Oneal and Russett operationalize trade interdependence as a contributing factor in the reduction in conflict by computing the mutual trade dependence of each state in a dyad by dividing total dyadic trade by GDP. For each dyad-year, this gives us two trade dependence measures, one for each state.

Neither the arguments, the operational methods they employ, nor the data used by Oneal and Russett are without controversy. In terms of the trade and GDP data, which are notorious for their unreliability, particularly in the early years of the data series, Oneal and Russett interpolate between observations to reduce missing data. It is important to note that in later years of the series, where they cannot reliably fill in gaps in the data, they recode International Monetary Fund (IMF) data originally labeled "missing" as zero trade. This is a particularly problematic issue regardless of one's solution. By dropping cases rather than assuming the trade to be zero, the loss of cases may introduce substantial selection bias into analysis. Alternatively, coding the data as zero may introduce substantial nonrandom measurement error if the two states actually had any trade. GDP data, which does not exist directly for most countries before World War II, comes from the estimates of economic historians, with key assumptions made to convert estimated relative growth measures to comparable dollar values.

Other scholars have used alternative measures, believing that dyadic trade divided by GDP is a poor measure of trade dependence (Barbieri 1996). In terms of the argument linking greater trade dependence to more quiescent international politics, it may be too simplistic to argue that trade provides incentives for states to avoid conflict. A state dependent on another may have incentives to provoke conflict if such conflict might improve terms of trade. Canada and the United States have been involved in trade disputes multiple times over the past forty years that escalated to the show of naval military force. By using their naval forces during a trade dispute, smaller countries such as Canada and Spain are able to demonstrate how seriously they take the trade dispute, which may be far more salient for them than it is for the much larger United States. Low-level conflict with a trading partner may also provide a means of signaling dissatisfaction with the relationship. Moreover, the cutoff of dyadic trade may not always lead to significant costs for either side of the dispute. Firms typically use multiple suppliers. The development of a multinational free-trade system means that states have ready alternative suppliers willing and able to substitute for trade lost during a low-level militarized dispute between two countries. This ability to substitute for lost trade with one partner lowers the economic costs of conflict associated with trade disruption (Brooks 2001). Finally, different types of trade, or trade in different types of goods with varying elasticity of demand, may be differentially associated with the economic cost of conflict (Crescenzi 2000). Raw materials are more substitutable than high-tech imports, for instance. This would suggest that total dyadic trade is, at best, a crude indicator of the likely cost of trade disruption.

Setting aside criticisms of measures and theory for the moment, we include two trade dependence variables in our analysis, one measuring dyadic trade as a proportion of GDP for the potential initiator and the second measuring dyadic trade as a proportion of GDP for the potential target. Prior work on trade (e.g., Oneal and Russett 1996) typically combines these variables and uses the minimum of the two trade levels in the analysis. This is largely because previous studies focused on nondirected dyad data, following the so-called weak link argument (Dixon 1993). As noted in chapter 3, in a nondirected dyadic analysis, we must transform the two variables somehow to remove the directionality of the initiator and target from the variables. The weak link assumption that accomplishes this argues that it is the less constrained of the two states in a possible conflict that will drive any conflict initiation and escalation. If one state in a dyad is highly trade dependent on the other, and therefore cannot risk losing this income from trade, it is likely (according to the weak link argument) to be more constrained than the less trade-dependent partner in the dyad. If the second state is largely independent of the first, as is often the case when great powers interact with small states, and hence trade is less salient than it is for the first state in the dyad, the second state will ignore the trade constraint on the first. Trade between the two may then appear to have no restraining effect if the second state is the aggressor. We include the measures of trade dependence separately for two reasons. First, because we have a directed dyadic design, we can easily include both measures. Second, we find the logic of the weak link argument applied to trade to be unsatisfying.

Even with the interpolations and data assumptions made by Oneal and Russett, there are substantially more missing data on trade dependence than is the case with any other variable in our data set. Because the trade data are not missing randomly, we are particularly concerned about how including trade may bias our other results (closed autocratic states do not report accurate GDP and trade data, and a large proportion of states have missing data before World War II). When we add the trade variables to our analysis, we lose 23 percent of the cases in our analysis of all dyads and 38 percent of the cases in our sample of politically relevant dyads. Such a major loss of data, particularly when it is systematic and correlated with other factors we wish to analyze, will likely bias our results on other variables. As a result, we add trade to our model in a secondary analysis after we analyze the larger, more complete data set.

INTERNATIONAL SYSTEM LEVEL OF ANALYSIS

The final area we investigate is the nature of the international system and its effects on the behavior of nation-states. Systemic theories of international conflict have a long history in the study of international politics. Realists traditionally start the discussion by noting what they refer to as the "self-help," or anarchic nature, of the system of states. Indeed, for many scholars, the defining characteristic or key feature that distinguishes international politics from any other variety thereof is the lack of central authority or binding contract enforcement mechanisms. The absence of a recognized central government with its own police power to enforce international law (and the anarchy this implies) leads some to then conclude that the distribution of power and beliefs about system-level power are where we should look to understand the behavior of states (Waltz 1979; Wendt 1999; Singer, Bremer, and Stuckey 1972; Morgenthau 1956). Perhaps the leading system-level scholar of the past fifty years, Kenneth Waltz argues powerfully that any theory or explanation of international relations that looks to levels below the international system level is no longer a theory of "international politics" but instead is merely a theory of foreign policy—implicitly, somehow less worthy of study. Waltz's argument begs the question of what the politics of nations are, however, and what determines the particular relations of states in the international system as compared to general levels of conflict throughout the system.

We take a somewhat different tack concerning system effects and their role in international politics. In our view, since international politics results from the interaction of states' individual and collective foreign policies, and the interaction of decisions and acts of foreign policy, there is no relevant distinction to make between foreign policy and international politics. This does not imply that we can safely ignore the effects of varying systemic characteristics. Rather, it suggests to us that to analyze the nature of international politics with a myopic focus on system structure, without reference to national decisions about foreign policy, would be folly. In the section that follows, we summarize the dominant and directly testable propositions or conjectures made by the leading international system-level theorists. By focusing on those that are directly testable, here we necessarily restrict ourselves to theories or arguments that focus on the material distribution of capabilities. Realist systemic explanations tend to focus on such capabilities, although Van Evera (1999) develops a notable exception. For an alternative view, based almost entirely on the subjective beliefs of the actors (which we cannot test directly), see Wendt 1999. To understand better the nature of the shifting beliefs to which Wendt and other constructivists refer but fail to specify in rigorous or testable fashion, see Savage 1954 and Converse 1964. We begin our discussion of system-level effects with the long cycle literature.

13. Economic Long Cycles/Kondratieff Waves

Some economists have argued that the world economy goes through long-term cycles of growth and stagnation (Kondratieff 1935). Building on the assumption that states need significant financial resources to prosecute interstate war, Joshua Goldstein speculates that there should be strong correlations between the international system's economic growth cycles and the relative likelihood of interstate war. He developed arguments about the effects of these economic cycles on international conflict through two mechanisms (Goldstein 1988, 1991; for a critique, see Beck 1991). First, as an exceedingly expensive activity, Goldstein argues that war requires economic prosperity, which is most common throughout the international system during periods of economic growth. Second, periods of systemic economic growth may also lead to heightened competition for world resources and markets. The ability (through prosperity) and demand (through competition) to fight for territory or resources may result in more and/or more severe wars during periods of prosperity, particularly among the dominant economies in the international system. Notably, Goldstein does not develop a detailed theory of war initiation. Rather than carefully developing a model of the causal path to war during periods of growth compared to periods of relative scarcity, he devotes the bulk of his work to developing the empirical basis for his claim that systemic economic cycles actually exist in the first place.

Goldstein found substantial evidence of long waves both in economic conditions and in wars but found less consistent evidence of a relationship between them. In particular, Goldstein found that, while major power wars were no more frequent during economic upswing phases than during other phases, they were more severe. Here we do not attempt to develop the missing theory that might help explain why several of Goldstein's hypotheses failed to work out. Instead, we aim to test more rigorously the empirical proposition that there are links between the system's economic growth cycle and interstate conflict.

We use Goldstein's (1988, 247) coding rules for periods of economic upswings and account for two representations of the "economic upswing" variable beyond 1975 when Goldstein's coding ends. His coding rules are somewhat problematic because he argues that there may be cycles within cycles. For instance, Goldstein initially codes 1968–75 as an economic downswing, which we project forward leading to a coding for 1968–92 as a global economic downswing. However, Goldstein also seems to suggest that the longer period 1940–80 is really a larger economic upswing (218). Therefore, we also test a coding rule of labeling 1940–92 as one long upswing. We found similar results regardless of which coding rule we employed. In our final analysis presented here, we include a dummy variable that distinguishes those years that were in an economic upswing (1) from those that were not (0) using the first of these two coding methods.

14. Hegemonic Stability

Much like the logic behind the various power transition arguments, the literature on the role that hegemony plays in international politics focuses on the pattern of changing capabilities among the top states in the international system. Hegemonic stability models focus on the effects of the presence or absence of a hegemon in international affairs (Kindleberger 1981; Gilpin 1981; Krasner 1976). Hegemonic stability scholars argue that the international system is most stable when one state controls a preponderance of the international system's resources and can impose its policies upon other members of the system. Periods of bipolarity or multipolarity, where there are two or more great power states of relatively similar size competing for dominance in the system, will be less stable than periods of hegemony. Hegemons are unable to maintain their position at the top of the international hierarchy forever, however (Kennedy 1987). Varying growth rates and/or the costs of system leadership lead to inevitable cycles of rise and decline, and conflict will eventually occur when the single great power is no longer able to ride herd on the other states in the system. From a related cyclic perspective on "power cycles," Modelski (1987) similarly argues that a cycle of power and wealth driven by the disparity between the costs and benefits of monopoly in the international system leads inevitably to the successive rise and decline of world powers, with periods of dominance being the periods of greatest stability.

Various authors have measured hegemony in a variety of ways, emphasizing different aspects of the phenomenon (for example, by measuring overall military resources, economic power, or naval power). We employ Gilpin's (1981) identification of the two periods of hegemonic governance in the international system relevant for our analysis. According to Gilpin, from 1816 to 1918 the system was under British hegemony, and from 1946 through the end of our study the United States was a hegemon. We include a variable marking the period of British hegemony to 1918; the post-1945 period of U.S. hegemony is marked in our analysis by the same variable marking the bipolar system. Because Gilpin codes the postwar period as hegemonic, we create a problem of collinearity in that Waltz and other scholars consider the same period to be bipolar.

With these characterizations of hegemonic versus multipolar periods or systems, our goal is to establish whether the postwar period has a different baseline risk of conflict compared to the interwar period and pre–World War I. For the moment, we ignore the inferential problems that Gilpin's and Waltz's dissimilar codings of the postwar period create. Note that the empirical prediction of these theories is that long time periods should be different from one another because of hegemony (bipolarity) or the lack thereof. This is a rather unspecific prediction, and there could be other characteristics of the system over long periods that make it more or less dangerous. The test is essentially, while controlling for other factors, whether the average baseline rates of conflict over these periods differ. This admittedly unsatisfying and overly broad test is where these loosely specified arguments leave us with regard to expectations about the incidence of interstate conflict and war. Hegemonic stability models typically predict that both the pre–World War I and post–World War II periods should be more stable than the interwar period, when there was not a clear hegemon.

15. International System Polarity

Waltz (1979) and other neorealists made three major modifications to the classical balance of power approach.[14] First, Waltz argues that states do not pursue power directly, but rather they seek to maximize their security. This subtle difference (subtle because power is an essential factor determining a state's national security) allows for the possibility that states will not constantly seek to expand nor to always choose guns over butter. Second, Waltz and other neorealists argue that polarity is the key attribute of the international system that critically affects states' pursuit of security. Third, Waltz conjectures that balancing—states acting to oppose potential hegemons—is automatic.

For neorealists, polarity or the number of large great powers present in the international system is of prime theoretical and empirical importance. In a bipolar system, where there are two major powers clearly separated from the other states in terms of relative capabilities, the major powers can achieve security through internal balancing. They do not have to rely on alliance partners who may prove unreliable or drag them into unwanted conflicts (Snyder 1984). In a multipolar world, though, the capabilities of several states simultaneously affect the security of any single state, forcing all states to mind the actions of all others and to pay much greater attention to alliances. The uncertainty inherent in this complex system may lead to a greater incidence of miscalculation, in turn leading to conflicts that would have been avoidable under the more transparent conditions of bipolarity. The evidence supporting this argument essentially boils down to the observation that there was no war between the United States and the Soviet Union during the forty-five years of the cold war.

Critiques of neorealist style arguments about the effects of system polarity come from several directions. The first wave of logical counterarguments came from Deutsch and Singer (1964), who argue that states would in fact be less likely to attack others under multipolar conditions, first, because uncertainty forced states to divide their attention among many potential foes and, second, because cross-cutting ties could exist between multiple states that would serve to reduce hostility. Divided attention would make it less likely that any state could be confident enough about winning that it would start a conflict that might inadvertently escalate into an unwanted war; cross-cutting ties would reduce overall hostility levels and provide positive incentives to avoid conflict. Wayman (1984) in turn argues that there were different kinds of polarity, what he termed "power polarity" and "cluster polarity," with the more nuanced characterization seeming to reconcile the competing arguments. Using finer measures of polarity, Wayman found evidence that bipolar systems were somewhat more peaceful than multipolar ones.

Criticizing polarity arguments from a different tack, Bueno de Mesquita (1978, 1981) argues that these simplistic system-level arguments about polarity were inadequate because they implicitly assumed that there is a dominant systemic risk attitude. According to Bueno de Mesquita's argument, Waltz implicitly assumes risk-acceptant decision makers who react to multipolar uncertainty by *starting* conflicts, while Deutsch and Singer implicitly assume risk-averse decision makers who *avoid* conflict under conditions of uncertainty. The reconciliation of the two perspectives plus concern for risk attitude required scholars to resort to a lower level of analysis, namely, the decision level. Huth, Bennett, and Gelpi (1992) and Huth, Gelpi, and Bennett (1993) tested some of these arguments about the interactive nature of polarity and risk-taking propensity and found that the interaction of risk attitudes and system structure did help to account for a larger proportion of international conflict initiation, but not conflict escalation. However, they also found that, when tested statistically, a single variable marking bipolarity did not correlate with conflict initiation.

Other evidence against Waltz's argument appears if we look at the length of time the system went without a war under bipolarity. When the system was bipolar, forty-five years passed (1946 to 1991) without a war between the poles. When it was multipolar, there were thirty-four years without a major power war between 1870 and 1904, thirty-eight years without a major power war between 1816 and 1854, and forty-four years without a war in Europe between 1870 and 1914. Critics of system structure stories argue that these numbers show that the pacifying effects of bipolarity have been overstated, especially given the much larger number of opportunities for war between major powers before 1945 (Hopf 1991).

Regarding the initiation and escalation of disputes among major powers, as well as the incidence of disputes among nonmajor powers, note that one of the reasons that a bipolar system is stable, according to Waltz, is that the two major powers will be vigilant and will respond quickly to any challenge by the other major power. Because they will respond quickly and because both states are resolved, war should not occur. Nevertheless, even if this logic is correct, this does not necessarily imply that there will be fewer disputes between the major powers in such a system. In fact, because they are acting to counter each other's moves quite quickly, there might be more disputes short of war than in other types of systems. If this were the case, then we would expect minimal reduction (or even an increase) in the risk of dispute initiation between major powers during bipolar periods and a negative effect only for dispute escalation. Extending neorealism logic to minor powers, the major powers may enlist the aid of proxies, whom they might encourage to fight (or resist) the other major power, leading to a further increase in disputes. According to this logic, there may actually be more disputes among minor power states during bipolar periods than during multipolar eras.

Again, as was the case with our tests of the democratic peace proposition, here we do not test the mechanisms claimed to lie behind the various polarity-based arguments and conjectures found in the literature. Instead, we more carefully test whether the post–World War II period was more or less prone to conflict than we would expect, given the effects of the various other factors believed to affect the likelihood of conflict. As mentioned previously, using the periods as delineated by Waltz and Gilpin, the post-1945 era is either bipolar or hegemonic, depending on whose classification one chooses. Our dummy variable marking hegemony will measure effects on conflict behavior common to both 1816–1918 and 1945, while the post-1945 variable will measure effects from 1945 on. If the post-1945 era is more peaceful than other periods, however, there is no way to tell whether the cause is hegemony or bipolarity (Gilpin's and Waltz's variables have no further variation). As a result, when we present our results we will discuss time periods rather than focusing on hegemony or bipolarity. We create a dummy variable to mark bipolarity, coding the variable as a "1" when the year of possible dispute was after 1945 and a "0" otherwise. We also created an additional variable by combining the post-1945 variable with one marking the U.S.-USSR dyad. That is, the variable was coded a "1" for dyad-years after 1945 between the United States and the USSR and a "0" for other dyad-years. According to Waltz's argument, this variable in particular should have a negative coefficient, although the coefficient on bipolarity alone might have a positive coefficient without violating the model's logic. Because of collinearity, we were unable to test this variant and so, confronting an early limit to knowledge, include only the broader measure, which differentiates all post–World War II dyads from others.

16. *Systemic Power Concentration and Movement*

Reacting to what they saw as flaws in the many arguments and measures relating polarity and power concentration in the international system to the incidence of conflict, Singer, Bremer, and Stuckey (1972) developed a set of sophisticated quantitative measures for various aspects of system structure, including a continuous measure of systemic power concentration that Mansfield (1994) recently reanalyzed. Following standard "realist" logic, Singer, Bremer, and Stuckey reiterated the oft-cited claim that the systemic distribution of military-industrial capabilities is associated with important effects on war and peace. Unfortunately, the precise causal mechanisms linking these systemic characteristics to state leaders' decision to go to war remain unclear in much of the literature on this topic. Singer, Bremer, and Stuckey argue that the concentration of power in the system should correlate with the uncertainty that leaders face when confronting international crises. The theoretical arguments linking uncertainty to war are not well specified. They require as yet missing linkages to state-level variables such as domestic political institutions and to individual-level variables such as risk attitude. Here we aim to clarify the empirical relationship between measures of system structure and the incidence of war and actual conflict behavior.

Both the earlier Singer, Bremer, and Stuckey study and Mansfield's recent work included three variables of capability concentration, change in concentration over time, and the temporal movement in power shares between states. Mansfield added the square of concentration to account for a potentially nonlinear fit between capability concentration and the onset of war. Despite using similar measures, the findings of these studies point to quite different conclusions. Singer, Bremer, and Stuckey found that power concentration and increases in this concentration have a negative association with annual nation-months of war for the entire period 1816–1965 but that movement in power share from one state to another correlates positively with war (although their findings reverse for the nineteenth century). After controlling for the related effects of hegemony and polarity, Mansfield found strong support for a positive relationship between concentration and war but a negative relationship between concentration squared and war that suggests an inverted U-shaped relationship between power concentration and war. He also found little consistent support for any particular relationship between power movement, changes in power concentration, and war. Unfortunately, Mansfield's results were inconsistent across different operational measures of system structure.

In our analysis, we include the three main variables of systemic power concentration, change in concentration, and power movement. We employ the "concentration" and "movement" measures for the interstate system defined in Singer, Bremer, and Stuckey 1972. This entails measuring each variable annually and then computing a five-year moving average. We recomputed the power concentration variables using the most recent COW data, and we use all of the states in the system for our coding. "Change in concentration" averages the annual change over the past five years. The value of the concentration index is 0 at an equal distribution of capabilities in the system and 1 when one state holds all capabilities; the related change in concentration variable is high when concentration increases. The value of the power movement index takes higher values when there have been more (and larger) capability-share shifts between states.

SUMMARY: THEORIES, HUNCHES, CONJECTURES, AND ARGUMENTS

This brings us to the end of our list of models and conjectures that we will test in the next chapter. In summary, in the analysis we will examine the following:

State Level of Analysis
 1. Democratization (six variables)
 2. Polity Change and Externalization of Violence (two variables)

Dyadic Level of Analysis
 3. Alliance and Defense Pact Membership (two variables)
 4. Arms Races (one variable)
 5. Balance of Power (one variable)
 6. Conventional Deterrence (one variable)
 7. Democratic Peace (five variables)
 8. Expected Utility (four variables)
 9. Geographic Contiguity (one variable)
10. Nuclear Deterrence (three variables)
11. Power Transition (three variables)
12. Trade Interdependence (two variables)

International System Level of Analysis
13. Economic Long Cycles/Kondratieff Waves (one variable)
14. Hegemony Stability (one variable)
15. International System Polarity (one variable)
16. Systemic Power Concentration and Movement (three variables)

Importantly, while these sixteen arguments represent just a sample of the numerous explanations of the path to war, they require thirty-seven variables to test them. Keep this in mind as we begin to confront some very real limits to our ability to make arguments about the origins of war in general as opposed to the particularistic origins of individual wars. If we find statistical support for just a few of these variables, we will be on safer ground claiming that there are a relatively small number of systematic causal factors leading to war. However, if we find that the majority of the factors identified in this chapter relate systematically to the incidence of war, confidence in our ability to generalize erodes substantially. Stating the puzzle in a somewhat different way, we next begin to tackle the question of whether the greatest common factor leading to war is that most wars have little in common with those preceding them. In the next chapter, we begin by testing to see if there is a statistically significant relationship between the variables associated with each argument and the presence and level of conflict behavior in each dyad. We then look more closely at the substantive effects associated with carefully controlled changes in the various operational measures.

5 FINDINGS

i do not know what i may appear to the world; but to myself
i seem to have been only like a boy playing on the seashore,
and diverting myself in now and then finding a smoother
pcbble or prettier shell than ordinary, whilst the great
ocean of truth lay all undiscovered before me.
—isaac newton

In this chapter, we test some hypotheses about the onset and escalation of interstate conflict. To do so, we look at the associations between the operational indicators of our various arguments and the dependent variable, thc values of which mark the status quo, dispute initiations absent military force, unilateral use of force, mutual uses of force, and war. We investigate the propositions first using the population of all directed dyad-years and second with a more limited subset of politically relevant dyads. To assess the models, we present a variety of information in several tables. In table 5.1 we present the results of a series of multiequation tests that provide the statistical significance for each argument's indicators based on likelihood ratio tests. In some cases, we tested individual variables, while in others we tested groups of variables. Testing multiple variables together allows us to assess the statistical significance of an argument comprised of a set of variables that should simultaneously affect the likelihood of conflict.

Even more so than with tests of statistical significance, it is difficult to interpret substantive effects in multinomial logit models by simply looking at the coefficients. In table 5.2, we summarize the changes in the relative risk of various levels of conflict as we allow the independent variables in the model to fluctuate. Risk ratios allow us to compare the proportional change in the outcome probabilities associated with comparable variation in the independent variables. For example, a risk of 1.20 for some outcome corresponds to a 20 percent increase over the baseline probability of observing that particular outcome.

At the risk of oversimplifying some findings, we also present a combined summary of the results from tables 5.1 and 5.2 in table 5.3, which gives a brief statement of our overall findings for each factor.

With these statistical results, we can address questions including the following:

1. Does each variable representing an empirical conjecture or proposition provide a distinct and unique contribution to our understanding of interstate conflict?
2. How large is the substantive effect associated with each variable/explanation, both in absolute terms and relative to other variables?
3. Do the direction and magnitude of a variable's/explanation's association with conflict vary across levels of conflict?
4. Does a subset of variables serve as a set of dominant indicators or suggest a dominant theory or approach to the study of international conflict?
5. How well does the model predict international conflict across the international system?

We begin with a summary of our findings and then turn to a detailed assessment of the variables corresponding to each set of arguments.

FINDINGS: OVERVIEW

Our first observation is that we find a large number of variables drawn from several explanations of conflict to be systematically associated with an increased or decreased risk of disputes occurring and their subsequent escalation to war. From the multiequation significance tests summarized in table 5.1, we can see that variables drawn from almost all of the arguments we considered have statistically significant effects on conflict initiation and escalation either in the all-dyads analysis or in the politically relevant subset. A notable exception is the curvilinear specification of the dyadic democracy-conflict relationship. In a few cases, a variable (or set of variables) appears to have a statistically significant effect in only one of the two data sets (balance of power and the global system-leader power transition). In the case of our power transition variables, we are unable to determine which of the set of variables is critical—we know that together the two dyadic power

TABLE 5.1. Multi-equation Tests of Statistical Significance, All Dyads and Politically Relevant Dyad Subset

Variables	Number of Variables	df	All Dyads (probability)	Politically Relevant Dyads (probability)
State Level				
All Democratization Variables	6	24	0.008	0.020
Democratization—Variance only	2	8	0.002	0.010
Polity Change	2	8	<0.001	0.089
Dyadic Level				
Dyadic Defense Pact	1	4	<0.001	0.002
Joint NATO Membership	1	4	<0.001	0.614
Arms Race	1	4	0.002	0.028
Balance of Forces	1	4	0.226	<0.001
Deterrence (initiator P(win))	1	4	<0.001	0.018
Balance of Forces and Deterrence (joint prob.)	2	8	<0.001	<0.001
Democracy	5	20	<0.001	<0.001
Curvilinearity of Democracy Relationship	1	4	0.392	0.098
All IIG Game Equilibria	4	16	<0.001	0.001
War Equilibrium Only	1	4	0.029	0.041
Contiguity	1	4	<0.001	<0.001
Nuclear Weapons—Both possess nuclear capability	1	4	<0.001	0.002
Nuclear Weapons—All variables	3	12	<0.001	0.047
Dyadic Power Transition (with satisfaction)	1	4	0.098	0.008
Dyadic Power Transition (no satisfaction)	1	4	0.148	0.186
Dyadic Power Transition (joint prob.)	2	8	0.025	0.042
Trade Dependence (initiator)	1	4	<0.001	<0.001
Trade Dependence (target)	1	4	<0.001	<0.001
International System Level				
Global Leader Power Transition	1	4	<0.001	0.998
Global Economic Upswing	1	4	<0.001	<0.001
British Hegemony	1	4	<0.001	0.001
Bipolarity	1	4	<0.001	0.092
System Structure—Concentration and Change	2	8	<0.001	<0.001
System Structure—Power Movement	1	4	0.007	0.028

TABLE 5.2. Predicted Outcome Probabilities: Relative Risk Associated with Change in Independent Variables

Variable: From/To Condition	Risk of Disputes without Force		Risk of Reciprocated Force Disputes		Risk of War	
	All Dyads	Politically Relevant	All Dyads	Politically Relevant	All Dyads	Politically Relevant
State Level						
Democratization:						
Mean Democratization, Mean Variance to Both Autocratizing (−1 SD), Mean Variance	1.12	0.83	0.98	1.39	1.27	1.17
Mean Democratization, Mean Variance, to Both Democratizing (+1 SD), Mean Variance	1.12	0.92	0.65	1.01	0.76	0.83
Mean Democratization, Mean Variance, to Mean Democratization, High Variance (+1 SD)	1.18	1.13	1.22	1.16	1.05	1.01
Abrupt Polity Change:						
Neither to change in initiator only	0.80	0.96	0.96	0.99	0.73	0.77
Neither to change in target only	0.74	0.69	1.00	1.10	—	—
Neither to change in both	0.59	0.67	0.96	1.10	—	—
Dyadic Level						
Dyadic Defense Pact: Absent to Present	1.39	1.03	0.53	0.45	0.61	0.50
Both members of NATO: Absent to Present	1.21	1.42	1.20	1.30	—	—
Arms Race: Absent to Present	1.32	1.25	1.06	1.01	1.93	1.86
Balance of Forces: Preponderance (1.0) to Mean (0.83)	1.28	1.59	1.48	1.53	2.22	4.94
Balance of Forces: Mean (0.83) to Parity (0.50)	1.18	1.36	1.29	1.32	1.69	2.85
Deterrence: 25% chance of initiator winning to 75% chance	1.29	1.24	1.26	1.20	1.11	1.01

Regime Type:						
Both Anocratic (mean) to Both Democratic (+1 SD)	1.00	0.84	0.98	0.89	0.25	0.25
Both Anocratic (mean) to Both Autocratic (−1 SD)	0.55	0.61	0.84	0.76	0.87	1.09
Both Anocratic to Democratic Initiator, Autocrat Target	1.61	1.67	0.95	0.88	1.89	1.74
Both Anocratic to Autocrat Initiator, Democrat Target	0.94	1.19	1.12	1.08	1.51	1.63
Expected Utility Equilibrium: Status Quo to War	1.66	1.58	4.04	4.46	2.20	2.07
Contiguity: Noncontiguous to Contiguous on Land	8.81	2.66	18.14	3.65	8.66	2.62
Nuclear Weapons:						
Neither has nukes to initiator only has nukes	4.05	0.99	1.51	0.53	—	1.21
Neither has nukes to target only has nukes	2.57	0.63	1.56	0.58	1.74	0.43
Neither has nukes to both have nukes	7.71	2.12	1.65	0.83	—	—
Dyadic Power Transition: −1 SD to +1 SD	0.95	1.04	0.78	0.97	0.89	1.01
Dyadic Power Transition, Varying Satisfaction: −1 SD to +1 SD	0.93	1.01	0.90	1.00	0.96	1.21
Initiator Trade Dependence: 0 to +1 SD	0.72	0.34	1.01	0.99	0.78	0.57
Target Trade Dependence: 0 to +1 SD	1.01	0.98	0.91	0.67	0.54	0.14
International System Level						
System Leader Power Transition: −1 SD to +1 SD	1.01	1.00	1.03	1.00	1.02	0.98
Global Economic Cycle: Downswing to upswing	0.89	0.95	1.68	1.71	1.98	1.79
Multipolar/British Hegemony: Pre-1918 relative to interwar	2.03	3.92	0.63	0.81	2.01	3.26
Bipolar/U.S. Hegemony: Post-1945 relative to interwar	0.32	0.38	0.67	0.84	0.08	0.02
Systemic Power Concentration: −1 SD to +1 SD	1.09	2.40	3.83	8.50	1.73	4.69
Change in Power Concentration: −1 SD to +1 SD	0.88	0.82	0.91	0.88	0.67	0.69
Power Movement: −1 SD to +1 SD	0.72	0.75	1.09	1.15	0.56	0.61

Note: Relative risk indicates the relative effect of changing values of the independent variables on outcome probabilities. Risk ratios greater than one indicate a higher risk of observing the outcome under the second condition; ratios below one indicate a lower risk. Data on trade dependence from secondary estimation on subset of cases; other effects from analysis without trade.

TABLE 5.3.   Summary of Substantive Results

State Level

Democratization	Generally supportive result: Democratization appears to (1) decrease odds of initiation and escalation to reciprocated use of force and war but (2) increase odds of low-level disputes. Variance (instability) in democratization has only a minor effect on risk of disputes escalating to war but increases risks of lower-level disputes by larger amounts. Weak to moderate effect.
Polity Change	Polity change lowers risk of conflict. However, cannot estimate all effects, particularly on escalation to war. Moderate effect.

Dyadic Level

Defense Pact	Mixed result: Among all dyads, more low-level disputes (without force) occur when two states are in a defense pact together. However, much less conflict occurs at levels escalating to a reciprocated use of force or war in dyads with a defense pact. Moderate effect.
Joint NATO Membership	Little substantive effect apart from that of defense pacts, although unable to estimate effect on war (collinear). Effects suggest that NATO membership increases risk of low-level disputes.
Arms Race	Supportive result: Increases probability of dispute initiation, but especially escalation to war. Moderate effect on disputes escalating to war.
Balance of Power	Result opposite Balance of Power prediction: Power inequality associated with less dispute initiation and escalation. Effect statistically uncertain in all dyads, but statistically strong in politically relevant dyads. Moderate to strong substantive effects.
Deterrence	Supportive result: The stronger the potential initiator relative to the target, the more likely initiation and escalation to all levels of violence. Weak effect, and the direct mutual deterrence effect of a power balance is clearly offset by dangerous effect of power equality.
Democracy	Supportive result: Democratic pairs have less conflict than autocratic or mixed pairs of states. Autocratic pairs also have less conflict than mixed pairs of states but effect is much smaller than joint-democracy effect. Autocracies tend to initiate and escalate more against democracies than other autocracies across levels of escalation. Democracies appear slightly more likely to initiate and escalate disputes against autocracies to war than autocracies vs. democracies. Generally moderate effect but very strong on joint democracy and war specifically.
IIG Game Equilibria	Supportive result: Conflict equilibria correspond to more dispute initiation and disputes that escalate to higher levels. Effects are clearest for the "war" equilibrium. Moderate to strong effect.
Contiguity	Supportive result: Increases conflict. Very large effect.
Nuclear Weapons	Effects unclear. While variables are statistically significant, estimated effects differ in direction across subsets and outcomes. Unable to estimate key effect on war probability. In general, dyads where either or both have nuclear weapons are estimated to have increased conflict among all dyads but decreased conflict among politically relevant dyads. Moderate effects.

TABLE 5.3—Continued

Dyadic Level

Dyadic Power Transition	Mixed/unsupportive result: Transitions have little estimated effect on war, and transitions slightly reduce disputes of all levels when estimated among the all-dyads data set. Weak effects.
Dyadic Power Transition (effect of satisfaction)	Mixed result: Increasing satisfaction appears to slightly reduce conflict at all levels of escalation among all dyads, but among politically relevant dyads, satisfaction appears to correspond to initiation and escalation of disputes going to war. Effects are rather uncertain.
Trade Dependence	Supportive result: Both initiator and target trade dependence decrease conflict. Effect on disputes escalating to war is largest. Generally moderate to weak effects, although effect on disputes estimated among politically relevant dyads appears very large.

International System Level

Global Leader Power Transition	Little apparent substantive effect.
Global Economic Upswing	Supportive result: Upswing increases chances of disputes that escalate to force or war. Moderate effect.
Eras: British Hegemony (pre-1918)	Mixed result: Pre-1918 period is most dangerous in having disputes without force, disputes with a one-sided use of force, and disputes that escalate to war, but period is safer than the interwar period or postwar period in having disputes where reciprocated force is used. Moderate effect.
Eras: Bipolarity/ U.S. Hegemony (post-1945)	Generally supportive of neorealism: Post-1945 is safest, with dramatic reductions especially in probability of disputes that escalate to war. The exception is disputes with a reciprocated use of force, which have their highest probability in the post-1945 period. Generally moderate effects, but strong effect on disputes escalating to war.
System Structure: Concentration	More concentration leads to higher chance of all types of disputes and war. Strong effect.
System Structure: Change in Concentration	Increases in concentration associated with higher odds of disputes with one-sided use of force but lower chance of disputes at all other levels of escalation. Weak effect.
System Structure: Movement	Movement associated with lower chance of both low-level disputes and disputes escalating to war. Moderate effect on these outcomes. Weak effect increasing the risk of conflict escalating to the reciprocated use of force.

Note: "Strong effects" denote effects that are roughly in the strongest one third of those we find and typically increase risk by 50 percent or more, while "weak effects" are in the weakest one third, with changes in risk of roughly 40 percent or less.

transition variables contribute to the model's fit, but collinearity between them makes it difficult to discern which (if only one) of the variables is of greater importance. These exceptions aside, the majority of the variables included clearly covary systematically with the incidence of violent international conflict in the equations tested here.

It appears that the majority of the many explanations of international conflict explains an independent or unique piece of the interstate conflict puzzle.

The conclusions we reach change only slightly if we compare our findings from the two data sets—the population of all dyad-years and the "politically relevant" subset. The explanatory power of the balance of power variable is stronger in the politically relevant data set, while the global system-leader power transition appears to have predictive power associated with it only among the set of all dyads. This is somewhat ironic in that it implies that what are essentially hegemonic power transitions influence conflict only among the politically "irrelevant" states. For most variables, however, our findings are quite robust across both data sets, with most variables having high degrees of statistical signifi-cance. That said, we show that the risk ratios estimated in the two data sets are sometimes rather different.

There are at least two reasons why a variable might have different effects in these two subsets of cases. First, it may be that the true association of a particular variable or explanation for conflict washes out when in the all-dyads data set because the model, while specified as a general argument, in fact only applies to a small subset of cases. For instance, we might expect the equilibrium predictions of our expected utility model (the IIG) to fit the data better in the politically relevant subset because many "irrelevant" international dyads simply are not engaged in interactions anything like those modeled in the game theoretic model. Second, and more likely, as recent literature on selection effects (e.g., Lemke and Reed 2001; Reed 2000) suggests, we should be concerned if we analyze only the subset of politically relevant dyads. Because this subset represents a truncated sample whose inclusion criteria correlate with the variables in our models—most important, the dependent variable—our parameter estimates in the smaller set may be biased.

We assess whether we observe the directional relationships hypothesized in our various empirical arguments by examining the risk ratios in table 5.2 (summarized in table 5.3). There we see if a positive change in some variable is associated with an increase or decrease in the relative risk of conflict. From the perspective of classical hypothesis testing, which focuses on whether an indicator has or does not have a statically significant directional association with the dependent variable (table 5.1), most of our results support the arguments from chapter 3. In a few cases, however, most notably for the balance of power, the direction of the change in the relative risk of war associated with the indicator runs opposite the direction of the standard argument. More generally, it appears that the variables marking the IIG equilibria, regime type, alliances, arms races, contiguity, polarity, economic cycles, and defense pacts are statistically significant and are associated with interstate conflict in ways generally consistent with the models or conjectures from which they draw, even after controlling for the indicators for the other explanations.

Some of the models did not fare so well, however. Our results are not particularly supportive for either the dyadic or the systemic implementations of the power transition models. Most of the operational variables associated with power transition arguments have substantive effects that are substantively quite weak, and a few of the variables employed to operationalize power transition arguments at the systemic level yield relationships opposite the model's expectation. Our results also offer quite mixed evidence for the predictions of hegemonic stability advocates. Regarding the dyadic balance of power arguments, our results run counter to predictions that relatively equal balances of material capabilities should correlate with lower levels of conflict. In the same way, contra the expectations found in the international institution literature, NATO membership does not appear to reduce low-level dyadic conflict behavior of its members beyond what we would expect for a less institutionally developed defense pact or alliance. Finally, it appears that the relationship between democratization and conflict is far more complicated than much of the previous research in this area suggests. We find that democratization lowers the risk of disputes that escalate to large-scale war, but it increases the risk of disputes that escalate to lower levels of force.

In addition to observing statistical "significance," our results also suggest that there is a wide range in the relative risk of conflict associated with the different variables. Table 5.2 presents the changing magnitude of each variable's associated effects on the relative risk of conflict. At the extremely risky end of the scale of association lies a factor that is immutable for most states. Geographically contiguous states face increased odds of conflict by at least an order of magnitude—contiguity increases the risk of war eight times and the risk of reciprocated force nearly twenty times over the baseline level of risk. Other variables are associated with an increase in the odds of conflict between less than two and up to four times or, in the case of variables associated with a reduction in the likelihood of conflict, a decrease in the odds to as low as one-tenth the baseline risk—a 90 percent reduction in risk.

It is important to keep in mind that the baseline risk for a large-scale war is extremely small, roughly 1 in 14,000 dyad-years. For most members of the international system, the risk of war is quite small. In each of the latter years in our data set, there are roughly thirty-two thousand individual directed dyads. This number of dyads continues to rise as the number of states in the systems rises over time. A doubling of the baseline risk would raise the general risk of war for any given dyad to 1 in 7,000 dyad-years—a substantial increase in the eyes of many—but, regardless, a war would still be an exceedingly rare event. To gain an intuitive sense of this scale, consider that in 1997, 43,200 Americans died in automobile accidents, out of a population of approximately 280 million. The baseline risk for an individual dying in an auto accident is roughly one per sixty-five hundred person-years. Obviously, this is a naive risk rate, as is the case for war. Just as not everyone rides in cars, some states never get into violent conflicts simply because they have no military, Costa Rica being a prime example of the latter. However, across the system, the odds of war for a randomly selected pair of states are comparable to the odds of death one faces annually in the United States when riding in a passenger car, a risk millions of people happily take daily.

Interestingly, we also see in table 5.2 that the marginal effects of several variables change in direction and magnitude across the various outcome categories. For example, changing the IIG equilibrium prediction from the status quo to war in the politically relevant dyad data set leads to only a minor increase in the risk of disputes without any force, an 85 percent increase in the risk of war, and a 165 percent increase in the risk of disputes with a reciprocated use of force. However, in the case of other variables, the direction of the effect on different categories changes sign, not just degree. Movement in power share across the international system, for instance (the last row of table 5.2), appears to increase slightly the risks of disputes involving the reciprocated use of force but appears to decrease the chances of both lower-level disputes and the risk of war. These differing effects for some variables across the escalation levels clearly suggest that the outcome variable categories are not ordinal in relation to independent variables and hence that our multinomial logit analysis was appropriate. This also suggests that theories or conjectures that assume a factor will simply cause "more conflict" without carefully specifying the logic at different escalation levels are underdeveloped.

The variation in the indicators' association with both increased and decreased risk of conflict and war provides empirical support for our selection of the multinomial logit estimator. It also suggests, however, that an even more sophisticated approach might be appropriate. Smith (1996a) and Signorino (1999) argue quite persuasively that our results may suffer from serious bias since we do not control for unobserved selection effects. To test for this sort of selection bias, we also estimated a similar set of models using Smith's Bayesian estimator (Smith 1996a). While we do not present the results of this analysis here (the output runs well over one hundred pages), in no event did the use of Smith's estimator change the fundamental tenor of any of our findings. The statistical significance tests were all similar. Using Smith's estimator led to some variation in the estimates of substantive significance but in no case did the change in substantive effect lead to a reversal of a parameter estimate's sign or its imputed casual direction. The range of these differences was no greater than the changes in relative explanatory power associated with simply changing the model specification while staying with the much simpler multinomial logit estimator.

We also estimated our logit model with a number of different subsets of independent variables to determine the robustness of our results. The coefficients in our model remained generally stable when we dropped individual blocs from our model. Substantive significance for each bloc did vary somewhat as the content of the statistical model changed, however. The results we present here represent the fullest, most inclusive statistical model. We strongly encourage readers to make use of the software and data available at www.icpsr.org, study number 1290.

CONJECTURES, MODELS, ARGUMENTS, AND THE RELATIVE RISK OF WAR

State Level of Analysis

I.   DEMOCRATIZATION

We find strong support for Ward and Gleditsch's (1998) arguments about the pacifying effects of institutional democratization. Our results in table 5.4 contrast sharply with Mansfield and Snyder's findings (1995), particularly when it comes to high levels of conflict. Dyads where both states are democratizing (change in polity toward consolidated institutional democracy as compared to other kinds of polity change such as semidemocracy to anocracy or oligarchy to autocracy) show 20–30 percent reductions in the risk of disputes that escalate to war relative to dyads that are becoming neither more autocratic nor more democratic. Such democratizing dyads have a 40 to 50 percent lower risk of disputes than dyads where both members are autocratizing. We find that the presence and rate of democratization appear more important than variation in the democratization pattern. For example, increasing the variance in democratization through our minus one to plus one standard deviation range increases the risk of war by 2 to 12 percent, depending on the level of democratization.[1] However, increasing the rate of autocratic regime change over a comparable range—from democratizing to autocratizing—increases the risk of conflict around 50 percent. We also find that democratization generally lowers the risk of disputes short of war.

These findings strongly contradict Mansfield and Snyder's (1995) main claim, as we find strong evidence that democratization is strongly associated with a reduction in the relative risk of war. Nevertheless, consistent with one of Mansfield and Snyder's observations, we do see that in some cases autocratizing dyads are safer than politically stable dyads when it comes to low-level disputes, that is, disputes that the states resolve far short of war. Examining the results of our analysis of politically relevant dyads, we see that dyads where both members are autocratizing are 17 percent less likely to have disputes where no force is used and about 34 percent less likely to have disputes where one side uses force than dyads where the states have stable regimes. Such dyads are much more likely to have more serious disputes, though, with a nearly 39 percent increase in the risk of reciprocated force disputes and a 17 percent increase in the risk of disputes that escalate to war.

2. POLITY CHANGE AND EXTERNALIZATION OF VIOLENCE

While we find that gradual and joint regime change in the direction of greater autocracy is associated with an increased risk of war, our results for abrupt political change may come as a surprise to those who argue that sudden domestic political instability is a common source of international violence. Table 5.5 illustrates the effects associated with rapid regime change. Counter to standard arguments about the political externalization effects of rapid political change, as compared to more gradual or evolutionary political change, sudden or abrupt regime tran-

TABLE 5.4. Predicted Probabilities for Dependent Variable Outcomes Given Level of Democratization

All Dyads

Democratization	Outcome	Variance: Low (0) Prob.	Rel. Risk	Mean (8.1) Prob.	Rel. Risk	High (26.7) (1 SD above mean) Prob.	Rel. Risk
	No Dispute	0.99754	1.00	0.99718	1.00	0.99677	1.00
−4.53	Dispute, No Force	0.00062	0.95	0.00074	1.12	0.00087	1.32
Both Autocratizing	Unilateral Force	0.00109	1.08	0.00119	1.17	0.00129	1.28
(1 SD below mean)	Reciprocated Force	0.00065	0.80	0.00079	0.98	0.00097	1.19
	War	0.00009	1.21	0.00010	1.27	0.00010	1.33
	No Dispute	0.99778	1.00	0.99744	1.00	0.99705	1.00
−0.0045	Dispute, No Force	0.00056	0.85	0.00066	1.00	0.00078	1.18
Both Stable	Unilateral Force	0.00093	0.92	0.00101	1.00	0.00110	1.09
(mean)	Reciprocated Force	0.00066	0.82	0.00081	1.00	0.00099	1.22
	War	0.00007	0.96	0.00008	1.00	0.00008	1.05
	No Dispute	0.99778	1.00	0.99747	1.00	0.99710	1.00
4.52	Dispute, No Force	0.00062	0.95	0.00074	1.12	0.00087	1.33
Both Democratizing	Unilateral Force	0.00111	1.09	0.00121	1.19	0.00132	1.30
(1 SD above mean)	Reciprocated Force	0.00043	0.53	0.00053	0.65	0.00065	0.80
	War	0.00006	0.72	0.00006	0.76	0.00006	0.80

Politically Relevant Dyads

Democratization	Outcome	Variance: Low (0) Prob.	Rel. Risk	Mean (6.0) Prob.	Rel. Risk	High (22.8) (1 SD above mean) Prob.	Rel. Risk
	No Dispute	0.98824	1.00	0.98700	1.00	0.98561	1.00
−3.64	Dispute, No Force	0.00320	0.73	0.00363	0.83	0.00410	0.93
Both Autocratizing	Unilateral Force	0.00449	0.62	0.00472	0.66	0.00497	0.69
(1 SD below mean)	Reciprocated Force	0.00359	1.20	0.00417	1.39	0.00483	1.61
	War	0.00047	1.16	0.00048	1.17	0.00048	1.18
	No Dispute	0.98628	1.00	0.98499	1.00	0.98355	1.00
0.10	Dispute, No Force	0.00388	0.88	0.00440	1.00	0.00498	1.13
Both Stable	Unilateral Force	0.00685	0.95	0.00720	1.00	0.00758	1.05
(mean)	Reciprocated Force	0.00258	0.86	0.00300	1.00	0.00349	1.16
	War	0.00040	0.99	0.00041	1.00	0.00041	1.01
	No Dispute	0.98824	1.00	0.98706	1.00	0.98575	1.00
3.84	Dispute, No Force	0.00357	0.81	0.00404	0.92	0.00458	1.04
Both Democratizing	Unilateral Force	0.00525	0.73	0.00553	0.77	0.00582	0.81
(1 SD above mean)	Reciprocated Force	0.00260	0.87	0.00302	1.01	0.00351	1.17
	War	0.00034	0.82	0.00034	0.83	0.00034	0.84

TABLE 5.5. Effects of Abrupt Polity Change on Outcomes

Polity change in:	Neither State	Initiator Only		Target Only		Both States	
Outcome	Prob.	Prob.	Rel. Risk	Prob.	Rel. Risk	Prob.	Rel. Risk
All Dyads							
No Dispute	0.99772	0.99832	1.00	0.99789	1.00	0.99847	1.00
Dispute, No Force	0.00068	0.00054	0.80	0.00050	0.74	0.00040	0.59
Unilateral Force	0.00100	0.00057	0.57	0.00107	1.07	0.00061	0.61
Reciprocated Force	0.00054	0.00052	0.96	0.00054	1.00	0.00052	0.96
War	0.00007	0.00005	0.73	0.00000	—	0.00000	—
Politically Relevant Dyads							
No Dispute	0.98778	0.98987	1.00	0.98859	1.00	0.99070	1.00
Dispute, No Force	0.00374	0.00360	0.96	0.00259	0.69	0.00249	0.67
Unilateral Force	0.00488	0.00304	0.62	0.00532	1.09	0.00332	0.68
Reciprocated Force	0.00317	0.00315	0.99	0.00350	1.10	0.00348	1.10
War	0.00043	0.00033	0.77	0.00000	—	0.00000	—

sitions almost uniformly appear to reduce substantially the chances of interstate conflict at all levels. However, we are unable to estimate the effects of such polity changes in the target or both states on the probability of disputes that escalate to war. There are sufficiently few wars combined with polity-change circumstances that we cannot estimate any systematic substantive effects. For the associations that we can estimate reliably, the estimated effect of polity change is weakest on the presence of reciprocated force disputes, with the estimated magnitude of the effect small enough to fall within the margin of error of the model. When it comes to lower-level disputes, however, where the abrupt policy changes do affect the likelihood of observing a dispute, polity changes appear to decrease the risk of conflict by an average of approximately 30 percent across categories and types of change. It appears from the analysis here that abrupt polity changes lead neither to states being the target of conflict initiation by other predatory states nor to diversionary behavior against others.

Dyadic Level of Analysis

3. ALLIANCES AND DEFENSE PACT MEMBERSHIP

Our results in table 5.6 suggest that both the NATO alliance (in particular) and defense pacts (in general) have distinct identifiable substantive effects on the outbreak and escalation of interstate conflict, although in the case of NATO the effects may not always be in the direction some institutional scholars might anticipate (Keohane 1984). First, regarding the potentially pacifying effects of defensive alliances, we find a consistent dampening effect on the risk of conflict associated with the presence of general defensive alliances. Within the "all dyads" set of cases the risk of disputes occurring that escalate to the level of reciprocated force or to war is 39 to 47 percent lower when two states

TABLE 5.6. Effects of Alliances on Outcomes

Joint Defense Pacts

Dyadic Defense Pact:	No	Yes	
Outcome	Prob.	Prob.	Rel. Risk
All Dyads			
No Dispute	0.99776	0.99782	1.00
Dispute, No Force	0.00062	0.00086	1.39
Unilateral Force	0.00096	0.00096	1.00
Reciprocated Force	0.00060	0.00031	0.53
War	0.00007	0.00004	0.61
Politically Relevant Dyads			
No Dispute	0.98739	0.99043	1.00
Dispute, No Force	0.00360	0.00373	1.03
Unilateral Force	0.00488	0.00395	0.81
Reciprocated Force	0.00372	0.00169	0.45
War	0.00041	0.00021	0.50

NATO Membership

NATO Membership:	Not Joint NATO Members	Both States in NATO	
Outcome	Prob.	Prob.	Rel. Risk
All Dyads			
No Dispute	0.99780	0.99713	1.00
Dispute, No Force	0.00065	0.00078	1.21
Unilateral Force	0.00095	0.00144	1.51
Reciprocated Force	0.00053	0.00064	1.20
War	0.00007	0.00000	—
Politically Relevant Dyads			
No Dispute	0.98812	0.98303	0.99
Dispute, No Force	0.00360	0.00512	1.42
Unilateral Force	0.00471	0.00772	1.64
Reciprocated Force	0.00318	0.00413	1.30
War	0.00039	0.00000	—

share a defense pact and is 50 to 55 percent lower when we estimate effects within politically relevant dyads. Interestingly, our results for the effect of defense pacts on low-level disputes run in the opposite direction, as we find that dyads with a defensive alliance are 3 to 39 percent *more* likely to initiate disputes that do not escalate to any use of force. It may be that, while states in defensive alliances have conflicts of interests and so sometimes raise them in the form of militarized disputes, they resolve these disputes before they escalate to higher levels of violence. These findings are consistent with Bueno de Mesquita's (1981) conjecture that allies may actually find themselves in conflict more frequently than will states that are not allies. When states share similar alliance portfolios, they may view possible future shifts in alignment as a source of risk and potentially of future conflict. States perceiving imminent shifts in alliance patterns may actually seek to forestall such shifts by engaging in conflict. Our empirical findings suggest that the presence of an alliance may actually make it more likely that states will engage in low-level conflict, possibly due to such fears of future policy change, although these conflicts do not escalate to war.

In the bottom half of table 5.6, we find that joint membership in NATO appears to have a quite different effect than defensive alliances more generally. Joint NATO membership is actually associated with an increase in the chances of all types of dispute short of war relative to membership in a non-NATO defense pact. Note first that since NATO is a defense treaty we must consider the joint effects of both defense pacts and NATO membership to ascertain the net effects on the probability of conflict in a dyad. NATO member dyads appear to be more likely than dyads with non-NATO defense pacts to engage in disputes that escalate to levels short of war. The size of these associated substantive effects is moderate (estimated at approximately 20 to 50 percent in the all-dyads sample and 30 to 65 percent in the politically relevant sample) and, in the case of all types of dispute except for those in which force is not used, is offset by the reduced risk due to the existence of a defense pact. However, note our inability to estimate the effects of NATO on disputes escalating to war. Because no two state NATO members have gone to war with one another, it is clear why we cannot estimate the effects of NATO in this category. NATO membership is a perfect predictor of peace between members, as there is no variance on the value of war between NATO members. There is simply no way statistically to estimate the relative magnitude of this possible association. This suggests that NATO may be having a strong pacifying force, helping prevent high-level conflict, although we cannot compute a numerical estimate of the magnitude of the effect. Our estimates of the effects on the risk of conflict associated with NATO point out an important limit to knowledge about the nature of cold war international politics and the tools we employ in this study.

One way to investigate the possible effects of NATO membership would be to conduct case studies focused on those states that engaged in conflict prior to joining, such as Greece and Turkey, and to look for archival evidence directly implicating NATO membership as a constraint on future disputes. Anecdotal evidence suggests that NATO does have this sort of pacifying effect—see, for instance, Russett and Stam (1998), who argue that joint NATO membership prevented Turkey and Greece from reigniting their ongoing disputes over Cyprus. While it is a bit tautological because of the fact that NATO members have not engaged in war, the apparent pacifying effect of NATO appears infinite. This is true for any explanation of peace that fits the data perfectly. If an independent variable is a perfect restatement of the dependent variable (peaceful when present and warring when not), we cannot estimate its effect relative to the other independent variables.

A similar sort of problem arises when using fixed-effects analysis, which privileges cross-temporal variation over cross-sectional. In fixed-effects analysis, time-series that have no variation on the dependent variable are dropped from the analysis. Statistically, this makes sense, but in doing so we wittingly throw away all the cases in which we are likely to be most interested, those cases where the two states never go to war. It is important to note that this does not preclude the fact that the factor dropped from the analysis (such as NATO membership) may truly have some pacifying effect. Rather, it simply points to an important limitation of this type of statistical analysis.

Finally, note that one reason we included a separate indicator of NATO membership was to provide an important control for our tests of the democratic peace proposition. Something resembling a consensus exists, suggesting that the democratic peace is stronger following World War II (Oneal and Russett 1997; Gowa 1999). There are several possible reasons for this finding, ranging from emergent postmaterialist values within wealthy liberal democracies (Kim 2001) to NATO membership. We find that even after we account for NATO membership and the presence of defense pacts more generally, joint democracy retains a strong association with lower risks of conflict—in particular, the risk of war—in both our samples.

4. ARMS RACES

In table 5.7, we find that the presence of an arms race, as measured here, significantly increases the probability of all types of disputes. Importantly, the strongest associations occur in disputes that escalate to war. For these disputes, we see almost a doubling of risk associated with an arms race being present. The increases in probabilities for disputes with lower levels of violence in the presence of an arms race are much more modest, ranging from 1 to 32 percent, depending on the outcome and the set of cases analyzed.

5. BALANCE OF POWER: NONDIRECTED DYADIC

We find highly statistically significant results on our power equality (balance of forces) variable within the subset of politically relevant dyads, although not in the population of all dyads. However, the direction of the effect on conflict is contrary to what realists, or balance of power theorists, might expect. Instead, in table 5.8 we find results consistent with some of the theoretical conjectures associated with some recent developments in the bargaining literature on war (e.g., Wittman 2001). As the balance of forces shifts from equality to inequality, the associated risk of disputes involving the use of force and those that escalate to war decreases dramatically, but the effect is clear only within the "politically relevant" sample. Looking at the probability of war among politically relevant dyads, we see that the risk of war drops 65

TABLE 5.7. **Effects of Arms Race on Outcomes**

Presence of Arms Race:	No Arms Race	Arms Race	
Outcome	Prob.	Prob.	Rel. Risk
All Dyads			
No Dispute	0.99789	0.99738	1.00
Dispute, No Force	0.00061	0.00081	1.32
Unilateral Force	0.00092	0.00114	1.24
Reciprocated Force	0.00053	0.00056	1.06
War	0.00006	0.00011	1.93
Politically Relevant Dyads			
No Dispute	0.98845	0.98626	1.00
Dispute, No Force	0.00348	0.00434	1.25
Unilateral Force	0.00455	0.00555	1.22
Reciprocated Force	0.00318	0.00322	1.01
War	0.00034	0.00063	1.86

percent when moving from a situation of parity to a mean level of balance in our data set (83 percent of capabilities for one side, or a 4:1 ratio). Moving to full preponderance (100 percent of the capabilities in one state) lowers the risk of disputes escalating to war to approximately 20 percent of the risk at parity. We observe similar effects (of slightly

TABLE 5.8. Effects of (nondirected) Balance of Power on Outcome Probabilities

Balance:	0.5 (parity)	0.83 (mean)		1 (preponderance)	
Outcome	Prob.	Prob.	Rel. Risk	Prob.	Rel. Risk
All Dyads					
No Dispute	0.99741	0.99782	1.00	0.99800	1.00
Dispute, No Force	0.00076	0.00064	0.85	0.00059	0.78
Unilateral Force	0.00106	0.00096	0.90	0.00091	0.86
Reciprocated Force	0.00067	0.00052	0.77	0.00045	0.68
War	0.00010	0.00006	0.59	0.00005	0.45
Politically Relevant Dyads					
No Dispute	0.99744	0.99826	1.00	0.99857	1.00
Dispute, No Force	0.00064	0.00047	0.74	0.00040	0.63
Unilateral Force	0.00121	0.00077	0.63	0.00060	0.50
Reciprocated Force	0.00062	0.00047	0.76	0.00041	0.65
War	0.00009	0.00003	0.35	0.00002	0.20

Note: All risk levels relative to parity.

Balance:	0.68 (1 SD below mean)	0.98 (1 SD above mean)	
Outcome	Prob.	Prob.	Rel. Risk
All Dyads			
No Dispute	0.99764	0.99798	1.00
Dispute, No Force	0.00069	0.00060	0.86
Unilateral Force	0.00101	0.00092	0.91
Reciprocated Force	0.00058	0.00046	0.79
War	0.00008	0.00005	0.62

Balance:	0.78 (1 SD below mean)	1.00 (1 SD above mean)	
Outcome	Prob.	Prob.	Rel. Risk
Politically Relevant Dyads			
No Dispute	0.99793	0.99854	1.00
Dispute, No Force	0.00054	0.00041	0.75
Unilateral Force	0.00094	0.00062	0.66
Reciprocated Force	0.00054	0.00041	0.77
War	0.00005	0.00002	0.38

lower magnitude) with all levels of dispute outcomes. Our findings clearly fit with the growing consensus that power preponderance, not power balance, helps to prevent the initiation and escalation of conflict.

As with the IIG war equilibrium (discussed later), the effects associated with our balance of power variable appear substantially greater in the sample of politically relevant dyads than among the populations of all dyads, although still substantial in the all-dyads set. Relative power is not likely to be of any consequence for many dyads not in the so-called politically relevant sample. In fact, within the population of dyads, the association between dyadic capabilities and war is not statistically meaningful, as seen in table 5.1. This is rather surprising given the extraordinarily large data set.

6. CONVENTIONAL DETERRENCE

In addition to the balance of power variable computed to measure nondirectional capability equality or inequality in a dyad, we also find that the initiator's subjective probability of winning is also associated with an important effect on conflict behavior. In table 5.9, holding the nondirected balance of capabilities constant, the more the potential initiator has the advantage, the more likely disputes are to occur and escalate. The magnitude of the effects are very similar across all levels of escalation, with changes in the probability of winning from 25 to 75 percent, leading to an 11 to 31 percent increase in the probability of conflict at various levels in the all-dyads analysis and a 1 to 30 percent increase in the politically relevant analysis. Initiators with more capability and/or more allies have a higher probability of conflict than initiators with less capability. This, of course, fits with the expectation of conventional deterrence arguments and the findings of empirical analysis (Huth 1988; Huth and Russett 1993) that have found an unfavorable capability balance to be a substantial (although not certain) deterrent to conflict initiation.

Together, our findings on the nondirected balance of power and the directed probability of victory initially appear contradictory. Increases in the nondirected dyadic balance of power variable (increased power preponderance) decrease the risk of war, while increases in the directed probability of victory *increase* the risk of war. How should we interpret the findings that nondirected parity in military-industrial capabilities increases the risk of conflict generally but that, for potential initiators, parity leads to less confidence in the ability to win and hence a lower probability that a state will initiate and escalate a dispute? Generally, shifting the directed odds of victory from the target (side B of the dyad) to the potential initiator (side A) increases the odds of the potential initiator starting and escalating a conflict. There is a corresponding change in the risk of war in the opposite directed dyad. The key to understanding these findings is to consider the net effect of both variables

TABLE 5.9. Effects of (directed) Conventional Deterrence on Outcome Probabilities

Balance:	1:3	1:1		3:1	
Outcome	Prob.	Prob.	Rel. Risk	Prob.	Rel. Risk
All Dyads					
No Dispute	0.99804	0.99778	1.00	0.99749	1.00
Dispute, No Force	0.00057	0.00065	1.14	0.00074	1.29
Unilateral Force	0.00085	0.00097	1.15	0.00111	1.31
Reciprocated Force	0.00047	0.00053	1.12	0.00060	1.26
War	0.00006	0.00007	1.06	0.00007	1.11
Politically Relevant Dyads					
No Dispute	0.98928	0.98803	1.00	0.98664	1.00
Dispute, No Force	0.00326	0.00363	1.11	0.00404	1.24
Unilateral Force	0.00418	0.00477	1.14	0.00544	1.30
Reciprocated Force	0.00290	0.00318	1.10	0.00348	1.20
War	0.00039	0.00039	1.00	0.00039	1.01

Note: All risk levels relative to 1:3 ratio.

Balance:	0.13 (1 SD below mean)	0.79 (1 SD above mean)	
Outcome	Prob.	Prob.	Rel. Risk
All Dyads			
No Dispute	0.99816	0.99743	1.00
Dispute, No Force	0.00054	0.00075	1.40
Unilateral Force	0.00079	0.00114	1.43
Reciprocated Force	0.00045	0.00061	1.36
War	0.00006	0.00007	1.15

Balance:	0.17 (1 SD below mean)	0.74 (1 SD above mean)	
Outcome	Prob.	Prob.	Rel. Risk
Politically Relevant Dyads			
No Dispute	0.98965	0.98671	1.00
Dispute, No Force	0.00315	0.00402	1.28
Unilateral Force	0.00400	0.00541	1.35
Reciprocated Force	0.00282	0.00347	1.23
War	0.00039	0.00039	1.01

taken simultaneously in a directed dyad. Only then can we judge the overall effects of different types of capability balances. In combination, the balance of power variable outweighs the probability of victory variable. The combination of the two effects leads to a net *reduction* in the risk of conflict as power becomes *imbalanced,* although if a conflict does occur, the state that is militarily advantaged by the power shift becomes increasingly likely to be the initiator. The most quiescent directed dyads are those imbalanced situations where the potential initiator is weaker than its potential target—large but militarily weak states such as China today generally do not start conflicts. The most volatile dyads are those with an equal balance of power combined with a potential initiator holding a military advantage. A middle level of risk of conflict exists where a potential initiator is stronger than its target.

7. DEMOCRATIC PEACE

Our results on regime type are quite interesting and support the observation that a regime's democracy level does not correlate uniformly with dyadic conflict across all dispute levels. Building on the highlights presented in table 5.2, table 5.10 shows the associated risks of conflict when we independently vary the initiator's and target's level of democracy. In table 5.10, moving across the rows increases the potential initiator's level of democracy, while moving down the columns increases the target's level of democracy. Changes along the upper-left to bottom-right diagonal in the table trace the effect of moving from joint autocracy to joint democracy. We computed the risk ratios relative to the baseline conflict level associated with a joint mixed-regime dyad, where both states have middle levels scores on the regime type variable. Some refer to these mixed regimes as oligarchies (Goemans 2000), while others refer to them as anocracies.

Focusing first on symmetric dyads (those where the two states are of the same polity type), we find that dyads where both states are either democracies or autocracies are less likely than our baseline mixed-regime dyads to engage in any type of dispute. Importantly, the associated risk reductions generally seem stronger for autocratic pairs than for democratic pairs (that is, their chances of conflict drop more than do the odds of conflict for democratic pairs) at all levels of conflict except one. The extremely important exception is the category of disputes that escalate to war. By our estimates, the risk of war in democratic-democratic dyads (defined as dyads where both states have a polity "dem" score of 6.3) is only 25 percent of the risk for joint mixed

TABLE 5.10. Effects of Democracy Scores on Outcomes

All Dyads		Initiator					
	Democracy Score:	−8.46 (autocratic)		−1.05 (mixed)		6.36 (democratic)	
	Outcome	Prob.	Rel. Risk	Prob.	Rel. Risk	Prob.	Rel. Risk
Target							
	No Dispute	0.99840	1.00	0.99808	1.00	0.99758	1.00
−8.47	Dispute, No Force	0.00036	0.55	0.00067	1.03	0.00106	1.61
(autocratic)	Unilateral Force	0.00072	0.94	0.00064	0.83	0.00072	0.94
	Reciprocated Force	0.00046	0.84	0.00052	0.94	0.00052	0.95
	War	0.00005	0.87	0.00009	1.58	0.00011	1.89
	No Dispute	0.99772	1.00	0.99797	1.00	0.99781	1.00
−1.05	Dispute, No Force	0.00054	0.83	0.00065	1.00	0.00090	1.37
(mixed)	Unilateral Force	0.00107	1.39	0.00077	1.00	0.00069	0.91
	Reciprocated Force	0.00057	1.04	0.00055	1.00	0.00055	1.00
	War	0.00009	1.61	0.00006	1.00	0.00005	0.83
	No Dispute	0.99701	1.00	0.99744	1.00	0.99811	1.00
6.37	Dispute, No Force	0.00062	0.94	0.00073	1.12	0.00065	1.00
(democratic)	Unilateral Force	0.00167	2.18	0.00116	1.52	0.00069	0.89
	Reciprocated Force	0.00062	1.12	0.00061	1.11	0.00054	0.98
	War	0.00009	1.51	0.00005	0.85	0.00001	0.25

Politically Relevant Dyads		Initiator					
	Democracy Score:	−7.86 (autocratic)		−0.40 (mixed)		7.06 (democratic)	
	Outcome	Prob.	Rel. Risk	Prob.	Rel. Risk	Prob.	Rel. Risk
Target							
	No Dispute	0.99122	1.00	0.98857	1.00	0.98610	1.00
−7.86	Dispute, No Force	0.00221	0.61	0.00375	1.04	0.00605	1.67
(autocratic)	Unilateral Force	0.00344	0.75	0.00386	0.84	0.00405	0.89
	Reciprocated Force	0.00277	0.76	0.00330	0.91	0.00321	0.88
	War	0.00036	1.09	0.00051	1.53	0.00058	1.74
	No Dispute	0.98662	1.00	0.98785	1.00	0.98780	1.00
−0.39	Dispute, No Force	0.00342	0.95	0.00362	1.00	0.00465	1.28
(mixed)	Unilateral Force	0.00590	1.29	0.00457	1.00	0.00390	0.85
	Reciprocated Force	0.00353	0.97	0.00363	1.00	0.00340	0.94
	War	0.00054	1.61	0.00033	1.00	0.00026	0.76
	No Dispute	0.98250	0.99	0.98590	1.00	0.99032	1.00
7.07	Dispute, No Force	0.00431	1.19	0.00424	1.17	0.00302	0.84
(democratic)	Unilateral Force	0.00873	1.91	0.00597	1.30	0.00335	0.73
	Reciprocated Force	0.00392	1.08	0.00363	1.00	0.00323	0.89
	War	0.00055	1.63	0.00027	0.80	0.00008	0.25

Note: Risk is relative to mixed-mixed dyad.

regimes (a drop of 75 percent) and, importantly, is much lower than the risk of war in joint autocratic dyads as well (where risk drops 13 percent). While we find evidence of pacifying effects associated with both democratic pairs of states and autocratic pairs, when it comes to war, the reduction in the risk of war associated with joint democracy is much greater than that associated with joint autocracy, with both being lower than the baseline level of interstate violence associated with anocratic dyads. At lower levels of escalation, particularly in disputes without the use of military force, the pacifying effects of joint autocracy are somewhat greater than joint democracy, but the difference is smaller than the apparent beneficial effect of joint democracy on the risk of full-scale war.

Keep in mind that we are not testing any specific theory that explains the causal foundation of these empirical results. Most of the theoretical work on militarized disputes does not develop any rigorous theory explaining why pairs of autocracies should get into relatively fewer low-level militarized disputes but relative larger numbers of wars compared to democratic regimes.

Our data also allow us to examine whether the political institutions of a potential initiator and target in a dyad correlate with the predicted directional risks of conflict, and here we report interesting new findings. The results we summarized earlier do not take into account which side (democratic, autocratic, and so on) initiates the dispute. They simply focus on the overall risk of a dispute. Turning to the question of who initiates the use of force against whom, we find in our data that democracies more frequently initiate disputes, both very low-level ones and those that escalate to war, against autocratic regimes. We also find that there is an increased risk of autocratic states targeting democracies relative to the baseline case. In particular, in a dyad with a democratic potential initiator and autocratic potential target, we estimate that it is about 75 to 90 percent more likely that a dispute will escalate to war than in a dyad where both states are mixed regimes. Democracies are also much more likely to initiate disputes not involving any use of force against autocrats than vice versa. This result stems in part from the frequent challenges by the United States against the USSR during the cold war, although it is less likely that democracies will initiate disputes against autocracies that end up in only a one-sided or mutual use of force without escalation to war.

Looking at autocratic initiator–democratic target dyads we see a risk ratio of 1.51. We estimate that disputes that escalate to war are 51 to 63 percent more likely than in dyads where both states are mixed regimes, and the risk of one-sided force disputes approximately doubles. Clearly, dyads where the two sides have different types of political institutions are more dangerous than dyads of similar states. It is also important to note in the context of recent scholarship on the war-fighting versus war-selecting characteristics of democracies that autocracies appear to target democracies less often than vice versa. The risk of war in both cases is greater than for joint anocracy dyads (e.g., Bennett and Stam 1998; Lake 1992; Reiter and Stam 1998, 2002; Reed 2000; Stam 1996). If democracies tend to win, both as initiators and as targets, then other states fearing risk of defeat should attack democracies less often, and this is just what we observe in the data here.

This discussion clearly indicates that the relationship between our democracy scale and dispute behavior is not linear in the context of either the potential initiator's or the potential target's regime type. For instance, the risk of disputes escalating to war decreases as the initiator's level of democracy increases—but only in cases where the initiator is facing a democratic or anocratic regime. However, this risk increases when the potential target is autocratic. For an autocratic initiator, the probability of a dispute escalating to war increases dramatically as the target moves from an autocratic to a mixed regime, but then it remains approximately the same (perhaps even decreasing marginally) as the democracy level of the target increases further. The probability of war would decline even further if we projected the level of democracy higher than seven, the top value presented in table 5.10.[2]

8. EXPECTED UTILITY

The likelihood ratio tests in table 5.1 show that the group of expected utility variables makes a statistically significant contribution to our model of international conflict. This is true even after controlling for other factors associated with an increased or reduced likelihood of war. When we separate out just the equilibrium prediction of "war," as a single predictor variable it is also highly statistically significant. In table 5.11, we present details of the probability of observing the different outcomes and the relative risk that they will occur under each of the equilibria. The war equilibrium, compared to the status quo prediction, correlates with higher risks of violent conflict, more than doubling the predicted risk of war in both data sets. The risk of disputes where both sides use force but stop short of war increases by over 300 percent in both data sets. We also see a higher risk of other types of disputes as well, but the magnitude of the effect is somewhat smaller.

Predicting how the other IIG equilibria correspond to conflict outcomes is difficult because it is not entirely clear how predictions of

TABLE 5.11. Effects of International Interaction Game Equilibria on Outcomes

Equilibrium:	Status Quo	Acquiescence by A		Acquiescence by B		Negotiation		War by A	
Outcome	Prob.	Prob.	Rel. Risk	Prob.	Rel. Risk	Prob.	Rel. Risk	Prob.	Rel. Risk
All Dyads									
No Dispute	0.99830	0.99940	1.00	0.99878	1.00	0.99760	1.00	0.99662	1.00
Dispute, No Force	0.00060	0.00014	0.24	0.00029	0.48	0.00074	1.25	0.00099	1.66
Unilateral Force	0.00085	0.00023	0.26	0.00060	0.71	0.00097	1.14	0.00148	1.74
Reciprocated Force	0.00019	0.00020	1.03	0.00031	1.60	0.00061	3.15	0.00079	4.04
War	0.00006	0.00003	0.45	0.00002	0.34	0.00007	1.26	0.00013	2.20
Politically Relevant Dyads									
No Dispute	0.99204	0.99168	1.00	0.99263	1.00	0.98740	1.00	0.98377	0.99
Dispute, No Force	0.00303	0.00253	0.83	0.00196	0.65	0.00384	1.27	0.00479	1.58
Unilateral Force	0.00367	0.00311	0.85	0.00305	0.83	0.00468	1.27	0.00661	1.80
Reciprocated Force	0.00094	0.00226	2.41	0.00220	2.35	0.00366	3.91	0.00417	4.46
War	0.00032	0.00043	1.36	0.00016	0.50	0.00041	1.30	0.00065	2.07

negotiation and acquiescence should correlate with our dependent variable, which measures interstate conflict. All of the IIG equilibria should predict non–status quo outcomes because all involve at least one player challenging the other, the necessary first step in a militarized dispute. However, while most of the equilibria do correspond to non–status quo outcomes, it is difficult to match each of the particular equilibrium predictions to the outcome categories in this analysis.[3] All of the equilibria other than the status quo correspond to an increased likelihood of disputes with reciprocated use of force, and the negotiation equilibrium correlates with a higher dispute frequency at all levels. Counter to what we might expect, though, the negotiation equilibrium more than triples the risk of disputes that escalate to the use of force just short of full-scale war. And predictions of acquiescence by either side correspond quite strongly to a reduced probability of all other types of disputes. This is not nonsensical, as this equilibrium suggests the lowest predicted level of non–status quo behavior; it is possible that acquiescence is in reality occurring before we observe the initiation of a militarized dispute. But this explanation clearly lies outside the bounds of our analysis and ex ante expectations. The predictions of the war equilibrium fit best with our expectations.

So what should we make of the risks associated with these measures of expected utility-based predictions of conflict and war? We can compare these increases in risk to another common and quite serious situation, the risk of cancer. Nonsmokers' lifetime baseline lung cancer risk is approximately 1 in 10,000, or .01 percent. For the case of war, the baseline risk is 1 in 14,000 dyad-years; for militarized disputes, the baseline risk is 1 in 500 dyad-years. Exposure to various conditions then modifies the risk of lung cancer for individuals. According to a recent World Health Organization study, nonsmoking subjects married to smokers were 1.2 times as likely to have lung cancer as were those married to nonsmokers. This risk ratio of 1.2 indicates the nonsmokers increased likelihood of developing lung cancer rising from 1 in 10,000 to 1 in 8,300. Smokers with an exposure of one pack a day for twenty years increase their cancer risk over ten times, with a corresponding odds change from 1 in 10,000 to 1 in 1,000. Smokers consuming two packs a day for sixty years face increased risk ratios between fifty and one hundred times, with a corresponding increase in the odds of cancer from 1 in 10,000 to approximately 1 in 100. While statistically significant, the substantive size of the risk of war associated with the game theoretic predictions (and most other variables) is closer in magnitude to the effect of exposure to second-hand smoke than to long-term smoking. While certainly not something we should ignore, second-hand smoke would probably not be the most profitable place to begin with if we were looking to explain human mortality. It appears that, as a universal data-generating process, Bueno de Mesquita and Lalman's (1992) operational prediction of war derived from their game fails to account for some of the fundamental aspects of international politics.

9. GEOGRAPHIC CONTIGUITY

As we might expect, the odds of a dispute, with or without the use of force, are much higher when states are geographically contiguous than when they are not. As the results in table 5.12 demonstrate, the association of contiguity and conflict is among the strongest of the variables included in our analysis. Within the set of all dyads, contiguous pairs of states are more than eight times as likely to enter into disputes escalating to war and are eighteen times more likely to engage in disputes where both sides employ military force of some level short of war. These substantive effects are somewhat smaller within the set of politically relevant dyads, where one of the selection criteria is contiguity. Using the politically relevant sample, we find that dyads involving contiguous states are still more than twice as likely to initiate disputes escalating to war than noncontiguous great power dyads and are more than three times as likely to have disputes that escalate to a reciprocated use of force. There is a somewhat oblique point here worth bearing out. Because states cannot really change their geographic position,

TABLE 5.12. Effects of Contiguity on Outcomes

States are:	Noncontiguous	Contiguous	
Outcome	Prob.	Prob.	Rel. Risk
All Dyads			
No Dispute	0.99869	0.98941	0.99
Dispute, No Force	0.00038	0.00335	8.81
Unilateral Force	0.00071	0.00344	4.87
Reciprocated Force	0.00019	0.00351	18.14
War	0.00003	0.00029	8.66
Politically Relevant Dyads			
No Dispute	0.99206	0.98053	0.99
Dispute, No Force	0.00240	0.00638	2.66
Unilateral Force	0.00380	0.00699	1.84
Reciprocated Force	0.00150	0.00545	3.65
War	0.00024	0.00064	2.62

some might suggest that we should leave it out of the analysis. It would be unwise to do so, however. First, many of the factors such as democracy that appear to dampen international conflict are not distributed randomly—they tend to cluster in some regions and not in others. Because these factors are correlated with each other, leaving contiguity out of the model risks biasing the parameter estimates for the variables we do include. In addition, because geographic proximity is such a powerful accelerant on the escalation of low-level disputes to war, the lack of war between NATO members provides circumstantial evidence that institutions such as NATO—whose conflict-dampening effects on war we cannot estimate directly—likely have powerful constraining or pacifying effects. This conjecture is consistent with Gowa's (1999) arguments that the democratic peace is an artifact of common interests and alliance patterns among the postwar European democracies, the results in table 5.10 notwithstanding. Contiguity provides a baseline estimate of the expected higher conflict rate among states such as NATO members. Absent some powerful constraining force such as NATO membership, we might otherwise expect to have observed large-scale war between the geographically contiguous powers in Europe at some point during the second half of the twentieth century. In addition, the effect associated with contiguity provides a baseline by which we can judge the relative explanatory power associated with other conjectures and their associated measures.

IO. NUCLEAR DETERRENCE

Our models suggest that the possession of nuclear weapons has a statistically significant association with the relative risk of various levels of interstate disputes. Our ability to estimate reliably the relative substantive effects of nuclear weapons on the probability of war or large-scale military force remains limited, however, because of the paucity of conflict between nuclear powers. As in the case of NATO membership, the absence of large-scale wars between nuclear powers makes it difficult to answer all of the questions we would like to address about the consequences of nuclear weapons in the international system, although this lack of war provides circumstantial evidence that nuclear weapons may have associated effects similar to NATO.

The results in table 5.13 suggest that nuclear weapons may embolden potential dispute initiators. Regarding disputes that fall short of war, the all-dyads analysis suggests that disputes of all levels are more likely when one or both states in a dyad possess nuclear weapons. This result goes against some of the standard nuclear deterrence arguments, although it is consistent with a rationalist moral hazard argument, assuming that states' leaders believe that nuclear weapons help make large-scale war impossible. Keep in mind, however, that these results estimate a correlation or association and do not provide a direct measure of a causal pathway. While the analysis of the "politically relevant" sample suggests that nuclear weapons dampen conflict incentives among this subset, in neither analysis can we obtain good estimates of the effect of the joint possession of nuclear weapons (nuclear deterrence) on disputes that escalate to war. While these conflicting results may appear at odds with one another, we can make sense out of them when we consider other factors that coincide or are collinear with nuclear weapons.

Within the set of all dyads, those dyads where nuclear weapons are present and conflict exists are either major power dyads (e.g., United States–USSR, United States–China, USSR-China) or contiguous dyads (e.g., USSR-China, Israel-Syria, India-Pakistan). In these cases, the states that pursued nuclear capabilities had significant ongoing disputes with one another. These circumstances in part drove them to acquire nuclear capability in the first place. Among the set of all dyads, the possession of nuclear weapons tends to correspond with countries that are conflict prone by their status or environment. The causality here may actually be opposite of that specified in chapter 4. The underlying implication of this is that the substantive effects we estimate may not be

TABLE 5.13. Effects of Nuclear Weapons on Outcomes

Nuclear Presence:	Neither	Initiator Only		Target Only		Both	
Outcome	Prob.	Prob.	Rel. Risk	Prob.	Rel. Risk	Prob.	Rel. Risk
All Dyads							
No Dispute	0.99807	0.99471	1.00	0.99548	1.00	0.99280	0.99
Dispute, No Force	0.00055	0.00223	4.05	0.00141	2.57	0.00424	7.71
Unilateral Force	0.00081	0.00231	2.86	0.00221	2.73	0.00214	2.64
Reciprocated Force	0.00050	0.00076	1.51	0.00078	1.56	0.00083	1.65
War	0.00007	0.00000	—	0.00011	1.74	0.00000	—
Politically Relevant Dyads							
No Dispute	0.98732	0.98992	1.00	0.99126	1.00	0.98398	1.00
Dispute, No Force	0.00370	0.00367	0.99	0.00233	0.63	0.00785	2.12
Unilateral Force	0.00495	0.00449	0.91	0.00415	0.84	0.00516	1.04
Reciprocated Force	0.00360	0.00191	0.53	0.00207	0.58	0.00300	0.83
War	0.00042	0.00000	—	0.00018	0.43	0.00000	—

causal at all but instead the result of a spurious attribution of the correlation with other unobserved or unmeasured factors.

As we noted previously, reliance on the so-called politically relevant sample induces selection bias, the effects of which we can see in the different results here. Within our unbiased population of cases, nuclear weapons are clearly associated with greater risks of armed conflict. By turning to politically relevant dyads, the sample that is limited to major powers and contiguous states, we effectively eliminate the correlation between major power status, contiguity, and nuclear weapons. Once we have removed these causally coincidental factors, we estimate that in most cases nuclear weapons do lower the risk of conflict escalation. In particular, states without nuclear weapons are much less likely to target states with nuclear weapons. When both states have nuclear weapons, disputes still occur more frequently than when both do not, but the effect is mainly limited to disputes that do not escalate to the use of any military force at all, suggesting that nuclear weapons may help to prevent dispute escalation.

There continues to be a limit to what analysts can honestly claim about the dampening effects of nuclear weapons and conflict at high levels, though. As with the relationship between NATO and war, and as we will later see about bipolarity and war, because we have not yet seen a large-scale war between states who jointly possess nuclear weapons (the India-Pakistan dyad notwithstanding), we cannot estimate what possible effects nuclear weapons have on the risk of war with the statistical tools we use here. Within the context of our results, such as the limited escalation in joint nuclear politically relevant dyads, it appears that nuclear weapons have some deterrent effect, but it is impossible to be sure using our research design. Detailed archival analysis may reveal whether nuclear weapons have the deterrent effect that we tend to associate with them (Tannenwald 2003).

11. POWER TRANSITION

Our findings regarding the various power transition permutations are weak and inconsistent across both data sets and measures. We start by noting that, as expected by power transition theorists and opposite the argument of balance of power proponents, static power preponderance is clearly more favorable for peace than is a static equitable balance. However, our variables that incorporate dynamic power changes in the dyad and satisfaction with the status quo do not add much to this finding. Our two dyadic power transition measures are individually statistically insignificant but as a pair are jointly significant. That said, the question of statistical significance is largely moot, as our tests of substantive significance suggest that the increase in relative risk associated with dyadic power transitions is quite small and sometimes appears to work in the direction opposite that expected by power transition proponents (Lemke 2002). Looking specifically in table 5.14, within the set of politically relevant dyads, for instance, we found that, when the dyadic transition measures indicated a magnitude of transition one standard deviation higher than usual (larger capability shifts over a shorter period), the chances of disputes ending with a one-sided use of force *decreased* by about 11 percent. The change in probability of other outcomes lies within the margin of error of our model.

Somewhat ironically, given Organski's (1958) claim that power transition theory described great power behavior, when we examined all dyads, the effects associated with the power transition variables were greater than in the smaller sample of politically relevant dyads (albeit that we must overlook the marginal statistical significance level of the dyadic power transition measure in the all-dyads set). In the population of all dyads, the probability of disputes leading to war dropped 11 percent with a higher value on the power transition variable, disputes with reciprocated force dropping 22 percent and disputes with a one-sided force use dropping 32 percent. These results run counter to power transition logic.

When we examine the standard power transition theorists' measure of satisfaction alone (section 3 of table 5.14), we find results more in line with their expectations. When we look within the politically relevant dyads, a standard deviation decrease in their measure of satisfaction increases the risk of disputes escalating to war by 21 percent and the risk of disputes with a one-sided use of force by 30 percent. The probabilities of other categories were essentially unchanged by this shift. Within all dyads, with similar changes in satisfaction, we see small decreases in the probabilities of disputes leading to war and reciprocated force use and an increase in the risk of disputes with a one-sided use of force, but the effects are small.

These inconsistent results leave us unable to draw supportive conclusions about the dyadic implementation of power transition arguments we employed here. They also point out an important limit to knowledge in our analysis. Even with the large number of cases we have, multicollinearity is still a problem for separating out the effects or predictions associated with some competing theories of explanations of conflict. Our power transition variables were highly correlated with

TABLE 5.14. Effects of Power Transition on Outcomes

Dyadic Power Transition

All Dyads

Magnitude of Transition:	0 (No transition)	0.11 (1 SD above mean)	
Outcome	Prob.	Prob.	Rel. Risk
No Dispute	0.99768	0.99818	1.00
Dispute, No Force	0.00065	0.00062	0.95
Unilateral Force	0.00103	0.00071	0.68
Reciprocated Force	0.00057	0.00044	0.78
War	0.00007	0.00006	0.89

Politically Relevant Dyads

Magnitude of Transition:	0 (No transition)	0.05 (1 SD above mean)	
Outcome	Prob.	Prob.	Rel. Risk
No Dispute	0.98783	0.98835	1.00
Dispute, No Force	0.00357	0.00372	1.04
Unilateral Force	0.00498	0.00441	0.89
Reciprocated Force	0.00323	0.00313	0.97
War	0.00039	0.00039	1.01

Note: Because 1 SD below mean falls minimum possible value, low value is 0.

Satisfaction (as part of Dyadic Power Transition)

All Dyads

Satisfaction:	0.32 (1 SD above mean)	0.64 (1 SD below mean)	
Outcome	Prob.	Prob.	Rel. Risk
No Dispute	0.99780	0.99779	1.00
Dispute, No Force	0.00066	0.00061	0.93
Unilateral Force	0.00094	0.00105	1.12
Reciprocated Force	0.00054	0.00049	0.90
War	0.00007	0.00006	0.96

Politically Relevant Dyads

Satisfaction:	0.30 (1 SD above mean)	0.71 (1 SD below mean)	
Outcome	Prob.	Prob.	Rel. Risk
No Dispute	0.98824	0.98675	1.00
Dispute, No Force	0.00362	0.00364	1.01
Unilateral Force	0.00458	0.00597	1.30
Reciprocated Force	0.00319	0.00319	1.00
War	0.00037	0.00045	1.21

(continues)

TABLE 5.14—Continued

Global Leader Power Transition
All Dyads

Magnitude of Transition:	0 (No transition)	0.003 (1 SD above mean)	
Outcome	Prob.	Prob.	Rel. Risk
No Dispute	0.99780	0.99776	1.00
Dispute, No Force	0.00065	0.00066	1.01
Unilateral Force	0.00096	0.00097	1.01
Reciprocated Force	0.00053	0.00055	1.03
War	0.00006	0.00007	1.02

Politically Relevant Dyads

Magnitude of Transition:	0 (No transition)	0.008 (1 SD above mean)	
Outcome	Prob.	Prob.	Rel. Risk
No Dispute	0.98805	0.98804	1.00
Dispute, No Force	0.00363	0.00363	1.00
Unilateral Force	0.00475	0.00476	1.00
Reciprocated Force	0.00319	0.00319	1.00
War	0.00039	0.00038	0.98

Note: Because 1 SD below mean falls minimum possible value, low value is 0.

one another. While power transition arguments distinguish between the effects of power transitions per se and power transitions in the context of a state's relative satisfaction, as well as the possible effects of whether the weaker state in the dyad was the faster growing state, the data do not allow us to draw any firm conclusions with the measures used here. The correlation of the transition measures, with and without satisfaction, is 0.98 in this data, and measures marking the identity of the faster growing state correlate at between 0.65 and 0.75. Statistically (in terms of the logged likelihood function), the two variables contribute marginally to the overall fit of the model. However, when we added the further interactions marking when the weaker state was growing faster, we could not obtain reliable estimates. Perhaps if we had been able to use a single measure that identified weaker and quickly growing challengers, the results would have offered more support for the model. Of course, the simplest and perhaps most satisfactory answer is that, counter to Lemke's (2002) claims otherwise, the power transition logic simply does not apply to pairs of states apart from global or regional leaders. In that case, however, we would still not have then expected to see the conflict-reducing effects that we did.

Findings

Turning away from recent attempts to transform Organski's power transition logic from a story of great power interaction to a general model of interstate relations, we now move to our variable that measured the magnitude of transitions among the system leader and other states. Here we again found quite small substantive effects, even though the variable in question had statistically distinguishable effects associated with it in one of our data sets. The increase in the probability of disputes and escalation to war associated with a system-leader power transition, as described by Organski and Kugler (1980), is between 1 and 3 percent as we move from situations of no transition to situations of higher than normal transition. The change in risk associated with system leader power transitions seen in table 5.14 is essentially zero.

Overall, these findings offer at best mixed support for these indicators of power transition theory. The results are inconsistent across various tests and after controlling for other explanations. Either the operational measures do not capture the key elements of power transition logic, in which case, as currently conceived, the variables and necessary operational measures provide an important limit to knowledge in our analysis, or of the theoretical arguments laid out by Organski and Kugler are wrong.

12. TRADE INTERDEPENDENCE

Arguments that trade interdependence contributes to peaceful relations between states have gained increasing attention of late (Oneal and Russett 2001). As we discussed earlier, however, there is significant missing data on trade flows and GDP. Such data only rarely run back to 1816 (the beginning of our analysis) and are widely available only since World War II. The available data are more accurate for Organization for Economic Cooperation and Development (OECD) states and other developed countries, and many GDP figures before World War II are estimates by economic historians. When we add trade variables to our model, we lose 23 percent of the cases otherwise included in our analysis of all dyads and lose 38 percent of the cases included in our analysis of politically relevant dyads. We are quite concerned about this sizable loss of cases, particularly since we know the distribution of missing data is not random. The cases that remain in our analysis after we include the trade data are disproportionately post–World War II cases and are, economically, disproportionately highly developed. This nonrandom sampling likely biases our results, as well as reduces our accuracy through lost information. As a result, we added trade to our model only in a secondary analysis. We report the results of that analysis in table 5.15.

We include two trade dependence variables in our analysis of trade dependence. The first measures dyadic trade as a proportion of GDP for the potential initiator and the second measures dyadic trade as a proportion of GDP for the potential target. Both the initiator's and the target's trade dependence was generally statistically significant. However, the significance of the variables is not uniform across the various dispute outcomes, leading to uncertainty about some key effects. In particular, focusing only on the highest level of escalation, both the initiator's and target's trade dependence appears to be associated with a diminished risk of war. However, while the target's level of trade dependence is clearly statistically significant, the initiator's level is not. While it has a large negative coefficient, it also has a large standard error, reflecting substantial uncertainty about how potential conflict initiators react to their own trade dependence. We observe this difference in statistical significance in both the analysis of population of dyads and the politically relevant dyads.

Although we are quite uncertain about the effect of the initiator's level of trade, the change in the relative risk associated with variation in both trade dependence variables is substantial. Table 5.15 presents the relative risk scores for the two trade dependence variables. Increases in trade reduce the risk of conflict at most levels by a substantial margin, whether the trade dependence of the initiator or target is increasing. In a few instances, we observe that increased trade dependence appears to correlate with slightly higher probabilities of some conflict outcomes, but these increases in risk are small compared to the large reductions in the other categories. Of particular interest is the risk of disputes that escalate to war. Increasing the target's level of trade dependence appears to cut the risk of disputes escalating to war by 22 to 85 percent, depending on the analysis. Further research might profitably focus on why trade dependence levels in the target state appear to have clearer effects than levels in the initiator, an observation masked in nondirected dyadic analyses that focus necessarily on the lower trade dependence in the nondirected dyad (Oneal and Russett 2001). In general, however, our findings support the argument that trade correlates with lower levels of conflict, albeit in a biased sample.

Adding the trade dependence variables to our analysis does not change the substantive conclusions associated with the other independent variables in many cases; for others the effects are problematic. Our findings on the balance of power, conventional deterrence, power

TABLE 5.15. Effects of Trade Dependence on Outcomes

All Dyads

Initiator Trade Dependence:	0 (minimum)	0.0175 (1 SD above mean)	
Outcome	Prob.	Prob.	Rel. Risk
No Dispute	0.99817	0.99829	1.00
Dispute, No Force	0.00054	0.00037	0.72
Unilateral Force	0.00075	0.00081	1.07
Reciprocated Force	0.00049	0.00050	1.01
War	0.00005	0.00004	0.78

Target Trade Dependence:	0 (minimum)	0.0175 (1 SD above mean)	
Outcome	Prob.	Prob.	Rel. Risk
No Dispute	0.99821	0.99822	1.00
Dispute, No Force	0.00048	0.00048	1.01
Unilateral Force	0.00075	0.00082	1.09
Reciprocated Force	0.00051	0.00045	0.91
War	0.00006	0.00003	0.54

Politically Relevant Dyads

Initiator Trade Dependence:	0 (minimum)	0.049 (1 SD above mean)	
Outcome	Prob.	Prob.	Rel. Risk
No Dispute	0.98734	0.98893	1.00
Dispute, No Force	0.00415	0.00250	0.34
Unilateral Force	0.00445	0.00460	1.06
Reciprocated Force	0.00370	0.00367	0.99
War	0.00037	0.00030	0.57

Target Trade Dependence:	0 (minimum)	0.049 (1 SD above mean)	
Outcome	Prob.	Prob.	Rel. Risk
No Dispute	0.98790	0.98839	1.00
Dispute, No Force	0.00347	0.00344	0.98
Unilateral Force	0.00425	0.00480	1.28
Reciprocated Force	0.00388	0.00319	0.67
War	0.00050	0.00019	0.14

Note: Because 1 SD below mean falls below data range, low value is 0.

transition, arms races, contiguity, nuclear weapons, hegemony and bipolarity, and global economic cycles are quite similar after we add trade. In one case, for the expected utility (IIG) equilibrium prediction of war, the estimated effect of the equilibrium on the probability of war increases dramatically after we add trade. For a few variables, adding trade reduces or eliminates their apparent effects. As anticipated by Gowa (1999), the apparent effect of joint democracy on reducing the risk of war is much smaller after we control for trade, with a shift from joint autocracy to joint democracy reducing the risk of war by 20 to 30 percent rather than the 80 percent estimated previously. The apparent effect of defense pacts in reducing the risk of disputes that go to war drops to zero. Finally, the estimates on democratization, polity change, and systemic power concentration and movement become rather unstable, with few clear patterns in the results. These changes are largely the result of losing a large number of important cases and, to a lesser degree, because of the high degree of correlation between trade dependence and the other variables in the model. The reductions in the effects associated with democracy and defense pacts both make sense, as we know that developed democracies are the most active traders in the international system, particularly after World War II. Many of these active traders are also members of NATO and so share common alliances. The net effect of adding trade is to reduce slightly the risk of violent conflict, but, more important, trade interdependence shifts the liberal institutionalist association away from democracy and alliances toward democracy and trade interdependence. Unfortunately, however, the data do not provide a clear way to distinguish which factors bear the causal burden.

International System Level of Analysis

13. ECONOMIC CYCLES/KONDRATIEFF WAVES

Consistent with Goldstein's (1988) arguments, we find periods of system-wide economic growth associated with increased risks of disputes escalating to all levels of disputes, including those involving the use of force and large-scale war. In table 5.16, we see that across all conflict categories, the increases in risk are generally of similar magnitude, with a 40 to 100 percent increase in the odds of conflict involving force during periods of economic upswing compared to periods of downswing. Only the probability of having disputes without the use of any force appears to drop slightly. A somewhat discouraging finding is that the associated increase in risk appears strongest for disputes escalating to

TABLE 5.16. Effects of Economic Cycles on Outcomes

| Global Economic Cycle: | Downswing | Upswing | |
Outcome	Prob.	Prob.	Rel. Risk
All Dyads			
No Dispute	0.99	0.99	1.00
Dispute, No Force	0.00068	0.00061	0.89
Unilateral Force	0.00084	0.0012	1.39
Reciprocated Force	0.00044	0.00073	1.68
War	0.00004	0.00009	1.98
Politically Relevant Dyads			
No Dispute	0.98	0.98	1.00
Dispute, No Force	0.0037	0.0035	0.95
Unilateral Force	0.0038	0.0062	1.60
Reciprocated Force	0.0025	0.0044	1.71
War	0.00028	0.0005	1.79

war, where the risk of such conflicts appears to be 80 to 100 percent higher than the baseline risk of war.

These results stand in contrast to debates in the 1980s and early 1990s over relative versus absolute gains. Regime theorists such as Krasner and Keohane argued that states, when concerned with absolute (as compared to relative) gains, would be less conflict prone. This set off a long-running debate about the nature of states' preferences, which in the end devolved to a discussion of whether there was really any distinction between the two, with the most rigorous theoretical analysis demonstrating that even absolute gains could only be measured in some context, a relative one (Powell 1991). Our results suggest that there is something of a Faustian trade-off between economic gains and the likelihood of war. During periods of sustained economic growth throughout the system, periods with absolute gains for all (or most) states, the incidence of war increases and rather dramatically so.

14 AND 15. HEGEMONY STABILITY AND INTERNATIONAL SYSTEM POLARITY

The estimated risk of disputes or war associated with the variables marking the pre-1914 and post-1945 periods provides little support for simplistic measures of hegemonic stability arguments, although the data do provide substantial, albeit, circumstantial support for Waltz's (1979) assertion that the bipolar period following World War II would be relatively more stable than other periods. In particular, table 5.17 illustrates that the risk of disputes escalating to war is much higher before 1918 than in either the interwar or the post-1945 periods. In the context of disputes escalating to levels short of war, the results vary somewhat across the data sets and specific outcomes. In general, both the interwar and the post–World War II periods seem to have a lower risk of other types of disputes as well as large-scale wars. During the pre-1918 period, the risk of disputes that escalate to war is roughly double that during the interwar period, while the relative risk of disputes leading to war after 1945 appears 95 to 99 percent lower than before 1918. We find strong support for the neorealist claim that interstate conflict should be less likely in bipolar systems. In contrast, there is little support for the hegemonic stability argument that conflict is relatively less likely whenever there is a clear system leader.

While these findings offer some support for the structural realists' arguments about bipolarity, the unsupportive results for simple measures of hegemony are in sharp contrast to the robust findings we have for the more sophisticated measures of systemic power concentration discussed later. It is true that the level of overall conflict varies tremendously from period to period. That said, we suggest that structural arguments that simply break the international system into periods of multipolarity or bipolarity add little to our understanding of the an-

TABLE 5.17.   Effects of Hegemony/Polarity on Outcomes

Time Period:	Pre-1918 U.K. Hegemony Multipolar	Interwar No Hegemony Multipolar		Post-1945 U.S. Hegemony Bipolar	
Outcome	Prob.	Prob.	Rel. Risk	Prob.	Rel. Risk
All Dyads					
No Dispute	0.99487	0.99628	1.00	0.99833	1.00
Dispute, No Force	0.00248	0.00122	0.49	0.00039	0.16
Unilateral Force	0.00181	0.00157	0.87	0.00076	0.42
Reciprocated Force	0.00047	0.00076	1.59	0.00051	1.06
War	0.00036	0.00018	0.50	0.00001	0.04
Politically Relevant Dyads					
No Dispute	0.99177	0.99665	1.00	0.99839	1.01
Dispute, No Force	0.00380	0.00097	0.25	0.00037	0.10
Unilateral Force	0.00110	0.00094	0.85	0.00074	0.67
Reciprocated Force	0.00046	0.00057	1.23	0.00048	1.03
War	0.00286	0.00088	0.31	0.00002	0.01

Note: All risk levels relative to pre-1918 period.

tecedents to disputes or wars. The major problem is that these arguments provide no explanation for conflicts that occur on a regular basis within each type of system, be it bipolar, multipolar, or hegemonic.[4] For example, Waltz (1979) argues that the system will tend toward an equilibrium of a balanced distribution of power, but this theory provides no explanation for which states will balance and which will bandwagon. He merely asserts a general tendency toward balancing behavior.

In each of these periods, a variety of other factors changes more frequently and rapidly than does this simply dummy variable indicator of time period. The coefficients that mark the periods of bipolarity or British hegemony capture the basic frequency of events, or baseline risk, during these periods not accounted for by other factors. Apart from judging this frequency, though, we still do not know *why* these periods have different baseline conflict rates. For instance, because we cannot obtain separate estimates for the effect of joint nuclear weapons possession on the probability of war, it could be that nuclear weapons are contributing to the relatively low risk of war after World War II. Similarly, it could be some other characteristic of the post-1945 system such as the presence of the United Nations, NATO, universal instant communication, or lingering memories of World War II causing the reduced risk of conflict. While the various structural arguments do predict that conflict will be more or less frequent in these periods, the prediction for the bipolar period is collinear with a host of other equally plausible explanations for conflict. More nuanced predictions about where conflict is more or less likely to occur during the various periods are necessary to help our understanding of the causes of war.

Finally, we note that, from a foreign policy perspective, polarity is also something that is relatively immutable in the short run, although recent research on system evolution suggests ways that the system may change from one type to another in ways divorced from change in material capabilities (Wendt 1999).

16. SYSTEMIC POWER CONCENTRATION AND MOVEMENT

From the perspective of classical hypothesis testing, our results suggest that the variables accounting for systemic power concentration have statistically significant effects on the incidence of conflict associated with them. Focusing on substantive, rather than statistical, significance, we find that, out of all the arguments we look at, the most powerful predictors of war are primarily associated with the concentration of power in the international system. Counter to power transition arguments, and consistent with system-level balance of power arguments (as opposed to dyadic conceptions of the balance of power), we find in table 5.18 that high concentrations of economic and military capabilities in the international system appear to be associated with a much higher incidence of all types of dispute and war. These results are consistent with our weak empirical findings for our power transition variables and run counter to power transition logic (power transition arguments suggest that increased concentration of power should correlate with lower rather than greater risks). We see the most dramatic results in the increased risks associated with power concentration and its effects on disputes short of war.

Concerning the risk of war and system power concentration, and consistent with system-level balance of power arguments, we estimate war to be three to six times (73 to 369 percent) more likely when the concentration of military and economic capabilities is one standard deviation above the mean compared to one standard deviation below. Dynamic changes in capability concentration have an opposite effect, though. Again, in direct contrast to power transition logic (which suggests that systemic power concentration shifts should lead to more conflict after controlling for the actual static level of concentration), we find that the probability of most dispute outcomes drops when system concentration changes (the exception is the unilateral use of force outcome). These effects are smaller than those effects associated with power concentration alone, though, so even sudden instability measured by rapid changes in power concentration will not counter the increased probability of conflict when the level of concentration is relatively high.

Our tests for a curvilinear relationship between system power concentration and war were inconclusive. We tried to add the square of concentration of capabilities to examine Mansfield's (1994) argument that concentration should have a curvilinear effect on war. However, in our sample, concentration and concentration^2 correlate at $r = 0.99$, too strongly correlated for us to be able to obtain robust estimates. When we included the terms in less fully specified models, the results suggested that both have statistically significant coefficients associated with disputes escalating to war. In contrast to Mansfield's expectations, however, in these models, we found results that suggested a U-shaped relationship between concentration and war rather than Mansfield's expected inverted U. In the models with a reduced set of independent variables, which allow us to estimate the changes in the relative risk of war associated with the curvilinear specification of power concentration, the coefficient associated with system power concentration is always strongly negative (-100 x) and concentration^2 is always strongly

TABLE 5.18. Effects of System Structure on Outcomes

Systemic Power Concentration

	All Dyads			Politically Relevant Dyads		
System Concentration:	0.27 (1 SD below mean)	0.33 (1 SD above mean)		0.28 (1 SD below mean)	0.35 (1 SD above mean)	
Outcome	Prob.	Prob.	Rel. Risk	Prob.	Prob.	Rel. Risk
No Dispute	0.99718	0.98599	0.99	0.98485	0.90940	0.92
Dispute, No Force	0.00067	0.00073	1.09	0.00415	0.00999	2.40
Unilateral Force	0.00139	0.01055	7.58	0.00627	0.04249	6.78
Reciprocated Force	0.00068	0.00260	3.83	0.00419	0.03563	8.50
War	0.00008	0.00013	1.73	0.00053	0.00249	4.69

Change in System Concentration

	All Dyads			Politically Relevant Dyads		
Change in Concentration:	−0.005 (1 SD below mean)	0.004 (1 SD above mean)		−0.006 (1 SD below mean)	0.005 (1 SD above mean)	
Outcome	Prob.	Prob.	Rel. Risk	Prob.	Prob.	Rel. Risk
No Dispute	0.99788	0.99773	1.00	0.98822	0.98795	1.00
Dispute, No Force	0.00069	0.00061	0.88	0.00398	0.00326	0.82
Unilateral Force	0.00080	0.00110	1.37	0.00394	0.00547	1.39
Reciprocated Force	0.00056	0.00051	0.91	0.00339	0.00299	0.88
War	0.00008	0.00005	0.67	0.00047	0.00032	0.69

System Power Movement

	All Dyads			Politically Relevant Dyads		
Level of Movement:	0.01 (1 SD below mean)	0.05 (1 SD above mean)		0.01 (1 SD below mean)	0.06 (1 SD above mean)	
Outcome	Prob.	Prob.	Rel. Risk	Prob.	Prob.	Rel. Risk
No dispute	0.99782	0.99771	1.00	0.98836	0.98737	1.00
Dispute, No Force	0.00077	0.00056	0.72	0.00409	0.00307	0.75
Unilateral Force	0.00080	0.00112	1.40	0.00403	0.00578	1.44
Reciprocated Force	0.00051	0.00056	1.09	0.00303	0.00347	1.15
War	0.00009	0.00005	0.56	0.00050	0.00030	0.61

positive (+150 x). The magnitudes of the associated risk ratios are dramatically larger than power concentration alone (.20 to 8) but are quite unstable, a sign of findings suffering from severe multicollinearity. As a result, we are unable to assess empirically Mansfield's argument about the curvilinear effects of power concentration.

Considering these results further, we note that because system power concentration values tend to shift very slowly over time, these measures suffer from some of the same problems as the broad measures of hegemony and polarity and are tapping some of the same effects as those variables. When we plot the data on levels of concentration over time, we find that the period of lowest concentration starts in the 1960s, following the period of highest concentration in the late 1940s. The mid-1800s and post–World War I eras also show relatively high system-level power concentration. Power concentration changed most rapidly because of, and immediately after, the world wars. With a large cluster of the highest levels of concentration occurring after World War II at the same time that we have relatively low incidence of war, the inference that power concentration is driving the level of conflict may be spurious. Other explanations such as war weariness are collinear with power concentration, complicating our search for the true causes of war.

Turning to power movement from one state to another in the international system (a continuous measure of power instability), we find that the effects of these power shifts on dispute initiation and escalation vary across the escalation levels of the disputes. The strongest effects appear to be associated with disputes that escalate to war. Periods with large power shifts between states experienced a 38 to 45 percent lower risk of disputes escalating to war than did periods where the power distribution across states remained stable. Looking at the distribution of movement data over time, this appears to be because power shifts were highest after the major systemic wars (that is, after 1918 and 1945, when there was also a period without war). Taken together, these results indicate that changes in the system's power distribution appear to lower the relative risk of conflicts that escalate to war, while stable periods of high concentration are the most dangerous. Again, however, these variables are collinear with other explanations not accounted for here, which may suggest problems with the inferences that we draw.

RELATIVE EFFECTS

One of the advantages of our research design is that it allows for the explicit comparison of the relative risk of disputes and war associated with the different arguments and conjectures we have examined. We believe strongly that it is not enough to say that most of the factors "make a difference" in the manner of classical hypothesis testing, noting that a variable either does or does not have an effect on the incidence of international conflict with some associated confidence interval. Simplistic hypothesis testing based solely on statistical significance does not allow us to assess the relative explanatory power of the arguments, one of our principal goals from the outset. Using the yardstick we developed in chapter 2, based on the population baseline risk of conflict for comparison, we present the effects on the relative risk of war associated with the factors we include in figures 5.1 and 5.2.

Table 5.2 demonstrates the direction and magnitude of the risk ratios associated with a one standard deviation change in the independent variables, illustrating the wide range in the size of the substantive effects associated with the various indicators. To simplify the interpretation, we present the risk ratios graphically in figures 5.1 and 5.2. In these figures, we compute and present the risk of conflict associated with changes in each factor across a comparable range of values. Figure 5.1 presents the risk ratios associated with our explanations of conflict in the context of the risk of disputes that escalate to war. Figure 5.2 presents the risk ratios for the variables associated with disputes that escalate to a reciprocated use of force, a substantially lower level of violence than interstate war. Both figures include risk ratios based on the two data sets we analyzed. We converted the absolute magnitude of all the risk ratios to be greater than one for illustration's sake. So, for instance, a risk ratio of 0.5 would have an absolute effect of 2 with this conversion. But further, factors that reduce the risk of conflict are displayed on the left side of the baseline risk level, while factors associated with increased risk of war are displayed on the right side. So a risk ratio of 0.5 is actually displayed as a −2 in the figures.

Most of the results are consistent across the two levels of violence and in the two data sets. There are a few notable exceptions, however, where the risk ratios vary greatly in the two data sets. The most obvious is contiguity, which appears to have a much weaker effect among the set of politically relevant dyads. This relative weakness is a direct result of contiguity being one of the selection mechanisms for creating that sample. Second, nuclear weapons appear to switch effects in the two populations, but as discussed this is partly a result of many politically relevant states being involved in repeated long-term conflicts, such as the United States and the Soviet Union, both possessing nuclear weapons. Third, the effects of trade dependence are estimated to be much higher when the politically relevant data set is used, perhaps suggesting that

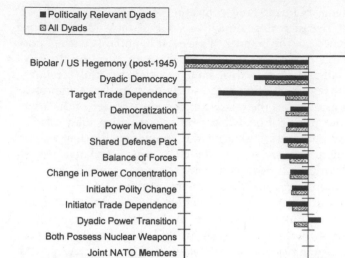

Fig. 5.1.   Relative power of variables on disputes escalating to war, sorted by all-dyads rank.

trade only serves as a brake on conflict when it is contiguous or otherwise relevant states that have decided to engage in it. Finally, changes in the risk of violent conflict associated with systemic power concentration variation appear to be approximately twice as strong within the set of politically relevant dyads.

Three insights follow from an examination of the figures and this range of effects. First, while the size of the risk ratios varies widely, most of the variables we include in the model have quite modest effects associated with them. Typically, the risk ratios indicate increases in the risk of disputes by 30 to 60 percent over the baseline risk of war (1 in

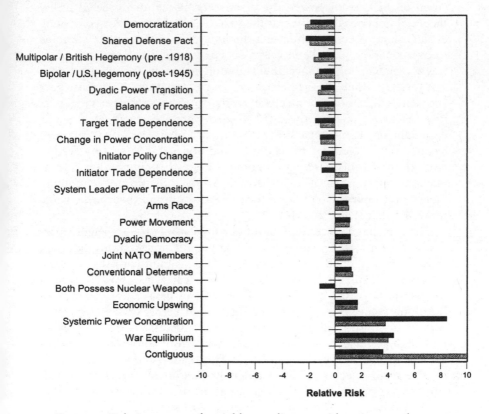

Fig. 5.2.   Relative power of variables on disputes with reciprocated force, sorted by all-dyads rank.

14,000 dyad-years). A few variables—for example, contiguity—are associated with increases in the relative risk of more than an order of magnitude. However, very few of the variables even double (or halve) the risk of conflict. Second, most of the variables have similar effects. The variables marking most arguments about the onset of conflict are quite comparable in their associated effects.

This leads to the third insight about the relative effects associated with the various indicators, namely, that there is no single overriding argument or variable that we can point to as the leading cause of international conflict either in general or in any single instance. None of the variables that serve as proxies for arguments posited elsewhere to be theories of international relations, whether they are arguments focused on balance of power, the democratic peace, or expected utility theory, dominates the effects of the variables accounting for competing explanations. A combination of a small number of factors can combine to overcome the increase in risk associated with changes in any other single variable. For instance, in a situation where the IIG equilibrium is war (perhaps doubling the risk of war), a combination of a defense pact and democratization (for instance) easily overcomes the associated positive incentives pushing the dyad toward war. The search for a single dominant or all-encompassing grand theory of international relations has not yet succeeded. This claim should not be taken as an assertion that no unified theory of war is possible but rather simply that current attempts fall short of the mark. Recent work in the field of bargaining theory holds out the best hope for this sort of grand theory to emerge (Powell 2002; Reiter 2003).

The fact that changes in most of our indicators produce small variation in the estimated relative risk of war is quite important to the study of international conflict more broadly. The magnitude of the risks associated with many of the "theories" of war we estimated here is roughly akin to the magnitude of the risk of cancer associated with breathing second-hand smoke, or the risk of breast cancer associated with birth control pills, or the risk of leukemia associated with living near high-voltage power lines. The findings from studies of these cancer risk factors are typically quite uncertain and produce very modest relative risk projections. For instance, studies of the effects of second-hand smoke produced relative risks of at the most 1.8, with the median result around 1.2. The risks associated with second-hand smoke are comparable to those of death from breast cancer for women using estrogen-based birth control pills. While there is a measurable increase in risk of death from breast cancer associated with the pill, for an individual woman who would otherwise bear a child, the risk associated with the pill is more than offset by the reduction of risk associated with carrying a fetus to term. In stark contrast, smoking a pack a day for twenty years leads to a lifetime increase in cancer risk of ten to twenty times.

One rule of thumb in epidemiology is that researchers look for at least a 2x increase (or 50 percent decrease) in relative risk before claiming that the effect of some hazard or treatment warrants serious attention in situations where the event is a relatively rare one. Studies showing risk ratios smaller than 2.0 are commonly "overturned" as subsequent studies frequently produce conflicting results. The general weakness of the explanatory effects we find here suggests a parallel reason for why repeated quantitative studies investigating the same source of conflict frequently find different effects. With multiple risk factors each with relatively small magnitude, even small changes in research design, variable construction, or variable specification may overturn prior findings.

DANGEROUS DYADS: COMBINING EFFECTS

Based on the individual conjectures of the onset of war, we can clearly see that some situations are more dangerous than others. Nevertheless, we have also found that the independent risks for the factors in our model tend to be quite small. Taken in isolation, these results offer only a little guidance to those seeking to predict when violent conflict is very likely to occur. These results do not suggest, however, that the risk of war is only marginally higher in the riskiest situations but rather that it takes a rare combination of multiple factors working simultaneously in any given dyad-year to push two or more states strongly toward a violent confrontation. In exploring further the interaction of factors needed for a dyad to have a high probability of war, we find that if we simultaneously set several variables to "dangerous" values then the estimated risk of war increases quite dramatically.

For instance, if we simulate a geographically contiguous dyad, with an IIG equilibrium of war, embroiled in an arms race, with a 2:1 initiator capabilities advantage, and with both states having become autocratic within the past ten years, the risk of war increases to nearly 40 times the baseline risk to roughly 1 in 400 dyad-years. The risk of reciprocated militarized disputes increases 32 times, to 1 in 60 dyad-years. If we further add the presence of an economic upswing cycle and assume the states in the dyad have no defensive alliances, the risk of war increases to about 55 times the baseline risk and reciprocated disputes increase to 45 times. If our two states had experienced a previous militarized dispute in the past five years, the estimated risk of war jumps to 70 times the baseline risk (disputes increase 50 times). Finally, if the previous dispute had occurred only two years ago, the risk of war actually jumps to 248 times the baseline risk, or 1 in 62 dyad-years (the risk of disputes jumps to 229 times the baseline risk). Note that the baseline probability of war in a single directed dyad-year is 0.000065; even a 248 times increase in risk keeps the annual probability of war for any dyad in this dangerous situation at less than 2 percent. The baseline probability of disputes is about 0.05 percent; with this increase, it rises to about 12 percent. Given that our data set contains over 33,000 dyad-years in every year toward the end of the time-series and that many of the risk factors are quite highly correlated (meaning that if you observe one, you are likely to see another), it is not surprising that we commonly observe many dyads having dangerous circumstances such as these. When risky conditions like these persist for several years, it becomes highly likely that a state will initiate a violent dispute with another state.

The fact that interstate war is a relatively rare event in the international system suggests that combinations of uncommon circumstances and dynamic interactions among them are the critical factors increasing the probability of war in any particular situation. Given multiple factors increasing the risk or incentives for war, the relative risk of interstate violence can rise very quickly. These results offer some support for Bremer's (1995) "concatenation of weak forces" conjecture. Bremer argues that only when "not-so-rare" events come together in unusual circumstances do rare events such as war occur. An important factor increasing the risk of conflict today is the occurrence of conflict in the recent past, something that helps distinguish long-term peaceful dyads from those likely to suffer from recurring conflict. A survey of international relations "theory," though, reveals that most explanations of war, particularly quantitatively oriented studies, ignore combinations (interactions) of circumstances except as afterthoughts.[5] Our inclusion of multiple variables as additive factors is the typical approach in the literature. The results here suggest we should have an increased appreciation of interactive effects between various situational or environmental factors.

Our results also suggest that investigating such interactions may be a fruitful area for further research. If we were to build in interactive variables exclusively, rather than simply adding variables as independent regressors, we would likely find stronger substantive effects associated with various combinations of factors we treat here as independent.

WHICH STATES ARE AT RISK?

Another means of assessing which dyads are the most dangerous is to examine those pairs of states that the model estimates as being at the greatest risk of war since 1816 and to examine which dyads the model predicts as most conflict prone in the early 1990s.

Looking at predictions from the analysis of all dyads, the top twenty most dangerous directed dyads of the past 175 years consist of Argentina-Chile in the late 1800s (with the peak probability of war occurring in 1899), Russia-China in the late 1890s (peak 1893), Italy-Austria in the late 1860s (peak 1867), Greece-Turkey (peak 1898), Austria-Hungary-Turkey (peak 1898), Germany-Russia (peak 1940), Germany-France (peak 1937), Yugoslavia-Rumania (peak 1914), Austria-Hungary-Russia (peak 1913), and Ecuador-Peru (peak 1906). All of these are, of course, dyads that experienced major conflict around these predicted peak periods. These same dyads appear to make up sizeable percentages of the most dangerous dyad-years as we moved further down the list of predicted dangerous dyad-years. Other notable dyads and time points appearing in the top one hundred include Guatemala-Honduras, Guatemala-El Salvador, Honduras-Nicaragua, and Honduras–El Salvador in the early 1900s; Germany-Belgium, 1937; Colombia-Venezuela, 1903; Britain-China, 1901; and United States–Mexico in the nineteenth century.

The model predicts the following as the most dangerous dyads (in terms of probability of war) in the last years of the model:

1990	1991	1992
North Korea–South Korea	North Korea–South Korea	Nigeria–United States
Uganda-Kenya	Uganda-Kenya	Kenya-Rwanda
Zimbabwe–South Africa	Burma-Thailand	Ecuador-Peru
Burma-Thailand	Uganda-Sudan	Sudan-Egypt
Iran-Iraq	Mauritania-Senegal	Turkey-Iraq
Swaziland–South Africa	Guinea-Bissau–Senegal	Guinea-Bissau–Senegal
Uganda-Zaire	Iran-Iraq	North Korea–South Korea
Turkey-Syria	Senegal-Mauritania	Uganda-Sudan

In 1992, we do in fact see disputes between North and South Korea and between Guinea-Bissau and Senegal. In prior years, we saw disputes in other listed dyads, including Ecuador-Peru and Turkey-Iraq in 1991. Other dyads topping the most dangerous list for 1992 include China-Taiwan, United States–Iran, Turkey-Iran, Thailand-Laos, Congo-Zaire, Afghanistan-Pakistan, and Israel-Syria.

PREDICTING SYSTEMIC CONFLICT

We conclude our final assessment of how well our model performs by predicting international conflict for the interstate system as a whole.

Waltz argues in *The Theory of International Politics* (1979) that any theory of international relations that includes domestic factors would devolve into reductionism and therefore would become a description of foreign policy and not be a theory of international relations. In this project, one of the implicit themes has been to argue that Waltz's dichotomy is a false one. The previous section demonstrated empirically, using measures derived from a variety of models and conjectures, that we can identify ex ante those particular dyads in the international system that are particularly at risk of entering into a dispute and of potentially escalating a dispute to the use of force. Some might characterize this type of prediction as foreign policy. What then of Waltz's claims about international relations? In our view, developing positivist expectations about "international relations" in Waltz's terms entails developing testable predictions about the overall risk or nature of conflict through the international system in any given year. Rather than focusing on the effects of the various arguments and conjectures on risk of war that individual states face, we now turn our attention to the international system as a whole. We approach Waltz's notion of international relations using the same models we used to develop our predictions of individual states' use of force.

Assessing the overall predictive power of any multinomial logit model, especially one with rare events, is not completely straightforward. First, we address how we should evaluate the overall fit of our models to the history of conflict over the past two hundred years. Then we look to see how the model performs on a year-to-year basis at capturing the overall level of conflict in the system as a whole. Recalling the arguments from chapter 2, if we assume a probabilistic world, combined with the nature of strategic choice driven by instrumentally rational actors, we must expect our model to be "wrong" most of the time. It is exceedingly rare, perhaps impossible, that we will predict probabilities nearing 50 percent (the point at which we might predict a "1" in a dichotomous logit context) or even 20 percent (a benchmark to predict any non–status quo outcome in our five category multinomial logit). While we do identify some dyads with absolute probabilities at these levels, and thus do better than those models noted by Beck, King, and Zeng (2000) as never predicting international conflict, we also need to be aware of the forecasting problem generated by rational leaders behaving strategically.

If we were to prepare a contingency table of predictions versus actual conflicts, we would underpredict conflict by a large margin in any of the dyad-years in which war actually occurs, in that the wars we observe occurred in situations where our model estimates the risk of war to be 50 percent or less. Our estimates for the system as a whole will be much closer to the mark than our predictions for any individual dyad. Aggregating the cumulative probabilities of war for all of the individual dyads will lead to predictions about the level of violent conflict in the system that are quite close to actual levels.

We focus our assessment of the overall fit of our model on an aggregation of the predicted probabilities of dyadic conflict in each year.[6] One problem with our dyad-year model is that even in the riskier cases the probability of conflict is typically relatively small. We do know, of course, that militarized conflicts occur on a regular basis in the system. Unfortunately, we cannot know with certainty which particular dyads will experience a war. This conjecture assumes that the actors are rational and are making purposive and not expressive decisions. That said, we are able to aggregate the multiple small probabilities of dyadic conflicts into an annual estimate of the aggregate conflict behavior for the entire system. We sum the probability of dyadic conflict in each of our four outcome categories across all dyads in each year. This yields the expected number of conflicts of each type in each year. We then graph this total number of expected conflicts per year alongside the actual number of conflicts in each year. This assessment presents a system-level summary of how well our model works over time.

Figures 5.3 to 5.6 graph the predicted and actual number of disputes at various levels of conflict from our analyses of the population of all dyads.[7] The graphs clearly show a close fit between our model's predictions for the system and the actual number of disputes and wars. Our discussion here will focus on two of these—disputes with reciprocated force and war—but all of the graphs of dispute behavior short of war show a quite similar fit. Looking at figure 5.3, which presents the predicted and actual disputes with reciprocated force for all states, we observe that, while there are individual years with more disputes than we predicted (e.g., 1919, 1940, 1962) and some with less than we predicted (e.g., 1945, 1970), the overall prediction of disputatious periods matches the actual periods with high dispute levels. The period 1848–50 shows a jump corresponding to an increase in dispute frequency, and an increase in predicted disputes starting around 1900 corresponds closely to actual events. The steady rise in predicted conflict in the interwar period and the post–World War II era corresponds to actual behavior (with dips that match the empirical record, notably in the early 1970s and after 1985). Figures 5.4 and 5.5 demonstrate similar fits to the data with the other low-level disputes in both data sets.

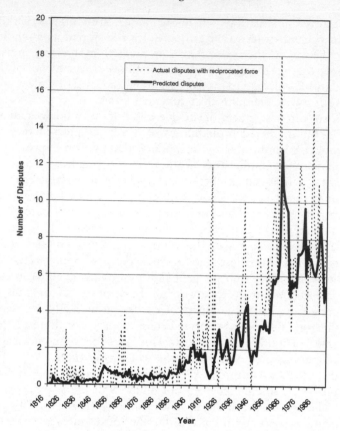

Fig. 5.3. Predicted and actual disputes with reciprocated use of force

As we turn to the cases of large-scale war, note that it is much more difficult to assess the fit to aggregate war occurrence because war is so rare. Figure 5.5 is much "spikier" than the previous figures. There are a handful of years where war initiations occurred in several dyads in a single year, although often these are only in one unified war. Normally, though, at most one or two wars begin in a year. Generally, in periods where our model predicts a higher frequency of war, we observe more of them. If we averaged the annual conflict data by making predictions for the number of wars in a ten-year period, the spikes that deviate from the prediction line would smooth out considerably. Our inability to make precise systemic predictions stems largely from the nature of the data we use. Most of the indicators tend to shift at a glacial pace,

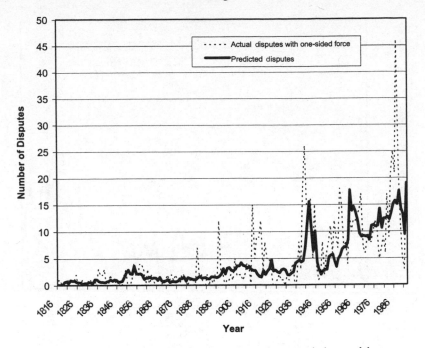

Fig. 5.4.   Predicted and actual disputes with one-sided use of force

while the factors that lead any individual dangerous dyad to escalate to war reflect variance in factors we cannot yet measure.

Our model does not predict years with more than two wars occurring at a time. The model does quite well fitting the mean number of wars over a period of three to five years but does quite poorly predicting the actual number of wars in any single year. In essence, our model smooths out much of the annual variance. For example, note in figure 5.6 the 1900–1914 period that corresponds to a number of actual war initiations, the interwar drop in expected war, and the uneven rise in war risk from the late 1920s through 1940. Three spikes in our predicted number of wars in the mid-1800s occur during a period of high war frequency as well. Overall, while imperfect, the model's predictions do correspond to periods of greater war frequency.

We assembled all of these figures using a very different approach than if we had set out to model the aggregate number of events in each year. A common alternative way to create this type of figure would have been to model the number of events in the system in a given year as a Poisson process, which might have yielded a better fit to the total number of

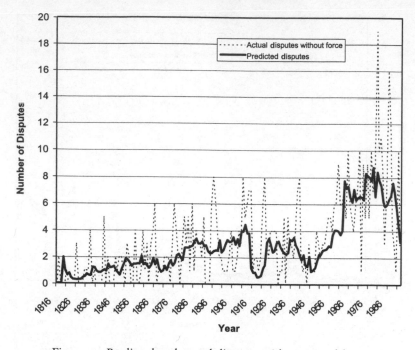

Fig. 5.5. Predicted and actual disputes with no use of force

events in a year than our results that emerge from dyadic logit estimates. Our point here is to demonstrate that the nature of the system as a whole and the policies of individual dyads are linked closely rather than representing fundamentally different data-generating processes to be theorized about in fundamentally different ways. Further, the concordance between the actual conflict data and the predictions generated by our model provides a strong rebuttal to the claim by Waltz (1979) that to include domestic-level variables in our models would result in a model of foreign policy but not international politics. Indeed, we find that the inclusion of information from multiple levels of analysis allows us to make plausible predictions about the relative risk of disputes within a particular dyad at a point in time and also to make plausible predictions of the amount of conflict expected throughout the international system on a year-to-year basis—a far more accurate prediction of system-level stability than we could generate by focusing an analysis solely at system level factors.

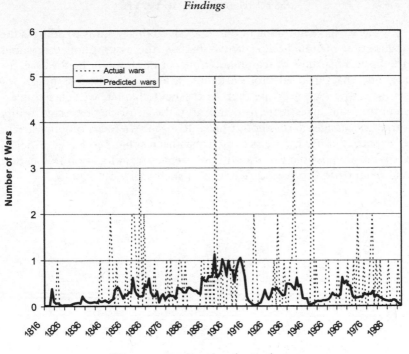

Fig. 5.6.   Predicted and actual wars

CONCLUSIONS

In this chapter, we have shown that many variables standing in for a large number of theoretical arguments and conjectures systematically covary with interstate conflict. We have shown both that these variables have effects on the probability of conflict associated with them even after controlling for other factors and that the effects are generally comparable, with no one factor accounting for an overwhelming proportion of the variance in our data. We have shown that we can make point predictions about the risk of conflict for individual dyads—illustrating those dyads that are at greatest risk of war in a particular year. We have also shown that we could successfully model aggregate conflict throughout the international system on an annual basis. Last, with our dummy variables for three separate periods—British hegemony, the interwar period, and post–World War II—we demonstrated that in different periods the system demonstrates different baseline conflict rates. During the cold war following World War II, conflicts that escalate to war were substantially less likely to occur than in the other two periods.

What we have not done in our analysis to this point is to address the assumption of unit homogeneity—that is, the assumption that states are states, regardless of region and time period. It might be the case, for instance, that our results for the democratic peace vary substantially for states in one region or another. In the next chapter, we relax this assumption and investigate in detail how the fit of our expected utility variables changes across both time and space. We focus on our variant of expected utility theory because it has been subject to harsh criticism for ignoring possible variation in preferences from location to location and from period to period. We turn to such variation next.

6 ASSESSING A MODEL'S RELIABILITY ACROSS SPACE AND TIME

the world's a scene of changes, and to be constant,
in nature were inconstancy.
—abraham cowley, 1647

When faced with an interstate crisis such as that leading up to the Falkland Islands War, did the decision makers in Buenos Aires make their choices in much the same way as did the decision makers in London? Did the leaders of the Argentine junta anticipate the same sequence of choices as did their British counterparts? Did the two sides share similar preferences for a negotiated outcome versus one that might entail the use of military force? Did these preferences in this case emerge from similar beliefs concerning the nature of national power, prestige, and domestic politics? When scholars working in the rational choice tradition confront the task of building a general model of interstate conflict and war, they must assume away much of the detail and nuance found in individual cases. They do this to build a model both that is tractable and that highlights the parts of the decision-making process they believe to be the most important. Critics of formal theory in general and rational choice models in particular find this process of stripping away the minutia profoundly disturbing, believing either explicitly or implicitly that the devil is to be found in the details—the facets of decision making often necessarily assumed away by formal theorists. Modelers typically respond to their critics by noting that logical consistency is a necessary condition for theory building and that the bottom line in evaluating the value of a theory or argument lies not in the nature of its assumptions but rather in how the theory's predictions perform in careful testing (Morton 1999).

Building and testing models of state behavior across the international system poses particularly thorny challenges; this is in part because of the tremendous variation in national culture and ideology across both space and time. Most models of interstate behavior must make sweeping simplifying assumptions about states' preferences and decision-making procedures. While many policymakers and analysts believe that the political world they inhabit is fundamentally different than the one in previous periods, political scientists using large-n statistical models typically assume the opposite—that our models will be just as appropriate for the early twenty-first century as they are for the late nineteenth century. This was our practice in the statistical analyses found in the preceding chapters, where we assumed unit and temporal homogeneity. We assumed that states were states, regardless of the point in history or their place on the globe, and so we assumed, for instance, that we could rightfully pool observations from the nineteenth century with those from the twentieth century. When scholars disaggregate their data into separate analyses for the nineteenth and twentieth centuries, or for pre– and post–World War II, they often do so without careful theoretical justification. In this chapter, we set out to test some commonly held assumptions about the universal applicability of the standard large-n social scientific approach to crisis decision making.

We examine the assumption of unit homogeneity over space and time by focusing on a particular theory, Bueno de Mesquita and Lalman's (1992) IIG and its associated empirical measures. We could analyze any of the large number of theoretical arguments, conjectures, and hunches we have explored here. Rather than choose one of the more commonly scrutinized conjectures such as the democratic peace, we focus our attention on a particularly well-developed variant of the rational choice approach. We do so for several reasons. Questions about the reliability of our models across space and time (along with a host of similar ones) lie at the core of one of the longest-standing debates in political science. Rational choice models of crisis behavior typically assume that a choice is a choice, regardless of whether the decision makers are in Europe, Central America, the nineteenth century, or the twenty-first century. Critics of the rational choice approach disagree with this assumption quite vehemently, arguing that crisis decision making is highly idiosyncratic, subject to various psychological pathologies, and may vary widely across regions and times (e.g., Lebow 1981, 1985). Moreover, Bueno de Mesquita (1981, 140) claimed explicitly in earlier work that his expected utility measures should fit the data just as well in one region as in another and in one period as in the next:

> To be sure, foreign policies in some regions—notably the Middle East—have yielded considerably more opportunities for war or

serious conflicts than have foreign policies in other regions (by containing a higher proportion of dyads with positive expected utility). Still, the propensity to require the same conditions has not varied meaningfully from region to region or from time to time.

This claim is not without controversy. As Jeffrey Friedman (1996, 4) points out:

It is only to be expected, then, that—to some extent—people will internalize and be guided by unselfish norms in non-economic realms. The extent of self-interestedness is therefore likely to vary historically as perceptions of appropriate behavior change. It would be foolish to deny the *possibility* that public choice theory will be applicable in a given instance, but it is equally unwise to assert in advance that it *must* apply in all cases merely because it applies in some.

We also focus on the IIG (in particular) and formal rational choice theories (in general) because many such models have not been subject to this type of testing to the same extent as other approaches (such as the democratic peace literature). As Kenneth Shepsle (1994, 217) points out in his reaction to Green and Shapiro's antirational choice diatribe, *Pathologies of Rational Choice* (1994), testing the standard implicit claim of universality is not a trivial task:

This is not as easy a theory-assessment regimen as it may first appear, for it requires the proponent of a novel theory to "nest" the relevant alternative theories into the assessment. Using a multivariate statistical instrument like ordinary least squares or logit as an assessment tool, for example, one would want to include variables not only from the novel theory but also from its strongest competitors; appropriate joint hypothesis tests permit assessments of the performance of the novel theory relative to its competitor.

To probe the universal nature of the performance of Bueno de Mesquita and Lalman's IIG, we use our interstate directed dyads around the world between 1816 and 1992 to examine the correlation between international conflict equilibrium predictions and actual conflict over time and across different regions while controlling for the other conjectures included in our previous analyses. Previewing our results, we find important differences both over regions and over time in how the predictions of the so-called expected utility theory of war fits actual conflict occurrence. This suggests an important direction for further research.

RATIONAL CHOICE AND THE PROBLEM OF
EMPIRICAL EVALUATION

Before setting out to assess the empirical appropriateness of the assumptions underlying the IIG, we begin with the observation we noted earlier that there has been only limited empirical evaluation of rational choice models in their most general setting. For example, while the development of game theoretic models of dispute initiation and escalation has proceeded rapidly during the past decade or more, much of the work relies on mathematical proof rather than empirical testing to establish its veracity (e.g., Brams 1995; Kilgore and Zagare 1991; Kydd 1997; Niou, Ordeshook, and Rose 1989; Powell 1990, 1996; Slantchev 2003; Smith and Stam 2002). While mathematical tractability ultimately limits the complexity of games that have identifiable solutions, data limitations have also limited our ability to test complex models of beliefs and behavior. Absent empirical testing, however, there are serious questions about what lessons we should draw from the game theoretic literature on conflict. As Powell notes about nuclear deterrence, "the models and analysis presented in the preceding chapters serve as, at best, sources of insight into the dynamics of nuclear confrontation" (1990, 185). Green and Shapiro (1994) emphasize this theme in their widely debated critique of the rational choice literature, in which they take issue with what they describe as the overly ambitious claims of rational choice, igniting a firestorm of faultfinding among rational choice scholars. They argue that the relative merit of the rational choice approach versus other approaches remains an open empirical question. Further, they claim that the rational choice body of scholarship is largely "much ado about nothing," with weak empirical support for formal rational choice models, which in turn suggests little connection between the "real world" and the world of formal theory.

Unfortunately, Green and Shapiro systematically exclude the international politics literature in their critical discussion of the degree of progress that rational choice scholars have made to date. They draw their examples from the American politics literature, specifically addressing the literature on voting behavior, interest groups, legislative behavior, and party competition. The exclusion of international politics poses something of a problem for Green and Shapiro's argument. Far from being a subfield worthy of exclusion from an empirical review of rational choice, international politics generally and international conflict in particular, we believe, represent areas where the strongest case for the effectiveness of the rational choice paradigm can be made and where we can easily examine assumptions of unit heterogeneity.

IN TESTING FOR UNIT HETEROGENEITY, WHY FOCUS ON EXPECTED UTILITY THEORY?

By focusing on Bueno de Mesquita and Lalman's game from *War and Reason* (1992), we hope to cover several bases. First, we hope to conduct a more careful evaluation of the theory. While Bueno de Mesquita and Lalman and subsequent extensions (Bennett and Stam 2000b, 2000c; Bennett and Rupert 2003) may present the most sophisticated large-n statistical tests of two-sided games in the international politics literature to date (Allan and Dupont 1999), the tests remain cast at the aggregate level; that is, they pool all regions and years. Second, by using the results from this analysis as a representative of some of the best formal theory in the international politics literature, we hope to provide circumstantial evidence to be able to address these concerns with other rationalist theories that we cannot test in such a direct fashion. For example, we later will discuss the implications that constructivist approaches or evolutionary theories of international politics have for how we should expect to see the IIG results change over time. While most rational choice scholars working on international conflict assume unit homogeneity, other approaches predict substantial variation across space and time. Only by disaggregating our results in chapter 5 by time, period, and region can we shed light on these other approaches to the study of politics. While we will have something to say about Bueno de Mesquita and Lalman's IIG, more importantly we also hope to be able to use the characteristics of their model's success and failures to say something more broadly about rational choice theory in general. Third, the substantive focus of this book, international politics, may represent the best case for testing expected utility models because the conditions for rational behavior posited by those advocating "procedural rationality" match well with the conditions under which leaders make key decisions in international politics.

While there is little scholarly agreement about the merits of the rational choice approach, some consensus does exist about the conditions under which instrumental rationality and procedural rationality are most likely to occur. Three factors appear to be among the most important. First, regardless of their views on rational choice, most scholars agree that the likelihood that an actor will behave according to the tenets of the rational choice paradigm will vary depending on the apparent stakes of the decision involved. As Fiorina points out, "Rational choice models are most useful where the stakes are high and the numbers low, in recognition that it is not rational to go to the trouble to maximize if the consequences are trivial and/or your actions make no difference" (1990, 90). Decisions in which a frivolous choice has no substantial gain or costly loss associated with it will be less likely to be associated with instrumental or goal-seeking behavior. Second, most scholars agree that decisions in which the interests of large numbers of people must be accommodated may also be unlikely to lead to rational, utility-maximizing choices. Logrolling models, other bounded rationality models, or psychological theories may be more appropriate in these cases. Third, in situations where rules, organizational structures, or standard operating procedures account for most of the variation in decisions, actors may feel that their own input is comparatively meaningless.[1] As such, they will be more likely to follow a decision process better characterized by a cybernetic model (Steinbrunner 1974), a dominant indicator model (Gartner 1997), or some other bureaucratic politics model (Allison 1971).

This list of three is by no means either an exclusive list or necessarily the correct one. For instance, Michael Taylor (1995, 224–26) lists five criteria, arguing that rational choice theory will be most productive when describing or modeling choices where

(i) the courses of action available to the actor are limited; (ii) the costs and benefits attached to the alternative courses of action are, to the agent in question, well defined and clearly apparent; . . . (iii) much for the agent, turns on his or her choice; . . . (iv) prior to the choice situation in question, there have been many similar or analogous occasions; . . . (v) the connections between the ends and means (which themselves are well defined) are transparent. (see also Taylor 1988, 1989; Gellner 1985)

We believe that leaders' decisions to use force in international politics fit these criteria (and also the three criteria listed earlier) as well as or better than most examples in other political science subfields.

Decisions in international politics generally, and particularly decisions about international conflict, appear to fit the conditions for instrumental and procedural rationality rather well. First, such choices are associated with very high-stakes events. State leaders rarely treat lightly the decision to initiate a war or break diplomatic ties, and so they would appear to be unlikely to behave in ways inconsistent with rational, interest-maximizing, instrumentally driven decision making. While getting to the voting booth and pulling a lever confers little apparent gain but entails some small cost to the voter, the choice to initiate war is a very costly one. Second, crisis decision making in international politics differs substantially from other issue areas in terms of the number of people involved in a decision. For example, modeling congressional voting or parliamentary government formation (frequent rational choice targets) requires the modeler to be able to predict the aggregate outcome of literally hundreds of individual choices made by actors whose preferences may vary widely. Each voter may be maximizing a number of interests, including the individual representative's or MP's political or economic interest, the interests of a larger organization such as the representative's political party, or even the so-called national interest.[2] The decision to initiate war, however, usually rests with a single leader (as in the case of dictatorships and some democracies) or with a small committee of powerful individuals (a politburo's or cabinet's inner circle, for example). Third, there are few enforceable rules in the international system serving to condition strongly the choices of the actors. In many of the cases studied by Green and Shapiro, rules either were the object in question or strongly conditioned the choice of the actors, as in the case of congressional committee selection. Within an international milieu frequently characterized as an anarchic system, there are few strict rules that force actors to give up their freedom to choose.[3]

SOURCES OF DISAGREEMENT ABOUT RATIONAL BEHAVIOR

The notion that existing formal rational choice models (such as the IIG) are valid universally, if at all, is not without its critics. Critiques of expected utility theory take several tacks. Many critics of rational choice models focus on the likely breakdown of procedural rationality, and/or agents' cognitive failure to be able to perform or even approximate the process that rational choice theory imputes to them (Rosen 2002). For example, psychologists argue that due to cognitive limitations humans simply do not make choices the way that we would expect actors to if they followed a rational choice process, even in crises (Janis and Mann 1977; Friedman 1996; Elster 1989; Abelson 1995; McDermott 2002). Others suggest that formal rational choice approaches rely too heavily on the assumption that all choices result from the self-interested pursuit of some end—behavior commonly referred to as instrumental rationality. For instance, Abelson (1995, 27) focuses particularly on the expressive behavior of actors, which is "action performed for its own sake with no apparent rational consideration of the material consequences for the actor." He finds numerous examples in which actors behave in ways that do not fit the prescriptive norms of the rational choice paradigm (see Kinder and Sears 1985; Sears and Funk 1990, 1991; Kinder and Sanders 1994).

Rational choice theory has also come under strong criticism for assuming actors' goals or preferences to be identical across all agents or decision makers. Scholars working in artificial intelligence, for instance, view choices and planning systems as designs to reach particular goals or a set of goals. This suggests that a solid understanding of an actor's goals is necessary to predict the choices that the actor will make, even if one is able to model adequately the process through which they reach their decisions. Models that ignore the characteristics of the systems in which autonomous agents make their choices tend to perform poorly compared to those that account for system characteristics. The frequent rational choice assumption that the ends are identical across agents ignores an important characteristic of the system that should help us understand individuals' choices (Conte and Castelfranchi 1995, 6).

A final and potentially more compelling criticism of universality assumptions typical to current rational choice applications in international politics has to do with potential differences in how different actors form preferences and how preferences or game structures may evolve over time. Making game structure endogenous to the process under study is on the current cutting edge of formal game theory. According to this criticism of universality, actors' decision making might in fact fit into a rational choice model, but if actors' preferences or decision-making processes are not fixed or easily predicted, then the rational choice approach will appear to fail in current versions (Lewis and Schultz 2002). In addition, if different types of states have different types of preferences across similar sets of outcomes, then those actors may interact with the international system structure in different ways (Wendt 1999). This chapter's empirical investigation focuses on these areas.

When applied in the international politics literature, these critiques of rational choice theory most often either are theoretical (e.g., Wendt 1994, 1999) or provide hypothetical alternatives and isolated examples with no systematic tests.[4] For example, and somewhat ironically, while Green and Shapiro find fault with the rational choice school for failing to provide adequate empirical and statistical tests of formal models, they provide no tests of their own. The critics neither demonstrate systematically the conditions under which existing rational choice models perform poorly nor advance general conditions under which we might expect rational choice theory to work best or fail most frequently. It would not be entirely unfair to argue, however, that the burden for this type of testing falls on the shoulders of the person presenting the model. The failure of many rational choice theorists to provide systematic tests that would demonstrate where and when instrumental rationality is present, and where it is not, seems particularly irksome to critics of rational choice approaches. Relaxing our assumption of unit homogeneity underlying the statistical tests we presented in chapter 5 and developing specific hypotheses about when, where, and how rational choice models may fail is our first task in analyzing the empirical application of rational choice models.

DEVELOPING AND TESTING HYPOTHESES ABOUT VARIATIONS IN PREFERENCES AND CHOICES

We develop several sets of testable hypotheses drawn from criticisms of rational choice models, specifically hypothesizing about the conditions under which the expected utility measures developed to test Bueno de Mesquita and Lalman's (1992) expected utility theory of war might be expected to make more or less accurate predictions about conflict. What we are ultimately interested in is whether we can use the same assumptions about preferences, utility functions, and the IIG decision tree to model behavior in dyads in different regions or periods. From the psychological and cybernetic perspectives, we might not be able to do this if some actors are rational and others are not. For instance, if one set of actors is playing a decision game characterized by goal-seeking behavior while some other mechanism dictates the behavior of other actors, a rational choice approach will likely fail. Rational choice models as implemented to this point might also appear to fail if all actors are rational but some are playing structurally different games than others. If one actor anticipates having a choice that an opponent is not aware of, then the actors will play a game that may bear little resemblance to the game we posited at the beginning of an interaction or even the individual games that each actor is trying to play. Finally, if our assumptions about preference commonality and stability are inaccurate, again, the universal application of rational models will fail. Bueno de Mesquita and Lalman's basic IIG, for instance, relies on a number of assumptions about states' preferences—for example, that negotiating is preferred to fighting—in order to deduce the outcome equilibria. If certain assumptions hold true only in certain regions or periods, then we would expect actors to *appear* less rational; that is, their behavior would not fit the predictions of the game in regions where the assumptions are not true. For example, historically in Southeast Asia in periods before our data set begins, nations commonly fought not over ideology but over the acquisition of labor (Scott 1976). In Europe, states traditionally fought over territory or capital (Holsti 1991). States may hold different preferences for the outcomes of the IIG depending on what it is they are trying to maximize. For instance, war might be less preferable when fighting for labor since waging war reduces the benefits of the spoils of victory. Alternatively, war might be more preferable if it is over territory, since war may drive away the citizens of the other state and leave the territory vacant for resettlement. Such differences may reverse assumed preference orderings.

Note that in these situations it is *not* that the actors are not rational, even though a universal model may fail. Rather, they simply are not playing the same game with the same preferences that we assumed at the outset. Nevertheless, empirical applications or tests in all cases will be similar: our predictions of conflict will be most accurate where actors are indeed playing strategically and where the game and necessary preference assumptions are what we assume them to be.

HYPOTHESES

Preferences and Game Trees Are Stable

H_1: The assumption of fixed and exogenous preferences can be sustained empirically.

According to most rational choice scholars, the assumption of fixed and exogenous preferences is theoretically essential and empirically sustainable. If true, there should be no significant regional or temporal variation in patterns of rationality as defined by the game and measures developed to test it, subject to adequate data. It is very important to keep in mind throughout this chapter that we are not testing the assumption of rationality. Nor are we testing whether or not actors are instrumentally driven. Rather, we are investigating a relatively simple assumption—that preferences or game trees are sufficiently stable over space and time in order to let us use a single game and ancillary measures to predict behavior universally. If the indicators of the IIG equilibria fail to fit the data in one region or period, it does not mean that the states' leaders in these regions or periods are not rational, nor does it mean that they did not make their decisions in instrumental fashion. Rather, it simply means that either their preferences differed or the game they faced (or believed they faced) was different from that posed by the game in our model. In a similar vein, to sustain the claim of universality, the degree of variation in the decision-making process should not exceed small and expected random variation across regions and across time when examining the relationship between measures of expected utility, conflict escalation, and the outbreak of war.

Preferences and Game Trees Vary as a Function of Culture and Time

H_2: Cultural differences in preferences, beliefs, or game trees lead to regional and temporal variations in behavior.

Following "second image" arguments, we hypothesize that states' preferences and expectations regarding their interactions with other states develop in the context of the states' domestic political and social culture. However, the distributions of cultures are not random throughout the system; rather, attitudes or preferences tend to emerge in clumps or regions (e.g., Granato, Inglehart, and Leblang 1996).[5] This implies that the cultural similarity (and shared preferences/beliefs) between states within the same region is usually greater than the cultural similarity between states in different regions. Culturally based explanations of preference differences should also be relatively time-sensitive since cultures presumably evolve over time. We should then expect to see significant variation both spatially (across regions) and temporally (across periods) in how well the equilibrium predictions of the IIG fit actual behavior.

Preferences and Structures Vary over Time because of Socially Constructed Beliefs

H_3: State behavior, preferences, and conceptions of rationality are social constructions and will vary over time, particularly the length of time a dyad has existed.

Constructivists argue that international systems and their constraining effects are intellectual, social constructions residing largely in the minds and belief systems of actors. Constructivism is in some ways "old wine in new bottles," as there is an extensive literature on the role that state leaders' belief systems play, and the effects of them, in shaping foreign policy and hence the nature of the international system (Almond 1950; Key 1961; Converse 1964; Holsti and Rosenau 1988; Murray 1996). Ironically, the earlier literature tends to be far more empirically sophisticated than the more "modern" replacement, constructivism.

Regarding leaders' beliefs about the underlying nature of the international system, Wendt (1992) maintains that the notion of anarchy in the international system is not a description of the state of nature but rather a description of the dominant beliefs in the minds of the system's political leaders. Only when leaders share similar beliefs or constructions of the system's nature will they act in accordance with predictions resulting from a single specified structure. Wendt (1999) also argues that state interactions at the systemic level can ultimately change states' identities and, as a result, their interests and preferences. Over time, Wendt argues, common interests and beliefs about each other can emerge and evolve—a mutual sense of "we feeling" can emerge between two actors, with an evolving common identity serving to ameliorate potential conflicts. If the nature of the international system (game structure and incentives) is actually a product of leaders' beliefs about each other's expectations, rather than reflecting observable factors such as power ratios or alliance patterns (or other materially based possibilities), then changes in beliefs can lead to changes in the assumed game structure or preference orderings needed for modeling decisions. Constructivists, at least those who argue that ideas "go all the way down" (Wendt 1999, chap. 3), would argue that a game tree simply represents the options the actors believe exist and hence is a social construction, subject to alteration, just as any other belief might be. Wendt implicitly argues against the standard game theoretic assumption that the structure of the IIG is fixed. Realists might also argue that game trees are mutable, but they come at the question from a somewhat different perspective. A realist, one whose beliefs about the nature of international politics are grounded in the preeminent role of actual material resources and not beliefs thereof, would nonetheless argue that features such as the availability of allies might easily alter the game tree.

If the game is not fixed, meaning that the options the actors can choose among come and go, we would then expect to see variation in the relationship between the IIG's equilibrium predictions and the onset of war as states continue to interact over time, what we refer to as dyadic aging. If the leaders' beliefs change over time to reflect a mutual recognition of common interests not captured in the IIG and auxiliary assumptions, then as dyads age, the fit between predictions of war and the onset of war should diminish, with peace becoming a more common outcome than expected, given a prediction of war. Under this and similar views, neither the states nor the physical character of the system need to change in order to see variation in state behavior. Rather, all that must change are the sets of beliefs in leaders' minds. Such shifts may occur quite slowly, however. Research in public opinion demonstrates that elites' normative beliefs tend to be quite stable over time in a variety of places and eras (Converse 1964; Murray 1996; Zaller 1992; Holsti and Rosenau 1988), and some argue that structures based on deeply held beliefs or attitudes rooted in cultural values are more resistant to change than any physical system.

H_{3a}: State behavior and conceptions of rationality are social constructions and may converge on a Kantian model of world politics over time.

If constructivists are correct in their view that the nature of the international system lies predominantly in the minds of the decision makers rather than its material attributes, then the system and its potentially constraining effects can also be transformed by wider shifts in, or the evolution of, leaders' belief systems. Such shifts or evolution of ideas does not require violent selection the way a Darwinian model implies, nor would it require contact and interaction with other states and systems the way an imitative learning model might suggest. The regional constructivist approach would imply that even isolated regions could evolve into peaceful systems (or might start out that way) simply because of shared beliefs in "friendship" (Wendt 1999). In turn, we might ultimately see regions or even the entire international system evolving toward the same set of normative beliefs and in particular evolving from what some constructivists often refer to as Hobbesian to Lockian to Kantian relations. Wendt argues that this evolutionary process, while not a sure thing, is likely irreversible. The "evidence" he provides, however, is the assertion that citizens in countries rarely, if ever, volunteer to give up voting rights once they are established (Wendt 1999, chap. 7). Empirically, this sort of evolutionary change would in turn be associated with a system-wide decline in the relationship between conflict behavior and Bueno de Mesquita and Lalman's expected utility predictions and measures thereof. While Bueno de Mesquita and Lalman argue that their model is testable with Kantian variants, simply by altering the preference ordering among the actors, Wendt and others are arguing for a somewhat different type of shift. Rather than simply preferring peace to war, or negotiation to capitulation, Wendt argues that, in Kantian systems, war is not a policy option ever considered between "friends." In Wendt's view, the changes in leaders' belief systems over time have pruned limbs off the game tree, not simply altered preferences across existing game tree nodes.

If substantial shifts in states' preferences and common beliefs are the norm rather than the exception, it could pose a problem for the rational choice paradigm. This is simply because ascertaining what states believe is in their best interests, or beliefs about what type of system they are in, may be difficult to determine ex ante and perhaps might only be known as states reveal these attitudes through the choices they make. Constructivists argue that we can know (and, by implication, build rigorous theoretical models of) these changing beliefs and that there are three major international systems, or worlds, on which we should focus. Substantially different reactions to similar situations or incentives characterize each of these worlds.[6]

In the world as many constructivists envision it, the system and the actors interact with each other and are mutually supporting, leading to a dynamic system in which norms (and the very games actors play) are endogenous and shift over time. Wendt argues that the initial international system or the state of nature existed as a Hobbesian world. Domestic and international society maintains a fragile or tenuous peace among members assumed to be atomistic and egoistic enemies. In the Hobbesian world, confederations (alliances) may exist among states to provide the conditions for survival. The assumption here is that, while individual states are necessarily hostile to one another, they are also mutually dependent. If an individual state, or some other relevant actor, drops out of the system or if international society casts them out, they cannot survive (Conte and Castelfranchi 1995, 79). A Hobbesian world is similar to the world that realists envision when they speak of an anarchic system with alliances.

In this Hobbesian world, states do not necessarily recognize the territorial rights of the others states and they are able to maintain their physical existence solely through militant vigilance and through confederations with like-minded actors. In a Hobbesian system, the moment a state lets its guard down it will become vulnerable prey for the other member states of this aggressive and potentially violent system. In this world, norms are the means by which actors solve collectivity problems. However, Conte and Castelfranchi argue that game theory fails both at providing a robust description of this sort of reality and at modeling evolving norms, in particular because rational choice approaches typically have a difficult time demonstrating or predicting the construction of external collectives outside of which the actor cannot survive. If this critique is correct, our measures of expected utility based on alliance politics should not work well in Hobbesian worlds. While Wendt argues that the European system evolved into a Lockian system before the initial dates in our data set, other regional systems composed of newly emergent states (or fascist leaders bent on world conquest) might resemble Hobbesian worlds.

In a Lockian world, the next step in Wendt's evolutionary path, states recognize the territorial integrity of fellow system members. Of course, some disagreements over territorial and other issues exist, and as a result wars occasionally occur. However, the default is not one where every border is up for grabs, and so war is not a frequent and ongoing event as in the case of the Hobbesian world (Wendt 1999). In the Lockian world, actors may perceive that they have some common interests with other actors beyond mere survival. States that see each other as "members of the same team" will not make the same purely egoistic calculation regarding each other's right to exist and will recognize that team members share the same right to exist as the state itself. These are different preferences than in the Hobbesian world, and as such we might expect a different set of outcomes when states confront similar situations. The European classical balance of power system is an example of a Lockian system. While states recognized the rights of other states to exist, they also competed for greater relative gains in pursuit of their national interests, as realists assert. Bueno de Mesquita and Lalman's IIG game should fit best for Wendt's Lockian system. In the Lockian system, states are not consistently aggressive (e.g., negotiation is assumed to be always preferred to war) but do not want to be taken advantage of (e.g., it is better to start a war than to be attacked) and are concerned about costs (e.g., acquiescence is assumed to be preferred to capitulation under threat).

In the final stage of Wendt's model of systemic evolution, mutually supporting multilateralism becomes the key to behavior. He argues that multilateralism, the core of the Kantian system, is a "very demanding institutional form" that is likely to evolve only over time. In the Kantian system, collective identity assumes full stature relative to individual identity. States' images of themselves become inexorably tied to the existence of all other states in the collective (Wendt 1999, chap. 3). In this type of world, states do not consider the elimination of others from the collective, nor do they even consider using force against one another to settle disputes. Obviously, preferences and the notion of what is acceptable behavior in this world are rather different from either the Hobbesian or the Lockian systems. The notions of utility and strategic behavior found in Bueno de Mesquita's IIG are at odds with the type of preferences and behavior that Wendt ascribes to states in a Kantian system. Given that he characterizes relations among the developed democracies today as a by-product of their changing beliefs toward a Kantian system, we would expect our utility-based predictions to fit poorly among modern postmaterialist democratic states.

Common Preferences and Decision Structures Are Revealed over Time

H_4: Conflicts and crises between states reveal private information about state capabilities and preferences, leading to less uncertainty, more predictability, and an appearance of greater rationality as dyads age.

Several types of learning may be relevant for assumptions, arguments, and tests of rational choice. Fearon (1995) argues, for example, that with risk-averse actors, war is possible only under conditions of uncertainty, incomplete information, or when actors cannot commit to or enforce bargains. As states interact more and for longer periods, there should be less uncertainty associated with any one interaction. Fearon's argument implies that, absent uncertainty, conditions related to the monitoring of bargains would then determine the apparent lack of cooperation. Over time, state leaders may learn about each other's capabilities and preferences. For example, Fearon (1997) argues that states may use force to reveal private information about their military capabilities. Decision makers may also learn what game (or games) they are playing against others, learn about others' preferences, and even learn about their own preferences. For instance, it may only be after a long-lasting bloody war such as the Vietnam War that decision makers learn that war carries with it a particularly high political cost. If we model and measure such costs before leaders knew of them or became sensitive to them, our model would predict poorly in the earlier periods. Absent good measures of uncertainty, we might therefore expect to see leaders appear to be more "rational" over time as uncertainty within a particular pair or group of states declines, because the use of force or other forms of information exchange reduce uncertainty. Following this line of argument, we would expect to see the fit between our equilibrium predictions of war and actual war improve as dyads age. We might also expect to see the incidence of war in particular dyads with repeated conflict decline over time (Smith and Stam 2002), a hypothesis we do not test here.

Darwinian Evolution or Learning Leads Preferences or Decision Structures to Converge

H$_5$: Convergence to one common set of preferences and decision structures occurs across regions over time as Darwinian learning (Hobbesian realism) selects out losers.

Classical realists suggest that states pursue their own national interest defined in terms of power. In this vein, setting aside liberals' concerns about emerging security dilemmas, more power leads to all things good in the world, so no great distinction or subtlety in preferences is necessary. If states do not pursue security rooted in materialist foundations in an anarchic system, ultimately their competitors will eliminate them. But in the original state of nature in the international system, perhaps harking back to the moment just after the Treaty of Westphalia had been signed, not all states might follow the precepts of realism. Newly hatched states and their leaders might have started out with different decision-making norms, held differing preferences regarding war and peace, or had different beliefs about which issues were or were not worth fighting for. However, given the assumed constant state of Hobbesian anarchy, those newly created states that did not rationally pursue power should not have existed in their original form for long. One of two things might happen with such states: either they could learn, with their beliefs evolving to meet the challenges and demands of the system so that they came to instrumentally pursue greater power, or they could be eliminated through war, with their preferences and beliefs in essence becoming extinct. As this process of learning or evolutionary defeat occurs, like-minded states that behave in an instrumentally rational manner with similar shared preferences for security maximization would come to populate the international system. This argument predicts that the fit between the predictions of expected utility theory and actual outcomes should increase over time and that the fit across regions, while varying initially, should converge as time passes.

H$_6$: Learning occurs through imitation or social contact. Regions will converge over time to look like the states that have existed the longest and with whom most interaction has occurred, the European "great powers."

An alternative to the Darwinian selection hypothesis invoking realism and conflict is a learning hypothesis based on imitative learning. In this model, states or regions that emerge or become independent (in the later years contained in our data set) would learn from and imitate the states that emerged first and were most successful (in our case, the European powers).[7] In order for the imitation to take place, contact has to occur, but the contact would not have to be violent or disputatious, as a Darwinian model would require. Trade or other intellectual exchange (e.g., the spread of European religious missionaries or attendance by students from peripheral states at universities in the core states) would suffice. Given that Europe has been the central region of the globe in terms of trade and international organizations for several centuries, and given that European states have been the most active in establishing military, cultural, economic, and religious contacts and centers around the world, movement toward the European model would be expected over time. The longer a region or group of states had been in existence, and the longer they had been in contact with the states to be imitated, the more their behavior would converge to a European model of decision making. The IIG may represent such an evolved version of an international interaction pattern, perhaps partially (even subconsciously) based on balance of power interactions such as those that have been seen in Europe for hundreds of years. In empirical terms, this means that the relationship between expected utility measures and dispute behavior across states and regions should improve over time as a function of state contact, even in the absence of conflict.

Rationality Varies as a Function of Stakes

H_7: Rational behavior varies as a positive function of the stakes.

To this point, we have argued that powerful assumptions commonly invoked about common preferences or decision-making sequences or games may not be empirically sustainable. Hypothesis 7 gets at a somewhat different problem. "Procedural rationality" assumptions imply a certain procedure to decision making, that actors will search out options and information (given time and cost constraints) and that they are able to "look down the tree." While not all rational choice scholars posit such behavior as a necessary condition to observe apparently instrumentally rational behavior, certain types of decision-making environments may affect actors' abilities to follow rational procedures due to psychological stresses or other constraints on their ability to process information in the manner theorists imply they should. In this light, actors may still be behaving in an instrumentally rational manner, but due to psychological factors and time constraints, their ability to follow "rational" procedures may be substantially degraded.

Since a careful, procedurally rational decision-making process involves costs, and sometimes quite significant costs (Gartner 1997), rational decision makers will focus more attention on the problem, conduct more elaborate information searches, and evaluate more carefully the costs and benefits of their actions when the stakes are high. The decision to initiate a conflict or to respond in kind to a provocative action by a potential opponent is a very high-stakes decision. Therefore, we expect that the higher the stakes are, the better the predictions of rational choice theories will fit behavior. In our data these would be cases of interstate war, compared to disputes.

H_{7a}: Instrumental rationality has a curvilinear relationship to the stakes.

While most scholars agree that low-stakes decisions are the least likely to be instrumentally rational, Lebow (1981) argues that irrational behavior might characterize intense crises as well. Lebow argues that time constraints in crises, along with the potentially high stakes, create a condition of cognitive or emotional overload, leading to failures of rational decision making. This raises the possibility that extremely high-stakes decisions (which also must be made quickly) will create conditions under which procedurally rational decision making is either impossible or highly unlikely. This suggests that the fit between expected utility theory and actual outcomes should decline at the highest levels of hostility.

RESEARCH DESIGN

The empirical evidence presented in Bueno de Mesquita and Lalman 1992 showed that the predictions of expected utility theory were highly correlated with actual dispute initiation and outcomes in Europe. However, by limiting their tests to a small number of cases in Europe, Bueno de Mesquita and Lalman limited the population of cases to which they can infer and could not analyze differences across regions. The subsequent tests use the data generated in chapter 4. We use logit analysis to examine whether the IIG war equilibrium predictions correlate with dummy variables, marking the occurrence of disputes that escalate to a level at which both sides use military force or go to war. As before, because the IIG makes equilibrium predictions of behavior in a directed interaction, our unit of analysis is the directed dyad-year. We analyze both the set of all dyads and politically relevant dyads between 1816 and 1992 where we have both IIG equilibrium predictions and complete data on a set of key control variables. We use standard errors corrected for clustering in dyads to deal with cross-unit heterogeneity and include a set of four "peace years" spline variables as suggested by Beck, Katz, and Tucker (1998) to deal with the effects of time dependence. We code dyadic outcomes (mutual dispute or war) for directed dyads A-B where A and B were involved on the initiating and targeted side (respectively) of a MID on the first day of the MID. That is, we create the set of dyads for each dispute as all combinations of "true" initiators against "true" targets, omitting joiners. Only these pairs reflect the IIG and empirical measurements; in many cases, joiners enter a dispute well after it has begun (even years later), and often after the outcome (highest hostility level) has already been determined. The strategic game for these joiners was not the same IIG considered by initiators, using very different information and projections. While excluding these states undercounts the interactions in large events such as the world wars, what those interactions require is a different game tree that awaits development and a set of different measures for empirical testing. Note that these "joiners" were often included in Bueno de Mesquita and Lalman's (1992) analysis, as they include all dyads in a dispute where at least one state was part of the dispute on the first day. As in our prior analysis, we drop dyad-years in which a dispute between the members was ongoing at the beginning of the year, unless there was another initiation in that year. Similarly, in directed dyad-years A-B with a dispute, we also drop the B-A direction, unless a dispute initiation occurs by B against A.

Dependent Variable: Disputes, Mutually Violent Disputes, and Wars

For the analysis in this chapter, we focus on two dummy dependent variables marking the actual occurrence of conflict outcomes following Bueno de Mesquita and Lalman (1992, 283–86). We use the COW MID data set coding of the highest level of hostility reached by each state in a dispute dyad. Cases in which both states either used force (level 4) or went to war (level 5) were coded as a "1" on the dependent variable "mutual force" or "mutual violence."[8] If no MID occurred in a directed dyad-year that reached the specified level, we coded a "0" for the dependent variable. Cases in which both states went to war (level 5) were coded as a "1" on the dependent variable "war," and "0" otherwise. Because these values are coded for directed dyad-years, a single MID may result in several directed dyad-years having values of "1" coded for the dependent variable when there are multiple initiators. Within the all-dyads set, 518 directed dyad-years had militarized dispute initiations that escalated to a level in which both sides used force and 74 had directed dyadic dispute initiations that reached the level of interstate war.

Independent Variables: Equilibrium Predictions

The independent variables used for testing hypotheses drawn from the IIG are dummy variables marking various dispute outcomes as the equilibrium of the IIG for a given directed dyad-year, as discussed in chapter 3. In this chapter, the key prediction we are interested in, and include in our analyses, is the equilibrium prediction of war (outcome War_A in the IIG).

Independent Variables: Time, Age, Region Stratification, and Interactions

We want to explore differences in how the rational IIG equilibrium predictions fit actual conflict behavior across regions, across periods, and as dyads age. For regional distinctions, we use the five regional categories described and used by Bueno de Mesquita (1981): Europe, the Americas (North and South), the Middle East, Africa, and Asia. Obviously, this is a highly problematic way to divide the world. For instance, to treat "Asia" as a single homogenous region borders on the ludicrous, although it is more reasonable than assuming the world is homogenous. Nevertheless, our aim here is not to find the "true" values that define the cultural contents of "Asia" but rather to demonstrate whether the degree of heterogeneity in the world system is sufficient to create problems for those who claim universal status to some expected utility models.

For time periods, we divided our dyad-years into the pre–World War I, interwar, and post–World War II (cold war) eras. To examine dyadic "aging," we code a variable that we label "dyadic duration," which marks the length of time both states in a dyad have been independent states. For states that were independent in 1816, we code dyadic duration as "0" in 1816 and incrementing annually thereafter.[9] For other dyads, the counter starts at zero the first year both states are system members according to COW.[10]

We include in our analyses the dummy equilibrium variables; stratification variables that mark regions, time periods, or dyadic duration; and the interaction between the equilibrium and the stratification variables. We also include a set of control variables, as discussed later. Given coefficients on each variable, we can then construct the estimated probability of conflict in different regions under conditions where the IIG equilibrium prediction was war, in different periods for each condition on the equilibrium variable, and at different dyad ages for each equilibrium condition.

Note that we do not disaggregate by conducting a series of subanalyses, one for each region, time period, or region–time period combination, but rather we build a saturated model using interaction terms. Once we disaggregate the data too far, it becomes impossible to obtain reliable coefficient estimates because of a smaller number of cases, and especially a smaller number of conflict outcomes, within each subset. The problem compounds once we add control variables to our model. Consider, for instance, the small number of interstate wars in Africa since World War II or the number of wars and disputes in Europe since 1945 and how their frequency and the time period might be collinear with nuclear weapons. Because of collinearity, we are unable to obtain estimates in several cases if we split the data into multiple subsets. Using the saturated model helps with this problem, although it cannot completely solve it, and we continue to have some analyses in which our estimates are not as reliable as we would like.

Independent Variables: Controls

Where possible, we also include a number of control variables in our analyses. While some rational choice scholars might maintain that "everything is in the utilities," meaning that the equilibrium measures we use here represent a complete data-generating process and provide a virtually complete explanation of state behavior, the results in chapter 5 indicate otherwise. What might appear to be changing preferences might simply be changing behavior that reflects changes in the material world or the context in which the decisions are made (Stigler and Becker 1977). Accordingly, consistent with the earlier analysis, we include indicators derived from other mainstream approaches.

ANALYSIS

We turn now to the results of our tests. We begin with a test that includes all regions and time periods, paralleling our analysis in chapter 5. Next, to test the more specific hypotheses about why the universal assumption might not hold, we turn to a more detailed examination of the relationship between the IIG equilibria and the data across regions and time. We focus on the predicted probability of war (or disputes that escalate to the mutual use of force) given a war equilibrium compared to the probability when the equilibrium is for a different outcome, as reflected in risk ratios. Risk ratios greater than one occur when the equilibrium is associated with more disputes or war, providing support for the IIG model.

Instrumental Rationality as a Universal Phenomenon

In table 6.1, we present broad baseline estimates of the relationship between the game equilibrium of war and the occurrence of disputes with a mutual use of force and war in the population of all dyads and the subset of politically relevant dyads. For comparison, we present results from a model where we included our set of substantive control variables and one where we did not. The right-hand columns show the increased risk of disputes and wars when the IIG predicts "war" compared to when it does not.

Looking first at the population of all dyads, we find statistically significant support for the equilibrium predictions that correlate positively with both the mutual use of force and interstate war. The effect associated with the war equilibria among all dyads is to increase the risk of conflict by 20 to 120 percent; similar effects appear within the subset

TABLE 6.1. Outcome Probabilities and Risk Ratios, Not Stratified

	All Dyads			Politically Relevant Dyads		
	War Equilibrium		Risk	War Equilibrium		Risk
	No	Yes	Ratio	No	Yes	Ratio
Mutual Use of Force						
No Controls Included	.00056	.00071	1.3	.0038	.0043	1.1
Substantive Controls Included	.00056	.0012	2.2	.0034	.0077	2.3
War Outcome						
No Controls Included	.000071	.000087	1.2	.00048	.00065	1.4
Substantive Controls Included	.000071	.00013	1.9	.00050	.00088	1.8

of politically relevant dyads. We also note that the inclusion of substantive control variables does not eliminate the predictive power of the equilibrium variable. In fact, in the population of all dyads, including control variables actually appears to enhance the strength of the war equilibrium prediction, perhaps by accounting better for variation in the many dyads in which we might not expect conflict to be a real possibility (e.g., noncontiguous dyads).

Preferences and Game Trees Vary as a Function of Culture and Time

Table 6.2 presents the fit of the IIG predictions to violent disputes and war across three time periods in history. The risk ratios presented in table 6.2 come from our model with control variables. For both the full data set and the politically relevant sample, and for violent disputes and war, the expected utility equilibrium of war actually does not appear to be associated with a greater risk of war before World War I. However, during the interwar and post–World War II periods, an equilibrium prediction of war is associated with a substantial increase in the risk of observing a violent MID. For the war outcome, we observe the expected relationship only following World War II. For the smaller scale use of force dependent variable, the strength of the prediction is actually greater in the population of all dyads than in the politically relevant sample. The negative (indeed opposite) findings for the pre–World War I period are one of the likely sources for the weak results in table 6.1. Note that, because there are so many more cases (dyad-years) in the post–World War II period, the results in table 6.2

TABLE 6.2. Outcome Probabilities and Risk Ratios by Time Period

	All Dyads			Politically Relevant Dyads		
	War Equilibrium			War Equilibrium		
	No	Yes	Risk Ratio	No	Yes	Risk Ratio
Mutual Use of Force						
Pre-WWI	0.0011	0.00030	0.27	0.0036	0.0010	0.28
Interwar	0.0010	0.0039	3.8	0.0041	0.0091	2.2
Cold War	0.00045	0.0011	2.5	0.0032	0.0086	2.7
War Outcome						
Pre-WWI	0.00016	0.000031	0.19	0.0007	0.0001	0.12
Interwar	0.00081	0.00033	0.41	0.0044	0.0008	0.18
Cold War	0.000027	0.000084	3.1	0.0003	0.0011	4.5

can easily aggregate in the full data set to the positive result observed in table 6.1.

The cultural variation hypothesis suggests that we next examine the relationship between predictions of war and MID behavior by region. Note that table 6.3 only includes risk ratios for the mutual use of force. This table illustrates our first run-in with a fundamental limit to knowledge—a problem of degrees of freedom. Our model with control variables includes a large number of independent variables. Recall that while we have close to 1 million individual observations, we observe fewer than eighty dyadic war initiations. The ratio of independent variables to the number of observations on the "war" dependent variable is so low that we can no longer generate the stable parameter estimates needed to calculate the risk ratios once we add controls for regions and the region/equilibrium interactions. As a result, we must focus our attention here on the "mutual force" dependent variable. Keep in mind, however, that the differences in the fit of the model for the two dependent variables were minor to this point; if more wars had occurred in the past, we might find the patterns in table 6.3 repeated among them, although we are unable to obtain evidence to assess this possibility. Looking at the results for the "mutual use of force" dependent variable, we find several substantial differences between regions. Note that, since we are not controlling for period, the results should be weaker than in table 6.2, which showed that some time periods had a much stronger fit between the game equilibrium and conflict. The game theoretic prediction of war correlates positively with mutual violence among all dyads in the Middle East, Europe, and Asia, while the correlation with dispute outcomes in Africa or the Americas (North and South) is the opposite of what the theory predicts. Among politically relevant dyads, the results are quite similar.

In table 6.4, we examine the fit to the data now by parsing our

TABLE 6.3. Outcome Probabilities and Risk Ratios by Region

| | All Dyads | | | Politically Relevant Dyads | | |
| | War Equilibrium | | | War Equilibrium | | |
	No	Yes	Risk Ratio	No	Yes	Risk Ratio
Mutual Use of Force						
Europe	0.00031	0.0010	3.2	0.0021	0.0048	2.3
Mideast	0.00084	0.0015	1.7	0.0044	0.0096	2.2
Africa	0.0023	0.00055	0.24	0.0061	0.0022	0.36
Asia	0.0014	0.0021	1.5	0.0069	0.0091	1.3
Americas	0.00038	0.00023	0.60	0.0030	0.0024	0.81

analysis simultaneously across both period and region. In this estimation, we again confront the problem of limited degrees of freedom given five regions, three time periods, and fifteen interactive variables. Due to the large number of combinations of region and time periods, many cells in this table are blank because no interstate wars and few disputes occurred in the particular region during a particular period. In the case of the model with substantive controls, because variables become collinear within a region and time period, it becomes impossible to obtain region- and time-specific predictions. Because of this, we had to drop our control variables to obtain the results we report here. Doing so reduces our confidence in the relative size of our estimates, but table 6.1 suggests that the differences between results with and without controls are not great.

For both the mutual use of force and the war outcome, we see substantial variation across both time and space (although we report only the model with force). In some regions and time periods the IIG war equilibrium corresponds to actual violent outcomes, while in others it clearly does not. Due to the small number of cases that essentially fall into each cell, some of the variable effects may be overestimated; it is unlikely, for instance, that the risk of violent disputes in Europe during the cold war actually increased by a factor of 220 given an IIG war equilibrium. Clearly, though, the effect in such a case is large and positive. It is not obvious in table 6.4 that there is a consistent pattern across time. For instance, the fit of the IIG to violent disputes appears to increase across the time periods in Europe, while in Asia the predictive power is strongest between 1918 and 1940. Overall, these results present a rather complicated picture of when the IIG war equilibrium actually corresponds to conflict. There is, however, substantial variation in the empirical applicability of the model in different subsets of cases, supporting hypothesis 2 and not hypothesis 1.

TABLE 6.4. Risk Ratios by Time Period and Region

	All Dyads			Politically Relevant Dyads		
	Pre-WWI	Interwar	Cold War	Pre-WWI	Interwar	Cold War
Mutual Use of Force						
No Controls Included						
Europe	—	27	220	—	8.4	23
Mideast	—	—	0.80	—	—	0.90
Africa	—	—	0.63	—	—	0.10
Asia	2.5	6.4	6.3	1.4	3.1	1.1
Americas	—	—	0.60	—	—	0.69

Preferences and Structures Vary over Time because of Socially Constructed Beliefs

COMMON PREFERENCES AND DECISION STRUCTURES ARE REVEALED OVER TIME

Rather than focusing just on time periods, hypotheses 3 and 4 emphasize change as the actors in a dyad interact over time. We explore this hypothesis using our measure of "dyadic duration," which measures the length of time in years that both members of the dyad were independent states. If a dyad can "learn" how to behave, or to emulate the behavior typical in another region, then we should expect that the fit of the game-theoretic prediction of war to conflict in the dyad will change as duration (and accompanying interstate interaction) increases.

In table 6.5 we present the probability of observing either a MID or a war given combinations of equilibrium predictions and dyad age. As we are no longer parsing our data into small subsets, we are again able to make some judgments about the universal aspects of the theory, although we must omit our controls to observe reasonable patterns. In both sets of cases, the all-dyads set and the politically relevant sample, we immediately see a common pattern: the risk associated with the prediction of war appears to decrease as dyads age for the war outcome and to increase for the mutual force outcomes. With the war outcome, since the risk ratios are dropping, this means that the strength of the relationship between the equilibrium and conflict is weakening over time.

TABLE 6.5. Probability of Conflict and Risk Ratios by Dyad Age

	All Dyads			Politically Relevant Dyads		
	War Equilibrium			War Equilibrium		
	No	Yes	Risk Ratio	No	Yes	Risk Ratio
Mutual Use of Force						
10	0.00046	0.0016	3.4	0.0040	0.0044	1.1
20	0.00051	0.0017	3.4	0.0039	0.0043	1.1
30	0.00057	0.0020	3.5	0.0037	0.0044	1.2
40	0.00064	0.0023	3.7	0.0036	0.0047	1.3
50	0.00072	0.0028	3.9	0.0035	0.0052	1.5
War Outcome						
10	0.000061	0.00019	3.1	0.00058	0.00062	1.1
20	0.000067	0.00019	2.8	0.00054	0.00043	0.80
30	0.000076	0.00020	2.6	0.00051	0.00038	0.74
40	0.000088	0.00021	2.3	0.00050	0.00036	0.71
50	0.00011	0.00022	2.1	0.00051	0.00034	0.66

We consistently find that the longer a dyad exists, the less likely are war outcomes associated with IIG conflict equilibria. For instance, among all dyads, we see that the risk of war under a war equilibrium is triple that of a nonwar equilibrium for ten-year-old dyads but is only double for fifty-year-old dyads (this is still large, but it is a significant drop, particularly since some dyads have existed for close to two hundred years). In addition, within the politically relevant dyads, the war equilibrium also actually shifts to predicting peace in "old" dyads. That is, at an absolute level, when the equilibrium is for war in some year, our empirical expectation is actually that there will be less war (all risk ratios less than 1.0 fit this category). At the same time, the IIG equilibrium predictions fit the data better (more strongly) as dyads age when it comes to predicting mutually violent disputes. This suggests that states may be learning to avoid serious conflicts and to settle existing differences over time and may even be moving into a so-called Kantian system, within which conflict outcomes become unlikely even given some incentives for conflict

Overall, then, our data lend support to hypothesis 3, somewhat less to hypothesis 3a, and little to hypothesis 4. There is systematic variation in the nature of the fit of the equilibrium to the data over time. However, the fit sometimes worsens over time. This implies that states are appearing less rational, given the IIG and its associated operational measures, or that state preferences are changing. Moreover, the trend is toward a weaker fit to the data, given a prediction of war (at least in terms of avoiding full-scale war). Such systematic shifts in the behavior of states and their common beliefs pose a potential problem for existing expected utility models.

DARWINIAN EVOLUTION OR LEARNING LEADS PREFERENCES OR DECISION STRUCTURES TO CONVERGE

Do the changes over time in regional differentiation correspond to the theoretical differences identified earlier? Our expectations would be that, if we assume that Bueno de Mesquita and Lalman based their model on a game and style of politics that developed in Europe and spread outward, the best fit between the predictions of the game and the actual outcomes should be observed in Europe and regions that were colonized early. The Middle East and the Americas had the longest colonial contact with Europe, while the Europeans colonized much of Africa only in the 1800s. Much of Asia never suffered under the yoke of colonization in the same ways as did the other regions, and Asian states more deliberately resisted foreign influences than did other regions of the world. For example, during the peak of British administration in India, the British relied on local rulers. They never had more than several thousand bureaucrats in the country (with a population of hundreds of millions) at any given time. Both China and Japan actively resisted the "contaminating" influence of Western culture. If any regions were to show different behavioral patterns (that is, less convergence over time to the European model), we would expect them to be Africa and Asia. By parsing the data by region as well as by age of the dyad in table 6.6, we can also provide a better test of Wendt's (1999) convergence argument. Again, though, because we run into issues with available degrees of freedom and conflict frequency over the age of various dyads, we had to omit the set of control variables in this analysis and only report the results for the occurrence of mutually violent disputes.

Overall, these results provide quite mixed results for the convergence hypotheses. We first observe that in Europe, the region that we consider a baseline on which others might converge, the fit of the IIG war equilibrium is quite strong and is increasingly so as the dyads age (old dyads are, of course, most common in Europe). However, in most dyads, the IIG actually does not do a good job of predicting conflict; it is strongest at predicting conflict among dyads in Europe and Asia. We note that the strength of the relationship changes in both regions as dyads age. In the other regions, the relationship is weaker, again with consistent decline over time and a relationship expected by the IIG only for young dyads in the Americas and Middle East. In Africa, the relationship is very weak for any dyads other than the youngest; when the IIG predicts war, we see a very low probability of conflict that is even less than the probability given an IIG prediction other than war. These findings may offer partial support to a hypothesis that Asia will look more like Europe over time, but we find no support for the argument that its behavior will converge on that of Europe. In fact, all of the regions outside of

TABLE 6.6 Risk Ratios by Region and Dyad Age

	All Dyads			Politically Relevant Dyads		
	10	30	50	10	30	50
Mutual Use of Force						
Europe	5.6	9.0	14	1.1	2.0	3.9
Mideast	0.98	0.62	0.39	1.4	0.89	0.56
Africa	0.93	0.11	0.014	0.13	0.07	0.04
Asia	6.7	5.4	4.4	1.3	1.40	1.50
Americas	0.36	0.30	0.25	1.1	0.78	0.55

Europe appear to diverge both from the pattern predicted by the IIG and from the European pattern. Note that the changes in the risk of conflict change in a rather dramatic fashion, with risk ratios dropping by 30 to 70 percent over a period of forty years in the ages we have projected. The effects we observe are not merely at the margins but are substantively very important.[11]

Overall, then, with this more subtle analysis, we again find continued support for hypotheses 2 and 3 (differences across age and region) and no support for hypothesis 3a (convergence to a Kantian system). We find only partial support for hypotheses 5 and 6. States in general do not appear to converge over time to a single simple rational pattern (that is, their behavior does not come to conform to the IIG), behavior is quite different across regions, and states' behavior appears to diverge between Europe and other regions. There is support for hypotheses predicting a better fit over time only in Europe, where the fit of actual events to the IIG improves over time.

RATIONALITY VARIES AS A FUNCTION OF STAKES

To investigate our final argument—that the stakes affect apparent rationality—we add an analysis of a third level of violence. In table 6.6, we presented the risk ratios across the regions and dyad ages for disputes that escalate to the level of mutual violence. In table 6.7, we extend this to the initiation of disputes, looking simply at the risk of dispute initiation without separating out high levels of violent behavior. Again, our analysis here does not include our set of control variables.[12]

If the data were consistent with our hypothesis that procedural rationality should increase with the level of the stakes being contested, we would expect that across differing conflict levels the fit of the IIG war equilibrium should be strongest with wars, then with disputes that esca-

TABLE 6.7.   Risk Ratios by Region and Dyad Age

	All Dyads			Politically Relevant		
	10	30	50	10	30	50
Dispute Initiation						
Europe	13	14	15	2.9	3.7	4.6
Mideast	0.80	0.75	0.69	1.1	0.86	0.68
Africa	1.2	0.46	0.18	0.24	0.20	0.16
Asia	5.7	4.8	4.0	1.3	1.4	1.5
Americas	0.46	0.50	0.55	1.1	1.1	1.1

late to force, then with disputes that do not escalate to violence. In general, though, the results we find across age and time are similar whether we look at dispute initiation or the development of disputes at higher levels. In Europe, extending the finding noted previously, the model fits as expected in the all-dyads sample, increasingly so for older dyads. The relationship is actually somewhat stronger for dispute initiations than for violent disputes. However, in Asia the reverse is true. For our high-stakes events, the mutual use of force outcome, the model's predictions are slightly more powerful than with dispute initiations. In other regions, the war equilibrium (given this specification) does not predict as well as we would expect with dispute initiations, as it did not for disputes escalating to mutual violence. Looking across the regions, then, we find little consistent support for hypothesis 7—that states will behave systemically either more or less in accordance with the model as the stakes change. Regional and time differences in the risk associated with a war equilibrium are at least as large as any differences across levels of violence (stakes). Of course, it may be that when leaders contemplate conflict initiation they are already behaving in a procedurally rational manner. However, given that this is the lowest level of conflict behavior we can examine using aggregate data, we find little further systematic variation as we move up the escalation ladder.

CONCLUSIONS

Clearly, Bueno de Mesquita and Lalman's IIG equilibrium predictions fit empirical conflict outcomes substantially better in some areas and at some times than others. One possible explanation for the different fit of the model to the data from parts of the world other than Europe has to do with the possible inaccuracy of data in other areas of the world. However, as long as the noise in our data is uncorrelated with the outcomes we are examining, we should expect such noise only to weaken existing relationships, not to reverse them. Thus, we cannot use this argument to explain the statistically significant negative relationships that we find.

The patterns that we observe fit more clearly with some alternative hypotheses than others, but in general they are consistent with Huntington's (1993) argument that significant differences in preferences for conflict exist across regions (or civilizations) compared to somewhat more sophisticated (but less nuanced) rationalist arguments such as Fearon 1994 and 1997 that would suggest convergence to rational behavior over time. Why is this? In following up on our hypotheses, we suggest a number of additional arguments to link systematic cross-regional and time variation to rational choice models. In general, none of these conclusions is antithetically opposed to a rational choice perspective, as all are potentially consistent with rationalist models. However, these possibilities suggest that we may not be able to make universal behavioral and preference assumptions but can only assume common beliefs or preferences to some smaller sample.

Talcott Parsons (1937, 57) argues that rational choice approaches—as implemented in most current models—undervalue the contributions of values and social norms as well as what he refers to as ritualistic choices, perhaps most common in preindustrial societies. Parsons anticipated the possibility of what we refer to today as endogenous preferences by pointing out that schemas of action link the ends that actors pursue to the means with which states (individuals) pursue them (58; more recent work such as Gerber and Jackson 1993 and Lewis and Schultz 2002 has also examined endogenous preferences).

Rational choice scholars often downplay the role of regional or national variance in what many anthropologists or sociologists refer to as "culture." Based on our results, however, it appears that idiosyncratic national or regional attributes may in fact provide a significant source of variation in beliefs, preferences, and even game trees. A number of more specific aspects of culture might plausibly link with decision making. Granato, Inglehart, and Leblang (1996), for instance, show that religious preferences and beliefs as well as attitudes toward education and postmaterialistic values might significantly accelerate or hinder a state's economic development. Granato and his colleagues argue that different social cultures help create different sets of preferences for the accumulation of wealth and savings in different countries. Turning to international conflict, religion has long been a central issue to many wars, such as the European Crusades to the Middle East in the fourteenth century. While state leaders' preferences shaped by religion could fit into a rationalist model, if these preference structures vary across interactions, then models built on an assumption of homogeneous preferences will work better in some cases and worse in others. The education of a country's mass publics is another important cultural attribute argued to be an essential component for the development of an advanced and enlightened society (North 1977). This development may serve as a necessary, but not sufficient, condition for the beginnings of the transition from a Hobbesian state to a more pacific Kantian state.

State leaders' and mass publics' attitudes toward violence may also systematically shape states' strategic decision-making institutions and their concomitant assessments of costs and benefits. Similarly, cultural attitudes toward violence vary tremendously across states and nations. The variance in levels of internal violence across states (which can be seen easily by examining levels of murder or incarceration rates, for instance) is tremendous, in some cases by as much as two orders of magnitude. Attitudes toward violence and the way a society reacts to it may affect the application of models of social choice to international politics in several ways. Some scholars have argued that these cultural differences toward violence may significantly affect a state's military power. For instance, Rosen (1996) points to the apparent weakness of the Indian army and demonstrates empirically the links between their battlefield failures and their sociocultural practices. Pollack (1996), making similar arguments, argues that Egyptian cultural norms limit their soldiers from being to able to take the initiative in combat, in turn limiting Egyptian power. Stam (1996) points out that class and racial biases particular to individual states systematically affect troop mobilization levels and efficiency and, hence, state power. Such factors might appear as systematic measurement error across states and time. Others have argued that communitarian societies (such as Confucian Chinese) value community preference over individual ones. This may in turn lead communitarian states, assuming they actually exist, to be more willing and able to bear costs associated with international conflict. In contrast, cosmopolitan states where individual rights are dominant may be more constrained in international affairs because these states are more sensitive to expected costs. Hence, leaders of cosmopolitan states may be more likely to prefer negotiated outcomes versus war outcomes. If large differences in preference orderings for the various outcomes of some hypothetical game tree occur across states or cultures, then imposing and making predictions based on an assumed single set of preference orderings are not likely to be very useful.

Many of the previous arguments focus on how the potential differences in preferences of different societies might lead to different estimates of the costs and benefits of conflict. Potentially, we could incorporate these factors into an empirical model by adding cultural variation to the measurement of utility or preference orderings. A second possible cultural effect would be more insidious and harder to take into account, however. We argued previously that states might need to learn the game that they are playing. If two states are playing different subjective games, or are playing a game that is different from the one that analysts expect, our empirical results would not match our theoretical predictions. It might be that culture influences the games states play. If some national or regional culture contained a norm of always accepting negotiation when offered, for instance, or if states' leaders never considered the option of acquiescence in some society, then the extensive form game tree we analyze might be different from the IIG. Differing informational discount rates, shadows of the future, or willingness to "look down the road" and a focus on long- versus short-term gains could also possibly affect a state's choices. If this is the case, then we might expect variations in the fit of the equi- librium predictions to our data across different periods or regions, even if we adjust our measurement for some elements of utility and preferences. The spring 2001 emergency landing of a U.S. surveillance plane in China and American leaders' subsequent apparent surprise at China's refusal to play the game the way the USSR might have played it during the cold war illustrate how differences in beliefs about the nature of the game can lead to unexpected outcomes.

These examples suggest ways in which national culture could in- fluence decision making and why states faced with the same sets of in- centives might make different choices. If this variation in choice is sys- tematic, then we can understand how games such as IIG come to predict outcomes better or worse in different situations. When we ex- amined increasingly complex models and interactions, we found that the fit of the expected utility model to the data is stronger in some re- gions and at some times in the life of a dyad than in others. We consis- tently found that political behavior in the Americas, the Middle East, and Africa fit the predictions of expected utility theory poorly, although the exact nature of the difference in fit depended on the specification and population of cases. However, even in Europe, the results are sen- sitive to time and differ by outcome. While in some instances the vari- ation in results is likely due to having relatively few conflicts to analyze, in others instances we believe that the differences represent complex re- gional and temporal variation in how conflict occurs.

Of course, a rational choice theorist might argue in response to our findings that the universality assumption is actually the best assumption to make in a case such as this, where we have complicated and in some cases inconsistent patterns among our various data subsets. For in- stance, the fact that our region and dyadic aging findings are similar on dispute initiation and disputes that escalate to the mutual use of force suggests that we need not look for differences across conflict levels. Moreover, the absence of clear patterns of behavior that consistently fit a single competing hypothesis suggests that our analysis is only picking up and amplifying small random differences in the distribution of cases across regions and time. Alternatively, it may be that we do not have the appropriate operational measures to capture the nature of power,

power projection, or exogenous regional features that need to be taken into account in order to clearly observe "rational" behavior patterns.

Our analysis also illustrates a problem in closely examining the assumption of unit homogeneity, namely, that we may be attempting to conduct too fine grained an analysis with limited data. Once we parse the data into region and time period, we create fifteen separate groups, captured in the saturated model by the addition of twenty-five dummy and interactive variables. Since duration is continuous, the model estimating duration effects required eighteen additional variables. We would expect some of these interactive variables (which capture all possible region and time differences) to be insignificant, but when searching for regional and time differences, existing theoretical arguments provide little guidance about which interactions we should exclude from the statistical model. If we actually thought that differences were subregional, or that time periods smaller than our pre–World War I, interwar, and post–World War II division were relevant, the problem would only become worse. If we must assume that every state possesses a unique culture, foreign policy bureaucracy, or set of rules governing its interaction with others, then the inferential problem becomes intractable if we seek to explain the rare occurrence of international conflict. The blistering criticism of Huntington's (1993) somewhat ad hoc categorization of states or regions into various "civilizations" gives us pause as we contemplate how those concerned with international politics should operationalize empirically distinct cultures, particularly when it comes to foreign policy behavior. There may exist a limit to knowledge both in how accurately we can conceive of the independent variable in question and in what types of tests we can reliably conduct.

In conclusion, we note that these results have important implications for specific hypotheses discussed in the initial part of this chapter. Generally, they suggest that assuming preferences are fixed, exogenous, and universal is problematic. Standard rational choice approaches to international politics (as well as most structural explanations) would have predicted little or only random variation in the fit of the expected utility model across different regions. Even if our measurement is not as good in some regions as others because of data concerns, this should generate only random deviations from successful predictions. However, whether the source is different game trees, preference orderings, assessments of utility, or some other cause, we find consistent, systematic, and potentially explainable differences across regions. This suggests that rethinking our claims of the scope of broad rational choice models (and perhaps other models) in international politics is necessary.

7 CONCLUSION

life's but a walking shadow, a poor player
that struts and frets his hour upon the stage
and then is heard no more: it is a tale
told by an idiot, full of sound and fury,
signifying nothing.
—shakespeare, *macbeth*

The analysis in the previous chapters fits into a research mosaic that has been developing over the past sixty years. The quantitative study of the origins and escalation of violent conflict between nations now has a history spanning nearly three-quarters of a century. Published behavioral works on the origins of war trace immediately back to a series of papers published in the 1930s by Lewis Richardson in the British science journal *Nature* and to Quincy Wright's *A Study of War* (1942). Both Richardson and Wright firmly believed that in order to eliminate the pox of war we would need to understand it better, both from a theoretical perspective and, as has largely been the case here, from an empirical one. Their work laid the foundation for several generations of scholars whose best efforts went to building and testing explanations of the onset of war, many of whose work we summarize here. Some have had greater success than others. Progress in social science, as in any science, comes from taking steps forward and backward—steps of building new ideas, refining old ones, and pausing for retrospection and reflection.

Among Richardson's (1960a, 1960b) most important conclusions based on his data was that chance, and not systematically identifiable causal relations, regulates the distribution of war with respect to both its beginning and its ending. The notion that chance, or the stochastic component of the war-generating process, plays a powerful force in determining war's onset thus has a long history. Historically, this has typically been an unsatisfying explanation. Consistent with John Donne's weary claim about all men that "Thou art slave to fate, chance, kings, and desperate men," Richardson's conclusion remains for many an unhappy one, as he began the process of discovering the limits to our knowledge about the onset of war. While Richardson was able to provide powerful descriptions of the wars that occurred in the past, he largely failed in coming to grips with the fundamental question that motivates many of those who study the deadly quarrels between nation-states, namely, what are the systematic causes of war?

The next generation of social scientists working on this puzzle greatly broadened the search for theoretical explanations of war. While doing so, they developed increasingly sophisticated statistical tests of their propositions. Current social scientists working in the empirical tradition owe a huge debt to J. David Singer, whose greatest contribution may have been to democratize the statistical study of war through the development and distribution of detailed data on many of the possible correlates of war (Singer and Small 1972, 1982, 1993). As we take our place at the contemporary end of this research program, we recognize that the questions we have posed and the answers we have provided differ more in manner of degree than in kind from those that precede this work.

If there were one single story to take from this book, it would be that there is no single story of war. In many ways, we are as uncertain about the causes and likely timing of any individual war today as we were in 1942 when Wright initially published his study of war. As our degree of certainty about the inherent limits to knowledge on the origins of war sharpens, we can see the proverbial glass as either half-full or half-empty—we can choose to be optimistic or pessimistic about the current and future state of knowledge and the nature of the unknowable.

As we move to discuss our general findings and the uncertainty associated with our attempts to evaluate the myriad arguments and empirical conjectures about the causes of war, it would be wise to keep in mind the following Socratic dialog that opens Richardson's *Arms and Insecurity* (1960b, overleaf):

Politicus: What are you trying to prove?
Researcher: In social affairs it is immoral to try to prove.
Fidor: Yes. One should have faith that God will provide. He that cometh to God must believe that He is and that He is a rewarder of them that diligently seek Him.
Researcher: I meant that in social affairs where proof is seldom rigid, and where prejudice so easily misleads, it is best not to

start with a fixed opinion. He that comes to research must be in doubt, and must humble himself before the facts, earnestly desiring to know what they are, and what they signify.

In the remainder of this chapter, suitably humbled by the facts as best we know them, we turn to a discussion of what they signify.

A CONSERVATIVE BUT OPTIMISTIC VIEW

One way to judge progress in any scientific endeavor is to pose the question "Which hypotheses perform best?" In this analysis, we have carried out a broader comparative test of many major international conflict hypotheses and conjectures using a larger data set than executed previously, and in doing so we have integrated information simultaneously across several levels of analysis, an impossible task using a qualitative approach. Analyzing the large number of observations and variables has given us many more degrees of freedom and a much improved ability to make carefully controlled comparisons than would be the case had we used other techniques and, correspondingly, more protection against spuriously attributing causal power to otherwise random correlations in the empirical results. The resulting models provide systematic descriptions of international conflict behavior, at the individual, dyadic, and system levels of analysis. Two major sets of conclusions emerge. First, we need to exploit information from multiple levels of analysis to understand the initiation of any individual conflict as well as to be able to understand the general level of violence throughout the international system. Second, not all theoretical arguments are equally useful or valuable. While this may seem an obvious point, it has failed to carry the day in the field of international relations theory. Some arguments are simply more powerful than others, particularly in terms of being able to predict the relative likelihood of future wars. For instance, recalling figure 3.3, the three most powerful factors associated with the onset of war are not among the five most commonly cited arguments in the literature. Many arguments such as balance of power assertions that are widely accepted as fact provide little if any systematic purchase on predicting future risk of violent conflict within the international system. By sorting out fact from fiction, we can also tease out limited, but carefully considered, policy recommendations based on the results of our models that summarize the nature of interstate conflict over the past 175 years.

Conclusion

The Need for Multiple Perspectives and Levels of Analysis

We found that a large number of factors suggested by multiple perspectives appear to influence the relative risk of international conflict, thereby simultaneously giving support to many conjectures of international conflict. Rather than there being any single dominant model of international politics, as advocates for some paradigms or perspectives maintain, multiple explanatory factors from multiple levels of analysis are necessary to understand best international conflict. Contrary to some claims, the wars we observe are not overdetermined—no single factor or explanation is fully adequate to understand the onset of large-scale war. None of the individual arguments we examined comes close to explaining the majority of international conflict or even a substantial proportion of it. Moreover, there does not yet appear to be any single grand theory that incorporates the predictions of the others. Instead, the key variables suggested by most approaches have relatively comparable and relatively weak effects on interstate conflict. This is an especially important observation when considering expected utility theories of war, sometimes presented as a complete data-generating process—an all-encompassing approach to the study of international politics. While it is theoretically possible to fit arguments about regime type, the balance of capabilities, economic expansion, and so forth into an expected utility framework, to understand the initiation of disputes and wars requires a wide-ranging combination of factors drawn from multiple analytic levels, something no extant expected utility model accomplishes. Recent work in bargaining theory holds out great promise in this regard (Powell 2002; Reiter 2003).

From the perspective that we need to understand the heterogeneity among our cases, multiple interactions of casual factors, and cultural context, a long bill to be sure, someone skeptical of statistical work might question whether an alternative to our approach, namely, a qualitative analysis, holds the answer. Unfortunately, while the careful analysis of a small number of wars, such as those studies focusing on the origins and prosecution of World War I, provides better opportunities to identify the causal processes that lead to the war in question, it does not allow us to consider baseline conflict rates or increases in the relative risk of war as we have done here (King, Keohane, and Verba 1999). Political scientists working in this descriptive tradition tend to see events as overdetermined compared to historians, who tend to take a more nuanced view of causality and motive (e.g., Van Evera 1999). Nor does a qualitative approach allow us to estimate the relative effects on the risk of war associated with variables drawn from the population of possible conflicts while simultaneously controlling for the effects of competing explanations.

The Relative Power of Theoretical Conjectures

While we find that multiple perspectives are necessary to explain any single conflict, we have also demonstrated that we need not weigh the empirical contribution of all these arguments equally, as the scale of the associated effects on the risk of war ranges widely. While none of the factors has what we would consider a dominating effect associated with it, the typical "real world" change in the risk of conflict associated with our different indicators is much larger for some than for others. All the same, in the context of a baseline risk of war of 1 per 14,000 dyad-years, even the most powerful individual explanation, systemic power concentration, raises the associated risk of war to a level no greater than about 1 per 1,000 dyad-years. Only when the effects associated with multiple perspectives accrue does the estimated risk of war mount to levels where we intuitively sense a high level of risk or danger. For the most part, statistically based explanations of international politics do not focus much attention on this type of interaction. Given the weakness of the relations between the operational indicators and the onset of war, our results suggest that increased attention to how multiple incentives and factors combine to increase the risk of conflict may prove fruitful. Based on our analysis, this path holds more promise for predictive power than a focus on any individual argument or conjecture.

Our analysis demonstrates that we have sufficient cases and data to estimate carefully the relative empirical effects of multiple variables on the outbreak and escalation of international conflict. However, we have also gone beyond simply recognizing that multiple variables contribute to international conflict to presenting a methodology and a set of findings on the relative effects of those variables on conflict. The directed dyad-year framework provides the ability to extend these analyses in the future to include a host of other factors from the various levels of analysis. Here, our models allow us to incorporate information from multiple levels of analysis to predict either dyadic conflict behavior or aggregate conflict throughout the international system.

We find that both system power concentration and the democratic peace proposition remain among the most powerful predictors of war and peace, even after controlling for a greater number of alternative explanations drawn from multiple levels of analysis than those found in previous tests. This suggests that previous results are not due to model misspecification or the examination of a limited region or period as claimed by some (Gowa 1999; Henderson 2002). At the same time, however, we find that variables used to operationalize the expected utility equilibria are not among the stronger empirical predictors of the likelihood of conflict as claimed by proponents of the theory (Bueno de Mesquita and Lalman 1992). In our models of war onset, dyadic democracy is the most powerful dyad-level explanation we find.

Policy Implication for the Epistemological Optimist

These types of predictions may be of some use in the field of policy analysis, where cost-benefit frameworks are becoming increasingly important. It is true that many of the factors identified, particularly those that have the most powerful influence on the conflict behavior of states, are either immutable (contiguity), shift at almost glacial pace (system power concentration), or appear to present something of a Faustian bargain (global economic upswings in development and wealth associated with increased risk of increasingly violent war). Nevertheless, we find solace in the fact that there are a few results with direct policy implications. The first and most obvious is the democratic peace finding, even though, as always, a caveat is in order here.

Since the mechanism that appears to lead to the absence of large-scale war between democracies remains elusive (whether it exists in their electoral constraints, in their shared norms, or in their similarity of interests), we need to be prudent about advocating plans to encourage the spread of democracy on security grounds. Note that we do not suggest prudence because we find the process of democratization to be destabilizing. Like Ward and Gleditsch (1998), our results strongly refute Mansfield and Snyder's (1995) argument that "democratization" per se is dangerous. Rather, recognizing the inherent pitfalls in the democratization process (Przeworski et al. 1999) and that the resources to support this type of enterprise are limited, the leading democratic states should place their democratization or state building bets carefully. The best gambles, and they are gambles to be sure, would be not only in those situations where the democratization efforts are likely to succeed but also in those areas suffering from the greatest risk of costly war. From the democratization literature, we know that for these pledges to succeed they must be made with long-term commitments to the development of stable democratic institutions and liberal political and legal cultures.

Our findings on system power concentration might be off-putting to some, as it would appear to be a gloomy result in these days of exceptional American economic and military power (Brooks and Wohlforth 2002). As Keohane (1984) notes, however, international institutions can play a powerful role in tempering the incentives for the use of force. These institutions may take the form of dyadic or multilateral defense pacts as we tested here, or they may take the form of multilateral economic trade institutions, whose indirect effects we also tested. While high levels of systemic power concentration create a relatively riskier environment, international institutions that attenuate incentives for the use of force can more than offset the higher levels of risk attributed to system-level characteristics. Institutions that restrain arms races, for example, belong in the category of policies worth advocating on both normative and positivist grounds.

When the United States moves to pull out unilaterally of long-standing arms control treaties, policy choices that threaten to reignite long-dormant arms races, the evidence clearly suggests that this raises the overall risk of conflict and war rather than reducing it. We also note that containment policies designed to create some sort of equitable regional balance of power in areas where conflicts loom are likely increasing rather than decreasing the future risk of war and violence. Rather than creating situations where all sides feel they have a reasonable chance to win a war should one occur, a more sensible policy would be for a powerful state or institution such as the United States or NATO to pursue a policy of extended immediate deterrence, along with concomitant building of democratic institutions. Consistent with work elsewhere (e.g., Huth 1988), potential aggressors seeking to alter a regional territorial or policy status quo are much less likely to escalate or initiate war if they fear losing that war. Creating locally equal balances of power increases these risks, while making credible deterrent commitments and establishing a clear leader reduces them.

For the scientific optimist, the bottom line is this: we need multiple theoretical perspectives to understand the onset of war, but not all theories or arguments are as valuable as others. Those whose scientific commitment is to comparative hypothesis testing as the path to new knowledge can take solace in the fact that progress is, in fact, being made. Moreover, our ability to anticipate future events improves by explicitly incorporating information from multiple levels of analysis simultaneously. However, this sort of monitoring of the scientific tote board is quite different than reaching a profound understanding of the causes of war, the principal goal of both Richardson and Wright. From this perspective, our analysis provides reasonable ground for serious skepticism.

Conclusion

A MORE SKEPTICAL INTERPRETATION

In our minds, there are two possible viewpoints from which one could judge the contributions to the state of knowledge made by this work. One view, that of the classical hypothesis tester, is quite optimistic. As noted previously, we have made great strides in winnowing through a vast sample of the potential correlates of war. That said, most of the conjectures we tested have no direct linkage to the causal processes generating the correlations we measured, a point that leads to our second perspective. The main goal from this viewpoint is to understand the underlying causal mechanisms that make war a more or less likely proposition. Without a carefully stated theory of why the factors we tested are associated with varying risks of war, we cannot be sure that we are not spuriously attributing causality where none really exists. An observer from this second viewpoint might have reason to be quite pessimistic, in part reflecting the skeptic's view that the outbreak of war is a seemingly random event or suggesting (as did Richardson) that chance powerfully tempers our knowledge about the onset of any particular war. In this view, our abstract models of organized violence amount to little in the way of systematic knowledge about the nature and timing of future violence. The person interested less in narrow hypothesis testing than in identifying the causal processes that lead to war may likely come away from this work dubious about the nature of our findings. This person is likely to conclude that we still know very little about the likely origins of individual wars and could reasonably be pessimistic about our ability to generalize about the causes of events, either those that have run their course or those that may occur in the future.

Running in Place?

The skeptic would note that in many ways we are still where we were twenty years ago in the study of causality and international conflict and that cumulative progress has been numbingly slow. This book points to three empirical conjectures associated with exceptionally strong explanatory potential: power concentration in the international system, arms races, and the democratic peace. In each of these cases, we have made little theoretical progress in the past twenty years toward an accepted understanding of the underlying causal processes involved. For example, the basic arguments found in the modern arms race literature draw directly from Huntington's work in the 1950s. The argument that the international system structure provides powerful incentives for or against the use of force is perhaps the oldest proposition in the study of world politics. The most widely accepted finding here, the democratic peace proposition, dates to the 1970s. Although there has been a growing volume of work investigating the underpinnings of the association to identify the causal processes at work, there is as yet no consensus on why liberal democracies have not gone to war with one another.

The Limits on Testing Explanations

While one can find solace in the fact that we succeeded in identifying numerous empirical regularities—that is, sets of variables associated with increased and decreased risks of conflict—if one is interested in gaining a deeper understanding about the theoretical underpinnings of the international system, then one would rightly be skeptical about the findings and implications of our analysis. The skeptic might note that, rather than presenting a grand test of myriad theories against one another, we have simply succeeded in testing a variety of empirical propositions linking operational indicators to the incidence of interstate conflict rather than testing the causal paths of even a single theory. From this perspective, then, the findings here constitute at best a road map of facts about the nature of conflict in the international system. And while we would argue that having such a road map is critical to making scientific progress, the skeptic would note that this analysis does not directly lead us toward a satisfactory explanation of the competing causal linkages implicit in the arguments, models, and conjectures we examined.

For instance, our empirical measures do nothing to help us evaluate the competing notions of liberalism found in the various electoral constraint mechanisms and the elite-level, norm-based explanations of the democratic peace proposition. In another example, regarding the association between military spending and the risk of war, while we find that arms races approximately double the risk of war, we have no means to distinguish between the psychological stories of arms races leading to security dilemmas (Jervis 1976) and various rational choice explanations of the association (Morrow 1989; Kydd 1997). Similarly, while we find a reduced rate of interstate conflict during the cold war as predicted by Waltz (1979), before jumping on the structural realist's bandwagon we note the inferential problem that the collinear and competing explanations of NATO institutions and nuclear weapons provide. Our inability to sort out these competing explanations must temper any claims about the actual predictive power of Waltz's parsimonious model. The committed skeptic could easily raise similar questions about any of the relationships identified in our empirical models.

Unfortunately, from the skeptic's perspective, sorting out where to go next is not a trivial task. When we cannot identify or measure causal factors directly, the observable implications of an argument about the origins of war may be quite distant from the supposed core arguments of our "theories" (Fearon 1996). If some variable does not fit the data in an analysis as expected according to some theoretical argument, it could be because of a flaw in the underlying causal chain, because of errors or omissions in the logic of the argument, or because of measurement error associated with some key concept. As we suggested earlier, we believe that such a tack must begin with greater care in theory development. For the most part, what international relations theorists call "theories" should be more accurately thought of as descriptions of a relatively few number of cases, and as such most of what constitutes international relations theory deserves the more precise label of conjecture, inductive empirical proposition, or simply "hunch."

From the optimistic perspective, we might think that this type of work is similar to medical research on the things that affect human health. There, the risk of disease across the population is commonly low, as is the case here with the risk of war. The beneficial effects associated with various treatment strategies are initially unknown and probabilistic in nature. Medical researchers also have a poor theoretical understanding of why many drugs work in some situations and not in others. Yet hope springs eternal in the field of medical research. Why should we not share the same sort of optimism about future payoffs with this type of large-n research? The key difference between research searching for new medical treatments and the efforts here is our inability to run experiments. The notion of random assignment of treatment—where some patients receive a drug and others receive a placebo but neither the patient nor the physician knows who received what—is the essential tool that separates the faith we have in so much of medical research and the skepticism we hold for so much of social science research. The ability to run randomized controlled experiments means that medical researchers do not need a real understanding of the causal mechanism behind improved human health in order to be able to judge the efficacy of a given drug or treatment. International relations scholars, limited to simulations and quasi-experiments, do not have the luxury of proceeding without a clear understanding of the causal process that generates the cases we study.

Unfortunately, because we are unable to run experiments on nation states, the only way we have to test conjectures about the onset of war or disputes is to look for real-world relationships between our dependent variables and the operational measures used as proxies for the various causal factors hypothesized to influence the onset of war (King, Keohane, and Verba 1999). With the statistical tools employed here, while we cannot directly examine many of the steps in some argument's alleged causal chain, the correlations between our final proxy variables and outcomes are all we have to go on. For the most part, the alternatives are worse. Counter to Walt's (1999) recent claims otherwise, even if some theoretical argument is useful as a heuristic tool for understanding previous and otherwise apparently idiosyncratic events, if its predictions do not fit to some systematically drawn random sample of the data, we must question its value for the purposes of creating new knowledge and making scientific progress. Aesthetics hold little value for us when it comes to judging the value of competing explanations of world politics.

Directly related to the problem of not resolving competing theoretical arguments is the problem of evaluating empirical assertions for which there is simply not enough evidence to judge which claim is correct. For instance, it is difficult to sort out the effects associated with NATO, nuclear weapons, and bipolarity on disputes that escalated to war during the cold war. With no wars occurring between either NATO members or the nuclear states, which could only have occurred during the post-1945 era, we cannot obtain reliable estimates of the effects associated with these factors. There is simply not enough evidence in our data set to judge what the source of peace is between the nuclear and/or NATO states. This is true regardless of the quantitative methods used to test the propositions, as there is not enough variation in the relevant variables for any technique to be able to judge the separate and independent effects of these factors. In these instances, we need either new indicators that will yield sufficient covariation to test the conjectures separately or new theories and appropriate data cast at a finer level of analysis. While we have established that there is a problem judging among these explanations, the skeptic notes that, given the tools at hand here, we cannot provide a solution.

While we find support for some arguments, the skeptic also notes that some key variables drawn from the most widely cited arguments do not have associated with them the empirical effects that many might otherwise expect. We recognize that in a probabilistic world no single test can provide compelling evidence for or against a casual argument. However, we believe that it is important for advocates of models that failed in our tests to explain why the empirical measures for their models have little apparent association with the risk of international conflict after we control for other explanations. Most notably, this is the case with our measures of power transition logic, for example, and the classic realpolitik argument that a bilateral or dyadic balance of power will restrain conflict. Both of these widely cited arguments receive no empirical support in our analysis. These findings beg an explanation from traditional realists because they undermine a basic assumption driving a large portion of the security studies literature and policy. It is unclear, for example, how debates about "balance of power systems" or about whether states "balance" or "bandwagon" can be resolved when the most basic premise of a dyadic balance of power (that an equal dyadic balance restrains conflict relative to imbalance) receives no support. The divergence between empirical regularities or lack thereof, arguments that refuse to go the way of the white whale, and our minimal understanding of the underlying causal processes leads the skeptic to question how much cumulative progress international relations "theorists" have made over the past forty years. The optimist notes that we now have a better established set of facts for theorists in various traditions to address. To the skeptic, though, the point that we are still establishing such facts rather than divining what the underlying causal processes are bodes ill for future progress.

Certainly, work remains to improve the econometric model developed here; it is far from perfect. A skeptic would suggest that the statistical models' inaccurate and relatively weak predictions are to be expected. Indeed, it may be impossible to improve them greatly, even if we dig more deeply into the data using alternative statistical or computational techniques. In one extension to our analysis, and in response to Smith's (1999) argument that strategic selection bias might plague our results, we replicated our basic analysis using a strategic Bayesian estimator of his design. After dedicating over sixty days of continuous computer processing time to running this large model, we generated new results that differed only in small degree from those presented here.[1]

A skeptic might also find it ironic that, while we have focused our attention in this book on estimating a more complete econometric model of interstate conflict, we end by suggesting the need for more theoretical work. Improved theory may help to enhance the statistical model by suggesting nonobvious interactions and nonlinear specifications of the existing variables. Similarly, we need more careful theorizing about the heterogeneity among cases, a serious and related confounding problem about which we should be much concerned. While the many structural-level explanations of international politics assume that "states are states" and that the effects of systemic anarchy swamp the causal effects of the varying internal characteristics of states, we hope the findings from chapter 6 will disabuse careful readers of this view.

Aside from the problem of unit heterogeneity, there are several possible reasons why, in the end, our statistical models suffer from serious limitations in predicting the onset of violent interstate conflict. Some of these reasons are typical of those caveats accompanying empirical analysis in any field. For example, we simply may not have the right variables in our model. Scholars may not have found the right measures or functional forms to specify accurately some particular expected relationship. Improved measures or instruments might improve the fit of our model to the data significantly. Another possibility is that we have not yet adopted the right theoretical perspective in our analyses and that some other explanations would produce the very strong findings about conflict we hope for, findings that would dramatically improve our predictive accuracy. Finally, our proxy variables for deeper concepts may be inadequate and fraught with error. Random noise in our measures can only hurt our model's fit, attenuating our parameter estimates.

None of these reasons is particularly satisfying, however; they sound to the skeptic's ear more like rationalizations rather than directions for future research. In our models, we included a major cross-section of the rigorously testable conjectures about the sources of interstate war. Most of the measures we used have been subject to multiple rounds of peer review and improvement for over twenty years. It is certainly possible that there is some dark-horse explanation or measure lurking somewhere in the literature, but this appears unlikely. Of course, it could be that there is not a single omitted strong argument but that several other theories or conjectures yet identified would each explain a little bit more of the conflict puzzle.

POSSIBLE WAYS OUT OF THE TRAP?

While the work in the preceding chapters continues the empirical tradition of the past sixty years, it also suffers from its inherent limitations. Given over a million observations and dozens of independent variables, might we reasonably have expected stronger results and predictions? Two powerful alternative tools hold much promise for the type of work executed here. On the empirical front, neural network models are quite promising because they offer the opportunity to estimate unconstrained models that allow for large numbers of interactions and nonlinear relations between the independent variables and the dependent variable. On the theory front, game theory offers a rigorous and deductive process to build real theory, something sorely lacking in the field of international politics. These complementary approaches are not without their flaws, however.

Neural Networks

One powerful empirical approach recently deployed is to use neural network models to find highly interactive sets of variables that together appear to predict outcomes relatively well (Beck, King, and Zeng 2000). Even this highly complex estimation method "is not a panacea" (22); while the method is quite effective at identifying patterns in the data, it allows us to explore the theoretical or casual structure of the conjectures included in the model only with great difficulty. We wonder whether using a largely unconstrained model is in fact any better for producing an understanding (rather than simply a complex description) of interstate conflict than the conjectures and hunches of which we have been so critical to this point. Based on this research, the best way to improve our understanding of the origins of war may not lie in the development of ever faster computers or more efficient and advanced statistical estimators. Rather, future advancement will most likely result from more detailed archival analysis of the data-generating processes that lead to the wars we observe, as well as those that never occur.

In addition to these basic problems, there are other, more fundamental reasons why this type of large quantitative analysis yields explanatory and predictive power that is lower than we would like. In presenting the advantages of neural network models, Beck, King, and Zeng (2000) argue that explanations for international conflict are likely to be highly contingent and interactive, demanding particularly close attention to interactions of circumstances and casual factors. If this is the case, then the approach of including multiple independent factors in additive fashion will surely prove inadequate. Unfortunately, systematic pursuit of the neural network approach confronts a fundamental limit to knowledge, the problem of limited degrees of freedom. Depending on how one defines the event of "war initiation," there have been roughly seventy-five to one hundred of them in the international system over the past 175 years, yielding a terribly skewed distribution with a small number of events to explain relative to the large number of nonevents.

When we begin to increase the potential interactions between our variables, the relatively small number of wars necessarily begins to limit the number of explanations we can consider simultaneously. In their neural network model, Beck, King, and Zeng (2000) included measures for alliances, geographic contiguity, dyadic balance of power, democracy, and the number of years since a previous conflict. Their model predicts well, in some ways better than the one presented here. For computational reasons, however, if they were to include measures for all the factors we know are systematically associated with war, they would quickly run short of the degrees of freedom needed to solve their model's simultaneous equations. This is because the neural net approach voraciously consumes data while sifting through a myriad combination of nonlinear interactions among the independent variables. Unfortunately, while the predictive performance of their model is relatively high, we know from our results that our ability to infer about the relative explanatory power of any one conjecture is highly contingent on what else is in, or out of, the statistical model. Similarly, if we believe that there is systematic variation in the fit of each explanation across regions and time periods (as our results in chapter 6 strongly suggest), we would need to include additional interaction terms. However, even if we could mark each argument with a single variable (something we know is not the case), we would quickly end up with significantly more variables than wars (5 regions × 3 periods × 16 conjectures = 240 variables).

In part, because most of our so-called theories are in fact inductive descriptions of a small number of events, we may never possess enough data to sort out empirically which set of variables and interactions among them provides the "best" fit to the data in general. As we noted earlier, knowing that democracy correlates strongly with the incidence of conflict is far different from understanding why this is so. Models exploiting large numbers of complex interactive measures (such as neural network models) help tremendously in establishing more fully the sorts of facts we lay out here. That said, these large, brute force attacks on the problem are not as helpful when it comes to answering theoretical questions, such as sorting out why democracies have different conflict propensities than other types of states or why NATO members have never gone to war but have engaged in mutually violent disputes just short of war. They can help us find and confirm empirical patterns, but they are not as well suited to helping us understand the theoretical mechanisms underlying these relations.

Is Game Theory the Solution?

Might the solution to these many problems, the majority of which are rooted in poorly or loosely specified theories, lie in more widespread use and development of formal mathematical models? Perhaps, but scholars building formal deductive models have not yet solved the puzzles found along the way in the quest to identify the true causes of war. Rational choice models may be subject to inherent epistemological limitations similar to those from which the brute force empirical approach suffers. A final limit to knowledge—a speed limit in a way, in terms of what we may be able to predict, particularly if the actors behave in perfectly rational ways—derives from Riker's (1980) pessimistic quip noted at the beginning of this book. Riker was pessimistic about the future ability of political scientists to predict successfully the behavior of strategic actors because he believed there might be no fundamental equilibria to identify. Following the logic of Arrow's theorem, Riker deduced that if there are multiple actors, with differing preferences, then there is no single equilibria, or core, that we can identify as clearly superior to others. How does this matter? In a recent paper, Lewis and Schultz (2002) show exactly how. They begin by building what we might think of as the world's simplest strategic signaling game—a game in which the two actors predicate their decisions to use force against the other on the "signals" one actor receives from the other actor about the other's intentions and expectations. From their Monte Carlo simulations, they reach the following somewhat unhappy conclusions:

> First, regardless of the solution concept employed, non-innocuous identifying restrictions must be made. For example, the effect of a covariate on a particular payoff generally cannot be estimated unless that covariate is assumed to have no effect on other payoffs. Second, the distribution of payoffs implied by a given set of outcome data strongly depends on the solution concept employed. Thus, even in very simple settings making inferences about payoffs from data on the outcomes requires strong and untestable identifying assumptions. This problem is exacerbated if the information structure is not known, in which case assuming the wrong information structure can lead to entirely misleading conclusions about payoffs and the effects of covariates on those payoffs. (Lewis and Schultz 2002, 1)

The issue is that different game theoretic solution concepts (Nash equilibria, perfect Bayes equilibria, quantal response equilibria, and so forth) can all lead to different equilibrium outcomes. Worse yet, these different equilibria are sometimes associated with wildly different comparative statics relationships among the variables that affect the likelihood of which equilibria will emerge, given the same game tree and similar sets of preferences. A solution concept is like a set of rules we need to follow to solve the game. The problem is that each of the solution concepts they explore is plausible—there is no compelling reason why we should prefer the Nash equilibrium concept to McKelvey's quantal response solution concept, for example. The real-world analogy is the following. Even if the two sides in a dispute are rational and agree that they face the same known sequence of choices, if they make their decisions in only slightly different but equally rational ways—in effect employing different equilibria solution concepts—then they may reach quite different conclusions about what is their best strategy. By "best strategy," we mean the best response to what they will rationally deduce the other side in the dispute to do. As a result, it becomes difficult both for the decision makers and for us as analysts to know what solutions present the best approximation of how decision makers may act in some particular situation. Empirically, we could test which sets of equilibria match real-world behavior best to help us understand which "style" of solution concept leaders tend to use most frequently. Somewhat ironically, however, that would be employing an inductive solution to a deductive trap—an approach of which advocates of game theory in particular and formal theory in general have been highly critical (e.g., Morrow 1993; Morton 1999). This is an area where experimental methods may prove tremendously helpful.

From a skeptical perspective on trends in the discipline, it appears that the promised gains from game theory and formal mathematical approaches remain as elusive as ever, assuming our interest is the generation of testable empirical propositions that illuminate novel and powerful causal arguments. While tremendous gains in computing power and software developments such as EUGene allow us to test arguments on the entire population of dyad-years (over a million observations), the payoffs from ever more sophisticated and complex models such as Bueno de Mesquita and Lalman's (1992) IIG are not clear. If anything, the most recent sophisticated work bodes ill for future progress in terms of game theory's contribution to our improved understanding of interstate violence (Lewis and Schultz 2002).

In the end, there may be actual limits to the degree of knowledge that we can distill from empirical observation of the events we wish to study. Following Gartzke's (1999) argument as developed in chapter 2, it will likely prove impossible to predict precisely the timing of individual international conflicts. If the incidence of war is a function of unobservable private information, even in part, then as analysts we can predict, at best, some relative likelihood of observing the initiation of war. If the theoretical upper limit of this forecasting probability is fifty-

fifty, or the flip of a fair coin, then the pseudo-R^2 summary statistics produced with our two models of 0.26 and 0.20 are quite good. This would likely be the case if state leaders were rational, if private information was the sole cause of conflict, if outcomes were win/lose, and if the choice confronting them was war/no war. These measures of aggregate model performance would then indicate that we are predicting roughly half of all that we can know ex ante about conflict initiation (again, assuming strategic and rational actors). If the decision makers are not rational, their behavior might be completely random, further lowering our chances of successful prediction. Alternatively, they might be irrational but in completely systematic ways, thereby raising the upper limit of predictability. While the view from the perspective of strategic rationality is not optimistic about anyone's ability to predict empirical behavior accurately, it may provide an understanding of the limited successes seen here.

WHERE TO GO NEXT?

Our results further point to focusing on differences between and interactions among states, their local and regional environments, and domestic politics as areas that need theoretical development. While recent work on the relationship between states' varying domestic political institutions and conflict behavior begins to relax the assumption of the state as a unitary actor, the inclusion of a single variable marking state type does not come close to capturing all of the potentially important differences across states and regions. Our results in chapter 6 demonstrate tremendous variation in the observed association between the expected utility measures and conflict behavior across regions and time periods. In results not reported here, we find similar patterns for variables drawn from balance of power approaches. Green, Kim, and Yoon (2001) have argued that the effects we associate with dyadic democracy, one of the more powerful pacifying factors, are also subject to substantial spatial and temporal heterogeneity. Related to our findings on trade and war, in another recent example, McGillivray (1997) shows that, if we want to understand tariff levels and states' general willingness to cooperate, it is not enough to account for regime type coded as democracy-autocracy. Nor is it sufficient only to distinguish between different democratic systems such as parliamentary or presidential systems (Garrett 1999; Busch and Reinhardt 2000). To understand the general demand and supply of protectionism—something going far beyond a narrow conception of a single state's foreign policy—we also need to understand the geographic distribution of industrial assets and actors in combination or interaction with a sophisticated notion of regime type. The weak and varying results we present for the expected utility model suggest that McGillivray and others who have developed sophisticated theories about the nature of government and private institutions and how these institutions interact with the geographic distribution of business and citizens' interest groups are clearly on the right track (Brooks 2001).

To those working in the field of comparative politics, it likely comes as no surprise that those who study international politics need a more sophisticated understanding of regime characteristics, regional differences, and the interaction of general factors with a more clearly specified notion of local contextual factors, otherwise known as "culture." Unfortunately, many international relations theorists choose to ignore the ways that the domestic affairs of state may alter or affect the policy choices we observe, using the presence of systemic anarchy as a basis for their claim that they can treat states as black boxes. Staking out an extreme view in this regard, Waltz (1979) and his followers argue that any theory of international politics that delves into the nature of domestic political systems immediately devolves into a theory of foreign policy and not international politics. If anarchy is largely what states make of it, however, this assertion is inadequate—moreover, recent work demonstrating the systematic effects of domestic politics on levels of conflict across the international system suggests that this assertion is patently wrong.

These pessimistic limits to our ability to forecast the future notwithstanding, with the analysis here, we provide a benchmark for further comparative tests of the power of multiple explanations for international conflict. Analysts who believe that different measures or additional explanations of conflict need to be included in analysis can easily extend our work using the software and replication data available at www.eugenesoftware.org, replacing or adding measures to reflect differing theoretical concerns. The key here is that the analysis of other variables and their permutations, interactions, and explanations proceed not in isolation but side by side with the multiple factors already known to influence conflict behavior.

We see at least three immediate directions for future research to expand upon our findings. New inquiries might fruitfully progress by seeking systematically to develop theoretical understandings of the heterogeneity among different dyads or regions we demonstrated in chapter 6. At this point, we do not have a good understanding of how we should conceive of international heterogeneity, even at the most basic level. States are all members of the international system, but they are simultaneously members of other types of systems as well: systems of regions, alliances, and dyads. As we showed in chapter 6, rational choice models of international politics fit the data quite differently across regions, time periods, and length of interaction; the same is true for other theoretical approaches such as liberal institutionalism (Ceder-man 2000, 2001). However, the appropriate level at which to model heterogeneity is unclear. If every dyad has a distinct baseline propensity for conflict, then we would want to use fixed-effects models for our estimations (Green, Kim, and Yoon 2001).

Related to this point are issues of selection bias in our studies of international politics. For example, analyzing samples known to be heterogeneous (such as "politically relevant" dyads), without understanding the selection mechanisms that generate such samples, risks producing parameter estimates that we cannot confidently use to make predictions across states and time. We need to consider whether and how our conflict models should apply to all cases or to nonrandom samples identified before the fact and how to integrate theoretical arguments that only apply to selected cases (such as power transition models of great power war) into the general approach we have advocated here.

Another important direction is to develop further a systematic understanding of how different models and explanations of international conflict interact. The infrequent confluence of a multitude of otherwise weak predictors of war may serve to explain the relative rarity of international conflict, as the large increases in the predicted risk we observed when combining changes in multiple variables suggest. It may also be the case that an additive approach such as the one we used here is simply inadequate to capture the contingent nature of most causal relationships, and we should therefore include a wider variety of interactions in our statistical models. For example, although we employed contiguity as an additive control variable, we may instead wish to include it as an interactive factor marking a concept such as "opportunity." However, we believe it is more appropriate to approach this issue from a theoretical perspective first rather than simply exploring the data or running saturated models to find variable interactions that are empirically powerful at predicting conflict in our data.

A final issue concerns the inclusion of more dynamic factors in our analysis. Our model does better at identifying conflict-prone dyads than it does at identifying the point in time when the members of a particular dyad will turn to war. One possible reason is that the models and hypotheses we tested are largely static and that the indicators included are largely structural rather than dynamic. Structural indicators are those that do not change as a conflict develops, while dynamic ones are those that can change rapidly, more accurately reflecting the policy decisions and choices that lead to the disputes and wars making up our dependent variable. Structural indicators are effective in predicting the behavior of a system if and only if the system is primarily in equilibrium (or close to it). However, if most social behavior is far from equilibrium, or has no fundamental equilibrium at all, then structural indicators will tell us relatively little about how the system operates in terms of the timing of individual events, which is the information we desire most.

Most of the variables in our statistical models do not change rapidly (e.g., capabilities), or else when they do, we often do not observe the changes measured on a time scale that will allow us to either make precise predictions about conflict timing or sort out the precise causal sequence leading to the outcomes we observe. For example, the fact that we must lag most of the variables we measure annually in order to avoid measuring factors after a conflict has already occurred contributes to this problem. Largely immutable indicators, such as polarity or power concentration, plausibly represent the structure of the system at the time of a series of dyadic interactions. As a result, they may affect the baseline risk of war, but they do not provide the day-to-day (or month-to-month) dynamic actions, reactions, and stochastic shocks to the system that represent critical flashpoints and proximate causes of violent conflict.

CONCLUDING THOUGHTS

In the end, what does all this mean for our general understanding of international politics? On the theory of international politics front, we have answered far fewer questions than those that remain outstanding. However, we have been able to present an assessment of the relative predictive power associated with a large variety of factors (some manipulable, some less so) purported to be causes or inhibitors of interstate conflict. We can also conclude that turning exclusively to a small-n approach will prove inadequate as an alternative to the kind of analysis we performed here. This does not mean either that we can rely on large-n studies to supply us with satisfying answers to the important questions about the theoretical bases of international politics. Instead, qualitative studies can provide a powerful counterpart or complement to this type of work; indeed, large-n statistical studies in the absence of controlled experimentation cannot provide the fine-grained information we need to understand fully events in the past as well as those that have yet to occur. It will likely be in detailed archival analysis that we will make progress in identifying the underlying causal mechanisms we have yet to put to any real form of test.

We close with a call for methodological pluralism. The skeptic is correct in noting that naive empiricism cannot provide the information we need to understand the causes of war. At the same time, our statistical optimist also rightly points out that purely historical research does not let us plausibly judge how the risk associated with one situation compares to the next. Moreover, we cannot rely on theory alone either; we also know that indeterminacies often riddle the equilibria derived from game theory models, the most rigorous theoretical approach we have at our disposal. The research efforts that will move us forward in the next era of peace research will likely combine aspects of all three approaches to the creation of new knowledge. Research into the causes of war has matured to the point where all of the comparatively easy tasks are done. Next comes the truly difficult work, work that will combine formal mathematical theory with archival work to establish causal pathways and complementary large-n tests where the data are available to enable carefully controlled comparisons to estimate the relative risks associated with the various indicators of interstate violence.

Looking with a retrospective view over the past sixty years of quantitative research, it seems clear that we have learned a great deal and have established several important facts relating arms races, domestic politics institutions, and the nature of the international system to the onset of war. It is also clear, however, that chance plays a powerful role in determining the individual events that shape our history and that many of the known leading indicators of international conflict have individually weak effects associated with them. As Bismarck noted in his memoirs, a ship's captain must keep an eye to the weather, as he cannot dictate the winds but rather must react to them. There will be times when the port of choice is out of reach because of the direction of the prevailing winds, and there will be times when favorable winds will carry a ship farther than anyone might have anticipated in advance. The truly wise ship captain also recognizes that, even with the best ship and finest crew, there will be times when no port offers a safe berth and that, at those times, prudence dictates sailing into the wind and waiting out the storm.

APPENDIX A
DATA DEVELOPMENT AND CUMULATION FOR
INTERNATIONAL RELATIONS: EUGene

The study of international relations using quantitative analysis relies, in part, on the availability of comprehensive and easily manipulable data sets. To execute large-n statistical tests of hypotheses, data must be available on the variables of interest, and those data must be manipulated into a suitable format to allow the inclusion of appropriate control variables as well as variables of central theoretical interest. Frequently, however, the process of preparing data sets for analysis is cumbersome, particularly data sets with many cases and with variables that come from a variety of sources. Frequently, control variables are excluded from analysis, not for theoretical or statistical reasons but simply because cumbersome data manipulation tasks preclude optimal test design. The somewhat daunting task of preparing large data sets can have the effect of turning scholars into technicians for substantial periods of time rather than remaining focused on theory development and research design improvements. When data sets are created, errors can creep in, miscodings can occur, and slightly different and poorly documented choices (for instance, how joiners or ongoing disputes are treated in different studies) result in nonreplicable data sets (sometimes by the data set creators themselves). For many scholars the barrier to entry into, and becoming competent in, the realm of quantitative research is sufficiently high to preclude any sophisticated analysis at all.

These issues are particularly serious when assembling data sets for comparative theory testing. Our data sets are dyadic, large, and contain many variables, and we made a large number of specific research design choices to fit our theoretical approach. But our data set is clearly not the last data set that will ever be required in international relations; to the contrary, we believe that changes, expansions, and extensions are essential to furthering the project we began here. While we believe our choices are the most appropriate for our task, others may disagree. Some may wish to use different rules for case inclusion and exclusion. Some may find other theories that we have not included particularly important and may wish to include them. Others may wish to operationalize variables differently for the theories we do analyze. Finally, new theories of conflict will certainly be developed in the future that scholars will wish to test against existing explanations for conflict. Making selected modifications while maintaining most of what we did is a daunting task.

To allow replication and easy extensions of our work, and to lower the barriers to entry in quantitative analysis, we have developed software designed to eliminate many of the difficulties commonly involved in constructing large international relations data sets, particularly dyadic data sets. Our software, titled EUGene (the Expected Utility Generation and Data Management Program), also generates the data necessary to test the international interaction game version of the expected utility theory of war developed in Bueno de Mesquita and Lalman 1992. EUGene is a stand-alone Microsoft Windows–based program for the construction of annual international relations data sets and is designed to make building such data sets simple. It accomplishes this by automating a variety of tasks necessary to integrate several data building blocks commonly used in tests of international relations theories. By reducing the time necessary to carry out routine data set construction tasks, EUGene allows users to proceed more rapidly to the analysis stage and allows scholars to spend more time on theory development and on asking new research questions than on data management. It also facilitates replication by providing a single program for data set creation that will produce the same results for all users, eliminating the problem of hidden or forgotten steps typically encountered when attempting replication.

Usage Overview

Updates, details, and the material needed to replicate our results are available free of charge from the Inter-University Consortium on Political and Social Research (www.icpsr.org, study number 1290).

Users will normally use one of three main choices when they enter the program. Most often, users will choose to construct an output data set containing any or all of the variables discussed previously by using the "Create Data Set" menu. A tabbed window provides the option for users to set the unit of analysis, population of cases, variables, and output format for their output data. EUGene also forces choices on a variety of critical but often unstated assumptions about the construction of key dependent variables and the inclusion of problematic cases that go into the construction of international relations data sets (how to treat ongoing disputes, for example). The program then assembles an output data set according to these user specifications, handling necessary merges between different input data sets and creating command files to automate reading the data into other statistical programs. Second, users may recompute expected utility data (or various components of it) under the "Recompute" menu. Usually users do not need to do this, as we have already precalculated data where appropriate, and all variables available for selection within the program are ready for output. The recalculation options exist for users who wish to create new data sets to examine the sensitivity of the results to various assumptions; submenus under "Recompute" allow users to specify some of those conditions, such as what distance discounting method to use. Recalculating these data, especially recalculating risk attitude data, is quite time consuming. As a third possibility, users may decide to upload or download new add-on data sets for EUGene under the "User Data" menu. Downloading new data makes variables from other users' data sets available in the program. Users may also upload their own data sets to www.eugenesoftware.org for eventual inclusion as possible downloads by others.

Unit of Analysis

The first choice made by users when creating a new data set in EUGene is the unit of analysis. Users choose to create data sets with the country-year, directed dyad-year, nondirected dyad-year, directed dispute-dyad, and directed dispute-dyad-year as the unit of analysis. By selecting these units of analysis, users can examine monadic time-series (by creating a country-year data set), examine dispute initiation from a condition of peace or examine the duration of peace (by creating a directed or nondirected dyad-year data set), examine the escalation of disputes (by creating a directed dispute-dyad data set), or examine the evolution and duration of disputes over time (by creating a directed dispute-dyad-year data set). Clearly, EUGene is particularly useful when creating data sets with the dyad-year as the unit of analysis. Scholars have increasingly come to use data sets based on the dyad-year to conduct quantitative analyses. This is because dyadic interaction lies at the heart of strategic international behavior and because it is possible to combine explanations from multiple levels of analysis in one quantitative study, as we have done here. Most scholars rely on annual data both because data is widely available at this level of temporal aggregation and because the year represents a natural political break due to budget cycles, electoral cycles, and the presence of winter or a rainy season that in many areas hampers military action.[1]

Variables

Users specify the variables that are to be included in the output data set by clicking on a set of check boxes. The program as currently distributed allows users to choose from a set of over sixty variables from several of the most important international relations data sets. Variables that can currently be selected for inclusion include Polity III democracy scores and ancillary components (Jaggers and Gurr 1995), COW project capability data (Singer, Bremer, and Stuckey 1972), data on interstate distances, alliance data, tau$_b$ scores, S scores (Signorino and Ritter 1999), risk attitude data, contiguity data, region, peace years (Beck, Katz, and Tucker 1998), expected utility values and international interaction game equilibrium predictions (Bueno de Mesquita and Lalman 1992), COW MID data (Jones, Bremer, and Singer 1996), and the Maoz dyadic implementation of them (Maoz 1999). Users may also download additional data sets that have been submitted to the EUGene Web site by other users of the program. They may also upload new data to our Web site for inclusion in EUGene. When such user data sets are placed in the appropriate program directory, EUGene automatically makes the variables that they contain available for selection.

Population of Cases

The scope of output data from EUGene may be set as either all dyad-years or some specified subset of countries and years. Users can specify a particular range of years for output (e.g., 1945–92 or 1816–1914) and can select from commonly used subsets of countries (e.g., all dyads, politically relevant dyads, major power dyads, contiguous states, or a user-selected list such as rivals). Alternatively, users may generate all dyad-years and include variables in the output (such as a "politically relevant" dummy marker) to allow selection at a later time. The creation of various case subsets allows users to conduct contingency analyses and to explore the sensitivity of their results to factors like era or region.

Case Inclusion Criteria and Assumptions

EUGene forces users to make specific choices concerning the inclusion or exclusion of potentially problematic data points related to dependent variable codings and case censoring. EUGene forces choices on three specific issues. The first concerns years with ongoing militarized disputes. EUGene allows users to either drop or include dyad-years where the countries begin the year with an ongoing dispute (users may want to drop such cases if they believe that a new initiation would be censored by the ongoing dispute).[2]

The second issue concerns the treatment of dyads where a state joins into a dispute that is already in progress. Should joiners be included for analysis in the same way as dispute initiators? We have argued that the information conditions faced by joiners into disputes is fundamentally different than the conditions facing the initial participants and omit joiners from analysis. Others may disagree. EUGene allows users to include or to drop such cases by selecting a check box.

The final issue concerns "target versus initiator" directed dyads. When one state initiates a dispute, it does so against a target state, creating a designated initiator A and target B. But when A initiates versus B, it is less than clear how to include the directed dyad B versus A, because true behavior in the B versus A dyad may be censored. EUGene gives users the option to include such target versus initiator dyads in the data sets it creates, to drop them, or to include them only if there is a subsequent initiation by B versus A.

Merging and Data Conversion

One difficulty with building data sets that combine variables is that input data sets frequently come with different units of analysis and in different formats, requiring conversion at a fundamental level in addition to simply merging. For example, many key IR data sets have the country-year as the unit of analysis (e.g., the COW national capability data, Gurr Polity data, or data on national risk attitude). Other data sets (or data constructions) have the dyad as the unit of analysis, such as distance data, the COW contiguity data set, or data on expected utility. Still other data sets are distributed in a hybrid form, such as the COW MID data set, which is dyadic and annual in its underlying form but comes distributed as three separate files that must be merged together. EUGene carries out necessary conversions among the formats, file structures, and differing units of analysis of these data sets automatically as part of the merging process.

Dispute Data Conversion to Dyads

The COW MID data set (Jones, Bremer, and Singer 1996) is commonly used to create most dependent variables in recent quantitative international relations studies. However, prior to 2003 the COW project has not distributed this data in a dyadic form. Converting the data to a dyadic format involves checking states for their involvement as originators or joiners, identifying states as initiators or targets (the initiator is the side of the MID that first crosses the militarized threshold, side A in the MID data), and pairing into dyads. Appropriately pairing states as "real" dyads rather than simply participants on opposite sides of a multilateral dispute involves checking to be sure that the states are actually involved on opposite sides at the same time (some simple conversions do not perform this check). The procedure to make appropriate pairings from the COW MID version 2.1 data set (Correlates of War 1999) involves reading data from three files, two of which have the dispute as the unit of analysis (one record per dispute) and one of which has the country involvement as the unit of analysis (one record per state involved in the dispute per dispute). Country-dispute-level information in the data set must be matched to the dispute-level data, and multiple country-dispute-level records must be matched to each other to obtain dyadic pairings. EUGene does this automatically.

Zeev Maoz has recently developed a dyadic version of the MID data (Maoz 1999) that is designed to correct problems involved in converting the original MID data into dyadic format. While Maoz begins by converting the original MID data sets into a dyadic format, much as EUGene does, he then conducts a variety of additional checks intended to verify that actual disputatious interaction occurred between the members of the dyad. Maoz's data are available as an alternative version of the dispute variables within EUGene.

Dependent Variable Coding

Scholars have made a number of arguments about the appropriate unit of analysis in international relations studies and about coding the origins of militarized disputes as a dependent variable in those analyses. In a directed dyad setting, the initiation of a dispute is the appropriate coding of dispute. The COW MID operationalization of initiator in practice is that the initiator is the "first mover," that is, the state who first crosses the MID threshold and makes the first threat or actual use or movement of forces. This definition of "initiator" gains clarity in terms of the temporal ordering of actions while losing any attempt to get at intent. An alternative image of the initiator that comes to mind is the predatory state that decides to engage in conflict against a state that wants to remain at peace. This may or may not be the state that moves first. EUGene allows users to specify an alternative coding for dispute initiators (which also comes from the MID data set) as those who are "revisionist" states.

A second issue has to do with whether the directed initiation of militarized disputes can be measured in a meaningful fashion (see the discussion in chapter 2). If users select nondirected dyads as the unit of analysis, the occurrence of MIDs is automatically measured and output as dispute "onset" rather than dispute "initiation" as it is in directed dyad data sets.

A final issue of dependent variable coding lies in the treatment of disputes that continue for more than one year. We have argued that only the first year of a new MID should be coded as a dispute initiation and that subsequent years of multiyear disputes should be dropped. Others who believe that our models should do equally well at predicting the continuation as well as the initiation of MIDs argue that we should code ongoing dispute years as a "1" as well as just the first year. EUGene allows users to specify either that only the first year of a MID is coded as a dispute initiation or that all years of a continuing MID are coded as dispute initiations.

Output Format and Use of Other Software

EUGene is not an analysis program but rather a data management utility. As a result, the merged data created by EUGene must be read into and analyzed by other statistical software. Users may then conduct analysis immediately or more likely will wish to compute additional variables on the basis of the data created by EUGene. EUGene's output files are created in a uniform format that can be read easily into any statistical analysis software. Data may be tab-delimited (tab characters are placed between values in the data file), space delimited, or comma delimited. EUGene also creates the command files necessary to import the data into SPSS, STATA, or LIMDEP; the command files both read the raw variables and set missing values appropriately. After creating a data set, users can then have the data up and running in these statistics programs in a matter of minutes.

Expected Utility Data

Users of EUGene may take advantage of the expected utility data sets and variables that come with the software. In its life as a data generation program, EUGene generates expected utility data for all dyads and years for which raw input data are available, following the methods developed in Bueno de Mesquita and Lalman 1992 and starting from first principles. Any interested user can view the complete code for these calculations in the form of EUGene's source code. EUGene actually has several intended uses vis-à-vis expected utility data. Most obviously, the availability of complete expected utility and IIG equilibrium predictions allows us to test arguments about the IIG and the expected utility theory of war in a much broader setting. A key goal was to implement the methods of previous expected utility calculations, which Bueno de Mesquita and others published across a number of books and articles, in a single, easily accessible package. Expected utility data is generated from first principles using the most recent updates to the COW alliance, national capabilities, and MID data sets to ensure that researchers have the most accurate expected utility estimates possible and to ensure transparency and further replication. By making data on all dyads available, EUGene also allows us to test previously unexamined arguments about expected utility. For example, with data generated by EUGene, it is possible to examine systematic differences across regions or time periods or to look for systematic variation in risk-taking propensities between countries.

Technical Information

EUGene runs under Microsoft Windows 95, 98, NT (version 4.0 or higher), 2000, and XP on IBM-compatible PCs with at least 16 MB of memory.[3] The program has a standard Windows program interface. EUGene is written in Borland, Inc.'s *Delphi* programming environment, an object-oriented Rapid Application Development package designed to create Windows programs, relying on a Pascal base. Version 2 of the program consists of approximately 36,000 lines of computer code split into eighty-five units and Windows forms. The program is copyrighted but is available as a free download from www.eugenesoftware.org. The downloadable program includes the main program executable file (about 1.4 MB), complete (eighty-page) documentation of the program, EUGene's source code, and the complete expected utility data described here. In addition to providing instructions for how to use the program, the program documentation further details the computations involved in making expected utility calculations, lists the variables available for output, and outlines key algorithms used in the program.

APPENDIX B
MEASURING EXPECTED UTILITY

A theory of particular interest in our analysis is the so-called expected utility theory of war (Bueno de Mesquita 1981, 1985a; Bueno de Mesquita and Lalman 1992). While being one of the most important current theories of international conflict, the general IIG variant of expected utility theory has until recently only been tested on a small set of cases.[1] This is because expected utility data has not been available for all dyads and over the full time span of most other international relations data sets (1816 through the 1980s or 1990s, depending on the data set). Replication of Bueno de Mesquita's data has been slow, in part because of substantial barriers inherent in replicating data construction algorithms and finding adequate computational capacity for creating this data.[2] EUGene (see appendix A) seeks to solve this problem by generating the data needed to test the IIG more broadly. This appendix details the operationalizations and methods followed to create expected utility data and IIG predictions.

The critical variables for testing the IIG version of the expected utility theory of war are the game-theoretic equilibrium predictions that emerge from the game structure plus data on the utility of the game outcomes. Making a prediction of the game's equilibrium at any point in time in turn depends on a variety of input data on national capabilities and alliances, which combine to create estimates of states' utility for outcomes.

STEPS IN EXPECTED UTILITY DATA GENERATION

EUGene takes as raw inputs a number of data sets, including national capability data, alliance data, country independence dates, contiguity data, and geographical location data. The program then computes the

COW national capabilities index, tau_b scores for all dyads, risk attitudes of all states for all regions, and finally states' expected utilities for war, negotiation, the status quo, and the other possible outcomes of the IIG. Finally, EUGene uses the states' utility scores to predict the outcome expected in equilibrium for each directed dyad-year in the interstate system. Appendix 1 of *War and Reason* (Bueno de Mesquita and Lalman 1992) contains the detailed formulas for the full operationalizations of the terms needed to estimate utilities and in turn the final IIG equilibrium predictions (with two clarifications made later). The software provides users with some options for modifying these calculations. For instance, users can modify the capability data used as input and regenerate utility predictions for sensitivity analysis and may choose to use either tau_b or Signorino and Ritter's (1999) S score as the measure of alliance portfolio similarity used in calculations. The steps carried out by EUGene to create final IIG equilibrium predictions are as follows (details of each part of the computation follow):

- The individual components of national capabilities are assembled into the COW national capabilities index for every country-year (Singer, Bremer, and Stuckey 1972).
- COW alliance data are used to calculate the tau_b score for each directed dyad in each year in the international system. Such scores are directed because the states included in computing tau_b scores depend on the region in which they are expected to interact (Bueno de Mesquita 1978; 1981, 94–97).
- Geographic location and contiguity data is used to create the distance between each pair of states, with changes over time due to major territorial changes taken into account.[3]
- Distance, tau_b, and capability data are combined to create an estimate of the expected utility of war for each directed dyad-year. The initial utility computation follows the methods in *The War Trap* but does not adjust expected utility for risk attitude using *The War Trap*'s risk method. That is, the scores generated are the sum of the bilateral and multilateral expected utility components (Bueno de Mesquita 1981, 59, eq. 6) but do not take the final step of introducing risk attitude. (These initial utility scores are necessary to estimate risk attitude by updated methods in the next step.)
- The initial expected utility values from the prior step are used to produce estimates of states' risk attitudes for all years and with respect to each region in the system following the methods of Bueno de Mesquita (1985a). First, alliance data and

expected utility data are used to generate actual (realized) national security portfolios for all state-years. Hypothetical alliance data is then used to generate potential maximum and minimum security portfolios for all state-years. The hypothetical security values are compared to actual security to compute each state's annual risk attitude; the closer a state is to its security-maximizing alliance portfolio, the more risk-averse it is.

- Tau_b scores and risk attitude scores are combined following the methods of *War and Reason* (Bueno de Mesquita and Lalman 1992, 293–94, eqs. A1.1–A1.6) to produce estimates of states' utility for the status quo, their most preferred international political position vis-à-vis the opponent, and their least preferred international political position. These are the estimates of $U^A(SQ)$, $U^A(\Delta_A)$, and $U^A(\Delta_B)$ for each directed dyad-year A-B.

- Tau_b scores, distance data, national capability data, and risk attitude scores (for state A, state B, and third-party states within the relevant region of conflict) are combined following equations A1.7 to A1.10 of Bueno de Mesquita and Lalman 1992 (294–97) to produce estimates of the probability of success P^A for state A in a military conflict against B, taking into account the likely behavior of possible interveners.

- The domestic cost term Φ is measured (Bueno de Mesquita and Lalman 1992, 297) as $U^A(SQ)$. Following the actual method of constructing variables that Bueno de Mesquita and Lalman used (Bueno de Mesquita, personal communication), the other cost terms α, τ, and γ are set to 1.0, because although these terms are defined theoretically and are included as part of the expected utility equations, Bueno de Mesquita and Lalman have no way to measure them empirically. Without this assumption, complete measurements could not be constructed.[4]

- The utility measurements $U^A(SQ)$, $U^A(\Delta_A)$, and $U^A(\Delta_B)$, the probability of success P^A, and cost terms are combined following table 2.2 of Bueno de Mesquita and Lalman 1992 (47) to produce estimates of the utility of each of the eight outcomes of the IIG for each directed dyad-year.

- The equilibrium outcome of the IIG played under complete and perfect information conditions is computed for each directed dyad-year, using the two states' utilities for each of the eight IIG outcomes. Equilibria were generated using backward induction; EUGene offers the option to follow equivalently the logical conditions in Bueno de Mesquita and Lalman 1992 (72–92).[5] For every directed dyad-year, the sixteen final expected utility values corresponding to the utilities of states A and B are used to compute equilibria.

In addition to final equilibrium predictions, most of the separate components used in computing them are available for output as separate variables from EUGene. In particular, tau_b scores, S scores, risk scores and underlying security values, and the individual expected utility components may be selected for inclusion in output data sets.

CALCULATIONS AND FORMULAS: DETAILS

EUGene undertakes a number of calculations leading up to the computation of expected utility values and IIG equilibria and uses a number of variables as follows:

National Capabilities/Percent System Capabilities

EUGene calculates the COW composite national capabilities index as developed by Singer, Bremer, and Stuckey (1972). This is an index of a state's proportion of total system capabilities in six areas: the country's iron/steel production, the country's urban population, the country's total population, the country's total military expenditures, the country's total military personnel, and the country's total amount of energy production. First, the state's proportion of total system capabilities in each area is calculated, and second, the average is taken across all of the areas for that state in which data is not missing. This variable can be computed from 1816 to 1993. (However, note that the data for 1991 to 1993 are *substantially* less complete in the COW input data files than for other years, leading to values for national capabilities that are quite suspect for those years.) EUGene does not systematically impute missing data, nor have we gathered additional data for this study, although we filled in missing energy data for Britain to 1850 (see on-line EUGene documentation for details and values; if users recompute national capabilities, they have the option of using the modified data on Britain). When data in one of the six capability areas are missing for a state, then that proportion is missing. We take the average for a state across all of the proportions that are not missing. So, if a state has no data on energy, for instance, its capabilities are the average across the five other areas.

Tau$_b$ Calculation

The Kendall's tau$_b$ correlation calculation performed by EUGene is based on the calculation used in Bueno de Mesquita 1975 and 1981. Here, the Kendall tau$_b$ is a rank order correlation for two states' alliance portfolios. The alliances of each state are combined into a 4 × 4 table where alliances are ranked as 1 (defense pact), 2 (neutrality pact), 3 (entente), and 4 (no alliance). Tau$_b$ is calculated from this 4 × 4 table and ranges from −1 to +1, representing totally opposite alliance agreement patterns to complete agreement in the alliances formed. The actual algorithm used to calculate tau$_b$ within EUGene was obtained from Hays 1981 (603–4).

When generating tau$_b$, EUGene generates what we refer to as both "regional" and "global" taus. The global tau is the tau$_b$ score when all states in the international system are included. The regional tau between states A and B is calculated from a 4 × 4 alliance matrix that includes only states in the "relevant region" of the directed dyad A versus B (the critical concept of "relevant region" is defined later). Bueno de Mesquita in his calculations uses only the regional taus; we follow this procedure. Global taus are calculated and are available for information only, as subsequent calculations use only the regional conception. Also note that in *War and Reason* Bueno de Mesquita and Lalman (1992, 291) modify any tau$_b$ equal to 1.0 to be 0.999 in expected utility calculations. We make the same modification when we compute utility and equilibria values. However, when tau$_b$ scores are selected as a variable in an output data set, we present the calculated values without this modification.

Alliance data from COW is available from 1816 to 1984. We use this data as corrected in Bennett 1997 to account for alliance terminations that were not correctly coded by COW. We also update this data using information gathered by Dan Reiter (2000) on new alliances and alliance terminations since 1984. Tau can then be calculated to 1992.

S *Calculation*

The S "similarity" calculation on alliance portfolios performed by EUGene is based on the formula developed by Signorino and Ritter (1999). Signorino and Ritter argue that S represents a significant improvement over tau$_b$ for measuring the similarity of alliance portfolios. In particular, they note that, while tau$_b$ is an excellent measure of rank order similarity, it has inherent flaws that allow a variety of alliance portfolios to have identical tau$_b$ results, which affect studies intended to look beyond rank order similarity. Like the Kendall tau$_b$, S evaluates the rank order correlation for two states' alliance portfolios. Unlike tau$_b$, S also takes into account both the presence and the absence of alliances in the correlation calculation. That is, the fact that a state has identical alliances with some states as well as no alliances with other states is accounted for by S calculation but not by tau$_b$.

Like tau$_b$, EUGene calculates S on both regional and global levels, with the same country inclusion criteria as with the tau$_b$ calculation (see previous discussion). In addition, S is calculated in both weighted and unweighted forms (the weighted version weights different alliances by incorporating country capabilities). The regional and unweighted S values are used for the construction of the expected utility computations used here. We calculate S for 1816–1992 using alliance data as discussed previously.

Relevant Region and Regional Identification

The concept of "relevant region" is necessary for almost all expected utility–related calculations about a dyad. Various expected utility calculations use information on the states defined as being "involved in" a region politically and refer to the "relevant region" for the directed dyad A versus B. Each directed dyad A versus B is considered to have a single relevant region where interaction is expected (see Bueno de Mesquita 1981, 97 n. 3); only countries for whom a region is relevant are included in related calculations. The general purpose of identifying the regions in which states are involved politically is to estimate the behavior only of relevant states in various calculations, taking into account only states somewhat likely to become involved or otherwise show support. For example, if tau$_b$ is calculated between the United States and Britain in 1880, it would be plausible to include countries in North and South America in the calculation, as well as all countries in Europe. It would be less plausible to include countries in Africa, because the United States was largely unconcerned with colonialism in Africa at that time. As another example, an alliance between Zaire and Zimbabwe is likely to be irrelevant for the behavior of Chile toward Brazil and should be ignored when computing the tau$_b$ score between Chile and Brazil. Bueno de Mesquita defined the concept of "relevant region" to exclude meaningless interactions from the computation of key variables (such as tau$_b$, S, and security levels) contributing to expected utility calculations.

The basis for regional involvement comes from the COW project's regional membership identification. States are defined by COW as belonging to particular world regions; states are always considered to be "involved in" any interaction in their home region. States are coded as being involved outside their home region following Bueno de Mesquita 1981 (95–98). For example, while the home region of the United States is North America, the United States is considered by Bueno de Mesquita to be involved in Europe from 1899 on. Dates of extraregional involvement are coded as follows:

Other states involved in the "Americas" region: Spain, Portugal, United Kingdom, France, Holland/Netherlands from 1816 to the present; Russia/USSR throughout the nineteenth century (i.e., 1816–99) and from 1946 to the present.

Other states involved in the "Europe" region: Turkey from 1816 to the present; United States from 1898 to the present; Japan from 1895 to 1945; China from 1950 to the present.

Other states involved in the "Asia" region: Britain, France, Germany, Holland/Netherlands, Spain, Portugal, United States, Russia/USSR from 1816 to the present.

Other states involved in the "Middle East" region: Austria-Hungary from 1816 to 1918; Italy from 1860 to 1943; United Kingdom, France, Germany, Russia/USSR from 1816 to the present; Spain from 1816 to 1936; United States from 1898 to the present; Greece from 1828 to the present.

Other states involved in the "Africa" region: United States from 1946 to the present; Italy from 1816 to 1943; Prussia/Germany from 1816 to 1945; Belgium, Portugal, Russia/USSR, Britain, France from 1816 to the present; China from 1946 to the present.

Once the regions of states' political involvement are known, the relevant region of a dyadic interaction may be precisely operationalized. Normally dyads have as the relevant region the region of the potential target, so in dyad A versus B, B's region is defined as the relevant region. An exception occurs in dyads where the (potential) initiator A and target B are from different regions and where the initiator is *not* involved in the opponent's region based on the criteria discussed previously. In this case the relevant region of the dyad is considered to be the initiator's region. So, for example, the relevant region for both Britain versus Thailand and Thailand versus Britain is Asia, and only countries involved in Asia in a given year would be included in tables for creating tau_b scores, risk scores, and so forth.

Uncertainty

Bueno de Mesquita and Lalman (1992, 298) operationalize uncertainty as the variance in risk-taking scores. EUGene computes this variance across all states in either the home region of an individual state or the relevant region of the dyad when a dyad (A versus B) is under consideration.

Distance

The EUGene method for distance calculation is a generalized, uniform version of the state-to-state distance calculation used in *The War Trap*. There, Bueno de Mesquita calculated actual port-to-port sea distances and capital-to-capital air distances from various reference sources. We compute distance by taking the latitude and longitude of international cities and applying the "great circle" navigation distance formula to compute distance (Fitzpatrick and Modlin 1996). This method has the advantage of consistency and replicability, avoiding a variety of issues in replicating shortest sea route distances given uncertain air and sea routes. Following Fitzpatrick and Modlin (xi):

$$Cos(D) = (Sin(L1) \times Sin(L2)) + (Cos(L1) \times Cos(L2) \times Cos(DiffLo)),$$

where

L1 = the latitude of place 1,
L2 = the latitude of place 2,
DiffLo = the difference in longitude between place 1 and 2,
D = the arc distance (in degrees) between places 1 and 2.

Within the formula, northern latitudes must be specified as positive and southern latitudes as negative; eastern longitudes must be specified as positive values and western longitudes as negative. Given the arc distance D, distance in miles can be computed by multiplying D by the average number of miles per degree, 69.16.

For most dyads, we used the national capitals as the ends of the curve to compute distance. However, in the case of the United States and USSR, we used multiple cities as described in *The War Trap*, using the shortest distance. States with land borders are considered to be zero miles apart because it is expected that states can readily move forces within their national borders. The 1993 version of the COW contiguity data set is used in these calculations.

Expected Utility Calculation (The War Trap)

The expected utility for war in each dyad calculated following the methods of Bueno de Mesquita (1981) is an important stepping stone to calculating risk scores as needed for final IIG utility and equilibrium computations. Expected utility following *The War Trap* methods is generated as the sum of the bilateral and multilateral expected utility components of the formulas in Bueno de Mesquita 1981 but without risk attitude taken into account (because the resulting estimates are used to compute risk attitude following improved methods!). These computed values (available as an output variable in EUGene) are not expected to equal exactly those reported in *The War Trap*, as we use updated data, and data in *The War Trap* use an early operationalization of risk attitude. The formula for the bilateral component of expected utility in a dyad i versus j is

$$\text{EU\_bilateral}_{ij} = P_i \times (1 - U_{ij}) + (1 - P_i) \times (U_{ij} - 1)$$

$$\text{(Bueno de Mesquita 1981, 47, eq. 1),}$$

where

$U_{ij} = \text{tau}(i, j)$
$P_i = \text{adj\_cap}_{ij} / (\text{adj\_cap}_{ij} + \text{adj\_cap}_{jj})$
adj_cap_{ij} is i's capabilities adjusted for distance to j, and
adj_cap_{jj} is j's capabilities adjusted for distance to j (which is a
0 adjustment).

The formula for adjusted capabilities is

$$\text{adj\_cap}_{ij} = \text{raw\_cap}_{ij}{}^{\log10[\text{miles/miles per day}) + (10 - e)]}$$

$$\text{(Bueno de Mesquita 1981, 105),}$$

where

raw_cap$_{ij}$ is the COW composite capabilities score,
distance is computed using the method given above,
miles per day equal 250 from 1816 to 1918, 375 from 1919 to
    1945, and 500 from 1946 onward.

The formula for the multilateral component of expected utility in
dyad *ij* is

$$EU\_multilateral_{ij} = \sum_{k}((P_{ik} + P_{jk} - 1)*(U_{iki} - U_{ikj}))$$

(Bueno de Mesquita 1981, 58, eq. 5),

where

P_{ik} is *i*'s perception of its probability of success versus *j*, given
    that state *k* aids *i*,
P_{jk} is *i*'s perception of its probability of losing versus *j*, given
    that state *k* aids *j*,
U_{iki} is *i*'s perception of *k*'s utility for *i* [= tau(*k*,*i*)]
U_{ikj} is *i*'s perception of *k*'s utility for *j* [= tau(*k*,*j*)].
The sum is over all third states *k* involved in the relevant
    region, that is, *k* involved_in relevant_region(*i*, *j*) and *k* <> *i*
    and *k* <> *j*.

P_{ik} and P_{jk} are estimated as follows (Bueno de Mesquita 1981, 108–9):

P_{ik} = (adj_cap$_{ij}$ + max(adj_cap$_{kj}$, adj_cap$_{ki}$)) /
        (adj_cap$_{ij}$ + max(adj_cap$_{kj}$, adj_cap$_{ki}$) + adj_cap$_{jj}$);
P_{jk} = (adj_cap$_{ji}$ + max(adj_cap$_{ki}$, adj_cap$_{kj}$)) /
        (adj_cap$_{ji}$ + max(adj_cap$_{ki}$, adj_cap$_{kj}$) + adj_cap$_{ii}$);

where adj_cap$_{kj}$ is *k*'s capabilities adjusted for distance to *j* and so
    forth.

The final expected utility calculation based upon *The War Trap* formulas combines the expected utilities for bilateral war and multilateral
war (Bueno de Mesquita 1981, 59, eq. 6):

$$EU\_final_{ij} = EU\_bilateral_{ij} + EU\_multilateral_{ij}.$$

Because this measure is dependent on tau$_b$ or *S* (and hence alliance)
data, it can be computed from 1816 to 1984 with the COW sequenced

alliance data or from 1816 to 1992 if Reiter's (2000) alliance data update is selected.

Risk Attitude

The calculation of risk attitude used in computing IIG equilibria is based on the method in Bueno de Mesquita 1985a. Risk scores are based on the sum of other states' utility toward a state and whether a state chooses to form an alliance portfolio that leaves it relatively vulnerable or relatively invulnerable to other states. If states form alliances that leave themselves relatively vulnerable, then they are said to be risk acceptant, while if they form alliances that keep them relatively safe, then they are said to be more risk averse. The risk operationalization begins with the concept of a "security level" for a state i, representing its vulnerability. First, define state i's actual security level as $\sum_{j \neq i} E(U_{ji})$, that is, the sum of all other states' expected utilities versus i. Then define $\sum E(U_{ji})_{max}$ as the security level associated with the hypothetical alliance pattern that would leave i most vulnerable to defeat (when i is vulnerable, the sum of other states' EU against i is large). Similarly, define $\sum E(U_{ji})_{min}$ as the security level associated with the hypothetical alliance pattern that would leave i least vulnerable to defeat, that is, in the best possible security position. Then,

$$\text{Risk}_i = \frac{2\sum E(U_{ji}) - \sum E(U_{ji})_{max} - \sum E(U_{ji})_{min}}{\sum E(U_{ji})_{max} - \sum E(U_{ji})_{min}}.$$

$\text{Risk}_i = R_i$ in the notation of Bueno de Mesquita 1985a. This formula is in essence the distance between a state's actual security level and its best and worst possible security level. This score ranges from -1 to $+1$, with -1 indicating a highly risk-averse actor and a $+1$ indicating a highly risk-acceptant actor.

Risk scores are computed for a state concerning each region of the world; a state may have a different risk attitude toward different regions (e.g., the United States might be risk averse toward Europe and quite risk acceptant concerning Africa). Since these scores are region based, the previous sums are over the set of states k, with k defined as the set of states involved in the region in question.

Bueno de Mesquita (1985a) further transforms R_i to r_i, where r_i ranges from 0.5 to 2. In the transformed r_i, a value of 0.5 corresponds to a risk-acceptant actor, while a value of 2 corresponds to a risk-averse actor; note that this reverses the "polarity" of risk acceptance and risk aversion. The variable r_i is used in calculations of expected utility, as per *War and Reason,* appendix 1. However, EUGene does not report r_i in its output. Because this measure is dependent on tau or S (and hence alliance) data, it can be computed from 1816 to 1984 if COW sequenced alliance data is used or to 1992 if Reiter's alliance data is used. Risk data computed using either tau_b or S are available for output. We use S-based calculations in generating the final data we analyze here.

Programming the algorithm to compute risk attitude scores following these definitions, and then generating actual risk scores, was perhaps the most challenging programming and computational task in EUGene. Finding the combination of alliances to maximize or minimize security scores as described previously is extremely difficult. An examination of any single potential alliance configuration in which i could find itself is not difficult, as it requires only the recalculation of each $E(U_{ji})$ and then a resumming of security, typically a computation and sum of about twenty-five countries (twenty-five countries would be typical of Europe). However, the number of *hypothetical* alliance configurations that a state could create (constituting the search space for the computation problem) is huge. The search space consists of all possible alliance patterns between state i and the other states involved in i's region; in a region of twenty-five countries and with four types of alliances (defense, neutrality, entente, or no alliance), the search space would be 4^{24} potential alliance patterns, or nearly 300 trillion combinations for a single country-region-year of data. Because it is impossible to examine exhaustively this space for even one country, let alone the 11,000 country-years that constitute the international system from 1816 to 1993, a search procedure is necessary. Bueno de Mesquita (1985a) computed hypothetical risk scores by sampling 30,000 configurations per year (not per country-year or per region-year) from this space and selecting the global minimum and maximum from this search as the hypothetical maximum and minimum for all states. We instead optimized our search by programming a genetic algorithm (Goldberg 1989; Holland 1975) that performs a more efficient evaluation of between 1,000 and 2,000 configurations per state per region per year. Our search examines roughly two orders of magnitude more hypothetical alliances, searches more "intelligently" with the genetic algorithm, and examines only alliance configurations that each state i could actually find itself in (other states' alliances are held constant). As a result, we identify different (and more accurate) best and worst security configurations, leading to slightly different risk scores from those reported in Bueno de Mesquita 1985a.

More specifically, in creating the data distributed with EUGene, we generated risk scores using the genetic algorithm with initial populations of between twenty and thirty alliance configurations, a mutation probability of 0.05 per state per alliance configuration per iteration, and assumed stability after eight generations without a change in the optimum security value found. We used a single crossover point and "cloned" the best two configurations from each generation to include in the subsequent generation. Variations on these parameters, in particular increases in population size, only occasionally improved the optima identified. After this best point was identified by the genetic algorithm, a random walk was followed to ensure that a true local optimum was reported (that is, an alliance configuration at which no adjacent configurations were better). Thus our optimization method was in the end a hybrid optimization method in which the genetic algorithm found the largest hills, and in the last iteration, a random search was used to follow that hill to its peak. When time and multiple computers are available, further work could repeat the optimization with bigger populations and longer stable time to increase further the accuracy of the maximum/minimum identification. EUGene can easily accommodate such changes in specification by the user. However, the program took approximately six months running on two 200 MHz Pentium Pro PCs to produce risk scores from 1816 to 1984, as used in initial publications in this project (e.g., Bennett and Stam 2000b, 2000c). More recently, it took six months to compute revised scores using S from 1816 to 1992 on a 600 MHz PC.

Utility (War and Reason)

Utility calculations are detailed in *War and Reason* (Bueno de Mesquita and Lalman 1992); the main expected utility formulas are given in table 2.2, while calculations are detailed in appendix 1. From the results of the measurements detailed there, the outcome utilities given in table 2.2 can be calculated empirically.

There are two important operational notes about those calculations specifically and about other items not initially relevant in Bueno de Mesquita and Lalman 1992. As mentioned previously, different values were not given to the parameters α, τ, and γ; Bueno de Mesquita and Lalman did not have empirical methods to distinguish between them. Although it is not entirely clear in the text, for operational purposes each of these parameters was set to a value of 1. Second, there is a slight inconsistency in the measurement of Φ, the domestic cost term in the utility equations. Theoretically, this cost term is expected to be positive and, more specifically, to range between 0 and 1. However, in the operationalization of the utility equations, the utility of the status quo is substituted to represent an increasing cost to a challenge as the status quo improves. As measured, the utility of the status quo ranges from -1 to $+1$. When this utility is negative, the calculations for other expected utility values may yield values that are inconsistent with the basic assumed preference orderings of the IIG detailed in Bueno de Mesquita and Lalman 1992 (47). This has an implication for generating predicted equilibria as described in the next section.[6]

Additional assumptions and explanatory notes are necessary as part of the extension of the expected utility computations around the world, as specific assumptions about regional inclusions are not laid out in Bueno de Mesquita and Lalman 1992. In the first case, consider the calculation of the initial utilities detailed in appendix 1 of *War and Reason*. $U^A(\Delta_A)$, $U^A(\Delta_B)$, and $U^A(SQ)$ refer to state A's utility for A's desired outcome, A's utility for B's desired outcome, and A's utility for the status quo, respectively. These utilities could be different between directed dyad A versus B and directed dyad B versus A. That is, A's utility for the status quo could be different when we consider A versus B than when we consider B versus A. The reason for this is that the relevant region of conflict for A versus B is sometimes different than the relevant region for B versus A. The risk scores of Λ (and B) could therefore differ in the calculation for dyad A versus B and B versus B, and similarly the alliance portfolio similarity values may differ.

We also need to make a particular assumption about regional relevance when considering the contributions of third states K to the expected utility of war for A versus B. For any dyad A versus B, there is a particular relevant region used for alliance portfolio similarity and risk scores. For figuring out the tau between some third party K and A, or K and B, there is also a relevant region. However, for those third parties K that must decide whether to support A or B in a conflict, the relevant region we use is not necessarily the relevant region for the primary dyad A versus B. Instead, we use the relevant region between K and A or K and B for making K-A and K-B tau calculations. The logic of this choice is that K is making a choice based on its policy preferences vis-à-vis A or B, which are related to a specific (relevant) region. K may not care about the region of conflict between A and B and so uses its own relevant region. As with calculations for expected utility following *The War Trap* methods, all states K that are involved in the relevant region of A versus B are included as possible supporters of A and B in the calculations. Again, though, when their alliance portfolio similarity scores with respect to A and B are calculated, the relevant region is considered to be region (K, A) or (K, B).

Normally, the utility values operationalized in appendix 1 of *War and Reason* are constructed so that the base conditions specified in table 2.3 are satisfied by construction. However, in a very few cases, due to rounding in the calculations, the value of negotiation appears to equal the value of acquiescence. The cases where this occurs are those where the probability of one side winning are so great that a negotiated settlement is only infinitesimally better than acquiescing.

Because the utility measure is dependent on tau_b or S (and hence alliance) data, it can be computed from 1816 to 1984 if COW data is used or to 1992 if Reiter's alliance data is used. In our earlier analyses, we used the unweighted version of S.

Equilibria (War and Reason)

Any combination of unique utility values will lead to one and only one expected outcome in equilibrium. It is this equilibrium prediction that makes *War and Reason* game theoretic rather than decision theoretic, as was *The War Trap. Equilibrium predictions should be used as predictors of outcomes rather than straight utility values.* Because this measure is dependent on tau or S (and hence alliance) data, it can be computed from 1816 to 1984 or 1992 using Reiter's data. Our equilibrium calculations run to 1992 and use the unweighted S scores.

Equilibria may be generated by either of two methods. First, for any given set of preference orderings (that is, given a set of computed utility values), backward induction may be used on a set of utility scores to solve the game and to predict the outcome. Second, the game may be solved to generate the set of logical conditions required for each equilibrium, and a case (set of utility values) may be evaluated against those conditions as to where it fits (this second method was used by Bueno de Mesquita and Lalman). EUGene allows equilibria to be generated using either method. Normally, these methods would produce the same result. However, because Φ ranges from -1 to $+1$ in the original operationalization employed in Bueno de Mesquita and Lalman 1992 rather than being strictly positive, as was assumed in specifying utility equations, some cases empirically appear to violate the basic assumed preference structure of the game. With phi used in this form, then, if the logical conditions from *War and Reason* are employed, *different equilibrium predictions may result than if backward induction is used.* When cases violate the basic preference orderings, then the logical conditions developed assuming that those basic conditions are met are the wrong conditions. EUGene provides a solution to this problem, as the user has the option under the "variables" tab of the main dyadic output window to generate equilibria either using the logical conditions given in Bueno de Mesquita and Lalman 1992 or using backward induction. If the user is concerned that the logical equilibrium conditions are not appropriate to the data, the logical conditions do not have to be used, given the option to carry out backward induction. We have found empirically that only a few cases are affected by this choice and that results do not change in the aggregate.

The logical conditions for each equilibrium predicted under complete information conditions are discussed in Bueno de Mesquita and Lalman 1992 (71–90). The combinations of preference orderings that must be satisfied to reach each equilibrium are as follows:

War_A (War started by A): Three conditions must all be met.

(1) $U_A(War_A) > U_A(Acq_A)$
(2) $U_B(Cap_A) > U_B(Nego)$
(3) $U_B(War_A) > U_B(Acq_B)$

Note that a fourth condition listed in Bueno de Mesquita and Lalman 1992 (72), $U_A(Cap_A) > U_A(War_B)$, must be dropped, because there is no way given current operationalization (where $U(War_A) = U(War_B)$) to simultaneously satisfy $U_A(War_A) > U_A(Acq_A)$ and $U_A(Cap_A) > U_A(War_B)$. Because this condition must be dropped, it is sometimes the case that a situation satisfies the logical conditions to be both a War_A equilibrium and a Status Quo (SQ) equilibrium. Users should think carefully about how to treat those cases where both equilibria are logically possible (for instance, by recoding the overlapping cases as SQ or War_A in sensitivity analysis). We treat these cases as War_A outcomes; the results are not significantly affected if we use the reverse coding.

War_B (War started by B): Never expected in equilibrium under complete information conditions.

Acq_A (Acquiescence by A): Either of two main sets of conditions may be satisfied that lead to Acq_A. Either

(1) $[U_A(Acq_A) > U_A(War_A)$ and $U_A(Acq_A) > U_A(Cap_A)$ and $U_B(Cap_A) > U_B(Nego)$ and $U_B(War_A) > U_B(Acq_B)]$

or

$[U_A(Cap_A) > U_A(War_A)$ and $U_B(Cap_A) > U_B(Nego)$ and *either*
(2.1) $U_B(War_A) > U_B(Cap_B)$ or
(2.2) $U_B(Cap_B) > U_B(War_A)$ and $U_A(Cap_A) > U_A(Cap_B)]$.

Acq_B (Acquiescence by B): Two main sets of conditions may be satisfied that lead to Acq_B. Either

(1) $[U_B(Cap_B) > U_B(War_A)]$
and either

(1.1) $U_A(Cap_B) > U_A(Nego)$ and $U_B(Nego) > U_B(Cap_A)$ and
$U_A(Cap_A) > U_A(War_B)$

or

(1.2) $U_A(Cap_B) > U_A(Nego)$ and $U_A(War_B) > U_A(Cap_A)$

or

(1.3) $U_A(Cap_B) > U_A(Cap_A)$ and $U_B(Cap_A) > U_B(Nego)$ and
$U_A(Cap_A) > U_A(War_B)]$

or

(2) $[U_B(War_A) > U_B(Cap_B)$
and
$U_A(War_A) > U_A(Cap_A)$ and $U_B(Cap_A) > U_B(Nego)$ and
$U_A(Cap_A) > U_A(War_B)$
and
$U_B(Acq_B) > U_B(War_A)]$.

Cap_A (Capitulation by A): Never expected in equilibrium under complete information conditions.

Cap_B (Capitulation by B): Never expected in equilibrium under complete information conditions.

SQ (Status Quo): Two conditions must hold: $U_A(SQ) > U_A(Nego)$ and $U_B(SQ) > U_B(Nego)$. Then, *one* of the following four conditions must also hold. Either

(1) $U_A(Cap_A) > U_A(War_B)$ and $U_B(War_A) > U_B(Cap_B)$ and
$U_B(Nego) > U_B(Cap_A)$

or

(2) $U_A(Nego) > U_A(Cap_B)$ and $U_A(Cap_A) > U_A(War_B)$ and
$U_B(Cap_B) > U_B(War_A)$ and $U_B(Nego) > U_B(Cap_A)$

or

(3) $U_A(War_B) > U_A(Cap_A)$ and $U_B(War_A) > U_B(Cap_B)$

or

(4) $U_A(Nego) > U_A(Cap_B)$ and $U_A(War_B) > U_A(Cap_A)$ and
$U_B(Cap_B) > U_B(War_A)$.

Nego (Negotiation): If the combination satisfies no other conditions, negotiation is expected.

NOTES

CHAPTER 1

1. Some recent theoretical and simulation-based research lends credence to Riker's pessimism. See Lewis and Schultz 2002.

2. For a detailed discussion of this debate and an alternative perspective, see Walt 1999.

3. See, for instance, Brooks 2000.

CHAPTER 2

1. Ray and Wang (1998) also advocate the use of dyads as a way of integrating levels of analysis in international politics. For a critical perspective on the use of dyad-years, see Raknerud and Hegre 1997.

2. Of course, many actual models are nonlinear in form; we use the typical regression equation to illustrate our argument.

3. There is a variety of statistical tests to help judge the severity of the problem, including the Hausman test, which we discuss in chapter 3. Unfortunately, the treatments are sometimes worse than the disease.

4. Of course, exceptions to this generalization exist. For example, Oneal and Russett (2001) go to some length to lay out the complementary effects of international organizations, democratic institutions, and international trade.

5. It would also be appropriate to use the median value as the baseline, as some of the variables have highly skewed distributions. For our analytic cut points, we used plus or minus one standard deviation. If we used plus or minus two standard deviations, the explanatory power of some of the variables would appear somewhat stronger.

CHAPTER 3

1. This approach does pose an interesting dilemma from the perspective of Kuhn's (1986) argument about paradigmatic shifts in the evolution of knowledge.

2. The list of books and articles that we associated with each theoretical perspective is in table 3.1, along with our annual count of citations.

3. Oneal and Russett (1999b) drop the ongoing years of the world wars,

leading to a data set with some, but not all, ongoing dispute/war years included.

4. We also considered Jackman's methods (1998, 2000). He examines several computational methods of dealing directly with errors and correlations over time in limited dependent variable data. Unfortunately, the solutions he presents are not practical, given data sets of the size we employ here.

5. See <http://www.stata.com/support/faqs/stat/repa.html>. See also Neuhaus, Kalbfleisch, and Hauck 1991, which considers the interpretations of the regression parameters in these two general approaches. Neuhaus, Kalbfleisch, and Hauck show that the parameters of cluster-specific (the fixed-effects estimator) and population-averaged models for correlated binary data describe different types of effects of the covariates on the response probabilities.

6. It might also be that the heterogeneity lies solely in the disturbance term. We discuss this possibility and corrections later.

7. Many statistics texts discuss multinomial logit in more detail, including Hanushek and Jackson 1977; Maddala 1983; and Greene 1993.

8. We use Stata 6.0 and 7.0 for our estimation. For the splines, our quartile cut points for the spline fell at six, fourteen, and twenty-six years.

9. More specifically, the steps involved in this procedure are as follows. (1) Start with the initial data and estimated coefficients. (2) Change the value on an independent variable of interest to a given value for all cases in the data. (3) Use the coefficients from the model to create predicted outcome probabilities for each case. Each case now has probabilities computed as if the case had the modified value of the independent variable of interest but with all other variables at their actual values. (4) Compute the average probabilities across the data set, giving an overall estimate of outcome probabilities at the specified variable value. (5) Repeat with different independent variable values and compare.

CHAPTER 4

1. For the first data sets on alliances, see Small and Singer 1969; Singer and Small 1966. On the size of alliances, see Olson and Zeckhauser 1966 for the seminal argument therein. For a complete survey of many of these issues, see Snyder 1990. On the origins of alliances, see Walt 1987. On the links between alliances and sovereignty, see Morrow 1993; Gartzke 1998; Siverson and Emmons 1991. For more on the pernicious effects of secret alliances, see Ritter 2001.

2. See Adler and Barnett 1998 and Deutsch 1957.

3. On the nature of signaling games, see Fearon 1994b, 1997; Morrow 1992; Schultz 1998; Kydd 1997.

4. See, for example, Lebow 1981 on the role of psychological processes in conflict escalation. For a more detailed explication of psychological constraints on decision making in foreign policy, see McDermott 1998.

5. We tried alternative measures, including a continuous measure and a three-year moving average, and obtained similar findings to those we report.

6. On risk-taking propensity and alternative views, see McDermott 1999. On satisfaction, see Lemke 2002; Lemke and Reed 2001.

7. For more detailed discussion of the role of norms, see Krasner 1983; Axelrod 1999; Cederman 2001; Risse-Kappen 1995b; Wendt 1999; Tannenwald 2003.

8. On institutional constraints, see Bueno de Mesquita et al. 2001. On audience costs, see Fearon 1994a; on signaling, see Fearon 1994b; Schultz 1999; Sartori 2002; Smith 1999. On problems associated with testing or differentiating signaling theories from other variants of linking democratic political institutions to conflict behavior, see Smith 1996a; Signorino 1999; Schultz 1999; Lewis and Schultz 2002.

9. Because they do not have a way to measure the magnitude of first-strike advantages, in a small number of empirical cases the status quo prediction and war prediction are not mutually exclusive. In such cases we assume that war is the equilibrium. This does not change our result (see appendix B, n. 5 for detailed discussion).

10. See also Henderson 1997; Maoz and Russett 1992.

11. Power transition models are closely related to hegemonic stability arguments, best known by the work of Robert Gilpin. We address this literature later. Brooks and Wohlforth (2002); Wohlforth (2000); Mastanduno (1998); and Keohane (1984) all address the effects of high concentrations of power versus systems characterized by more diffuse distributions of power.

12. Note that, although the model focuses on decisions, this conception of power transition theory is at odds with current formal bargaining theories of war, which in one variant argues that the simple dyadic balance of power should be unrelated to the incidence of conflict (Fearon 1996; Gartzke 1999). For a bargaining model consistent with some variants of power transition logic, see Wittman 2001.

13. In a variant on this test, we substituted joint satisfaction with the system leader for the pair's mutual satisfaction (dyadic tau_b) and obtained similar results to those we report.

14. For a recent review and update of polarity-based theories of international relations, see Schweller 1996

CHAPTER 5

1. A range of plus or minus one standard deviation corresponds to a change of -3.64 and $+3.84$ on the polity scale over ten years, respectively.

2. For space reasons, we present little discussion on the nature of individual variable distributions. This is a particularly interesting topic in the context of institutional democracy using the Gurr, Jaggers, and Moore (1989) measures. For more on this, see Gleditsch and Ward 1997. We also do not present results for fixed-effects analysis here, although we do address this question at length elsewhere and find little support for Green, Kim, and Yoon's (2001) claim that the democratic peace is simply an artifact of the typical study's focus on cross-sectional variance (Bennett and Stam 2000a).

3. The analysis in Bennett and Stam 2000a and Bennett and Rupert 2003 constructed the dependent variable specifically to more closely match the IIG's outcome categories. The downside of those efforts was that they were not able to control for the various alternative explanations that we are able to here. See also Morton's (1999) detailed discussion of issues with testing game theoretic models, which goes beyond the scope of the analysis here.

4. For a study in where this is more explicit, with the goal of assessing change in major power dispute behavior over time, see Pollins 1994.

5. Exceptions include the empirically driven rivalry literature (e.g., Bennett 1996; Diehl and Goertz 2000) and the theoretical work on war settlements, including studies by Fortna 2003; Werner 2000; and Smith and Stam 2002.

6. In terms of judging how well our statistical model fits the data, our choice of estimator limits the summary statistics we might normally use. Since we are working with a categorical dependent variable, conventional statistics such as the R^2 are unavailable or suspect. When we do employ the best measure for our situation, the McFadden "pseudo-R^2," we find a pseudo-R^2 for our models of 0.27 for the all-dyads analysis and 0.20 for the "politically relevant" dyads. This suggests a fit comparable to many other ordinary least squares (OLS) models in political science, and generally much better than competing models of international conflict fit to large data sets. Nevertheless, while suggestive, these figures still do not convey very well how we are doing in terms of predicting conflict, and the meaning of pseudo-R^2 measures is subject to debate (McFadden 1973). See Veall and Zimmerman (1996) for a discussion of various proposed pseudo-R^2 measures. They conclude that, for multinomial models, many pseudo-R^2 measures apart from the McFadden ones are not applicable, including the McKelvey and Zavoina (1975) pseudo-R^2, which otherwise performs the best out of a variety of options in mirroring the OLS R^2 (e.g., Windmeijer 1995). They also note the differences in interpretation that we could ascribe to the meaning of R^2 and in particular suggest that the use of R^2 to assess goodness of fit be seen in the context of a stream of research. For instance, they note that a researcher estimating econometric OLS regressions across countries might expect an R^2 of 0.8 or 0.9, while in other research an R^2 of 0.1 or 0.2 might be typical. In international relations research, a low R^2 is common and, in fact, is rarely reported in dyad-year analyses. As a way of making a more inclusive assessment of fit, we turn to graphic illustrations.

7. We only present figures with information for the all-dyads analysis. The differences between the figures here and ones for the politically relevant dyads are unremarkable.

CHAPTER 6

1. For a view that organizational decision making provides a hotbed of rationalist optimization, see the special issue of *International Organization* on rational institutional design (autumn 2001). For an original critique of rationality and large institutions, see Allison 1971.

2. In economics, preferences are assumed to be distributed normally, so while economists recognize that individuals' preferences may vary somewhat regarding their demand for objects that can be purchased with money, the extremes cancel each other out, allowing them to sleep at night while assuming the markets remain rational.

3. Certainly, some constraints on state action exist, but we argue that these are not formal rules that can be enforced by an actor outside the game. This also ignores the large literature on norms as representing formal rules and constraints on state behavior.

4. Lewis and Schultz's (2002) work is a notable exception and provides a rather damning critique of game theoretic approaches to international crisis bargaining models.

5. For a rather extreme version of this claim, and a discussion of possibly pernicious effects of regional "clumping of cultures," see Huntington 1996.

6. It is interesting to note that in general Wendt (1999) is not sanguine about our ability to test constructivist or social theory propositions, which is part of what we aim to do in this study.

7. An alternative view of this type of convergence might best be referred to as "cultural imperialism."

8. Bueno de Mesquita and Lalman label this category "war." We believe this label is inappropriate, because the category includes both wars (in the Singer and Small sense) and disputes short of war.

9. There are several possible start dates for dyadic interaction. One could argue, for instance, that the counter should begin in 1648 with the signing of the treaty of Westphalia. We follow the COW convention of 1816.

10. We cannot include a variable "year" to examine the evolution of the international system or specific dyads because we know that there are more disputes over time because there are more dyads.

11. These results are rather sensitive to the means used to generate the equilibria and to the controls included in the model. Given the difficulties in estimation we face once the data is divided into regions and periods, issues clearly exist with empirically examining the universality argument. In previous work (Bennett and Stam 2000b), we generated results using Bueno de Mesquita's tau$_b$ measure of alliances similarity as opposed to Signorino's S an improved measure that we use here. Using tau$_b$, we also found variation across space and time, although the specifics differ somewhat.

12. In this case, we are able to obtain good estimates even after including controls, but we report these results to maintain comparability to table 5.6. The results with controls are very similar to these.

CHAPTER 7

1. Models were run on a 1.0 GHz Pentium-based machine running Gauss code of Smith's (1998) design.

APPENDIX A

1. If scholars wish to use data sets with a subannual level of temporal aggregation—for example, the quarter—EUGene is not an appropriate tool. But if scholars wish to create data sets with a longer aggregation time period (for example, the decade), EUGene will create an annual data set that can be read into other statistical programs and then aggregated by the user (for example, by using the "aggregate" command in SPSS or "collapse" in STATA).

2. EUGene also allows users to code ongoing dispute years as either dispute initiations or noninitiations for purposes of the dependent variable, as discussed later.

3. As a standard Windows thirty-two-bit executable program, EUGene should run on future versions of Windows as well. However, the program has only been tested on those platforms listed.

APPENDIX B

1. Bueno de Mesquita and Lalman's data in *War and Reason* (1992) were limited to 708 observations in Europe. EUGene generates expected utility data on over one million directed dyad-years between 1816 and 1992.

2. Because of the complexity of operationalizing expected utility, Bueno de Mesquita initially developed a software program for the IBM PC known as Tolstoy (Horn 1990) to generate expected utility data. The goal of this software was to facilitate the output of data that could be easily transformed into estimates of conflict initiation and escalation probabilities. However, Tolstoy could not be used to obtain accurate data for the Bueno de Mesquita and Lalman 1992 IIG. Largely because of technological limitations that existed when it was written, Tolstoy implemented only expected utility calculations as presented in Bueno de Mesquita 1985a and was unable to produce estimates of expected utility for all dyads and time periods (errors and incorrect values were sometimes created by the program). Hence the need for new software, developed as EUGene.

3. *War and Reason* did not incorporate distance discounting into its calculations because the empirical analysis was purely within Europe, where all geographic distances are relatively small. Since we are analyzing dyads worldwide, we reintroduce the distance discounting methods of *The War Trap*. We discount capabilities in each dyad ij so that (1) the capabilities of the challenger i are adjusted by the distance to the target j and (2) the capabilities of potentially involved third parties k are adjusted by the shorter of the distance to i or j.

4. An additional implication of setting $\alpha = \tau$ (and so not measuring the magnitude of a first strike advantage) is that the utility of War_A and War_B is always equal. The fact that α, τ, and γ are set to 1.0 allows us to make unique equilibrium predictions for each dyad (with the exception mentioned in note 5), enabling us to avoid most of the problems discussed by Signorino (1999) of dealing with unknown cost parameters, at least in practical terms.

5. Because the utility of War_A and War_B is always equal (because $\alpha = \tau$, note 4), there remains one indeterminate situation in solving the game. Bueno de

Mesquita and Lalman's Domestic Proposition 3.1, the "Basic War Theorem," specifies that logically a war will be started by state A if and only if the conditions $U_A(War_A) > U^A(Acq_A)$, $U^A(Cap_A) > U^A(War_B)$, $U^B(Cap_A) > U^B(Nego)$, and $U^B(War_A) > U^B(Acq_B)$ hold. However, with $U(War_A) = U(War_B)$, the first two conditions are incompatible, as they together imply $U^A(Cap_A) > U^A(War)$ $> U^A(Acq_A)$, which violates the basic theoretical condition of the game that $U^A(Acq_A) > U^A(Cap_A)$. Because of this, the condition $U^A(Cap_A) > U^A(War_B)$ is omitted for purposes of generating the war equilibrium (see Bueno de Mesquita and Lalman 1992, 76 n). However, with this condition omitted, it is possible for a directed dyad-year to satisfy the conditions for both the War_A and Status Quo equilibria. We assume these cases to have a War_A equilibrium; in analyses we have undertaken elsewhere (Bennett and Stam 2000c), the results do not change significantly if we treat these cases as having a Status Quo equilibrium prediction instead of a War_A equilibrium.

6. It is important to note that this is a problem neither of the theory nor of the operationalizations alone, but with the fit of one element of the operationalization to the theory's assumptions. The fact that Φ was allowed to range from -1 to $+1$ in *War and Reason* could actually be viewed as making the operationalization more general than the theory, since the operationalization of Φ_i to include negative values in effect allows for an externalization boost as a domestic "cost."

BIBLIOGRAPHY

Abelson, Robert. 1995. "The Secret Existence of Expressive Behavior." *Critical Review* 9 (winter–spring): 25–36.

Adler, Emanuel, and Michael Barnett, eds. 1998. *Security Communities*. New York: Cambridge University Press.

Allan, Pierre, and Cedric Dupont. 1999. "International Relations Theory and Game Theory: Baroque Modeling Choices and Empirical Robustness." *International Political Science Review* 20, no. 1 (January): 23–47.

Allison, Graham. 1971. *Essence of Decision: Explaining the Cuban Missile Crisis*. Boston: Little, Brown.

Almond, Gabriel. 1950. *The American People and Foreign Policy*. New York: Harcourt, Brace.

Axelrod, Robert. 1984. *The Evolution of Cooperation*. New York: Basic Books.

Axelrod, Robert. 1997. *The Complexity of Cooperation*. Princeton: Princeton University Press.

Axelrod, Robert, and D. Scott Bennett. 1993. "A Landscape Theory of Aggregation." *British Journal of Political Science* 23:211–33.

Babst, Dean V. 1964. "Elective Governments—A Force for Peace." *Wisconsin Sociologist* 3:9–14.

Barbieri, Katherine. 1996. "Economic Interdependence: A Path to Peace or a Source of Interstate Conflict? *Journal of Peace Research* 33 (February): 29–50.

Barbieri, Katherine. 1998. "International Trade and Conflict: The Debatable Relationship." Paper presented at the annual meeting of the International Studies Association, Minneapolis.

Beck, Nathaniel. 1991. "The Illusion of Cycles in International Relations." *International Studies Quarterly* 35:455–76.

Beck, Nathaniel. 1996. "Reporting Heteroskedasticity Consistent Standard Errors." *Political Methodologist* 7 (spring): 4–6.

Beck, Nathaniel. 1998. "In (Partial) Defense of Logit Dyad-Year Analyses of International Conflict." Paper presented at the annual meeting of the American Political Methodology Association, Boston, August.

Beck, Nathaniel, and Jonathan Katz. 2001. "Throwing Out the Baby with the Bath Water: A Comment on Green, Kim, and Yoon." *International Organization* 55 (2): 487–98.

Beck, Nathaniel, Jonathan Katz, and Richard Tucker. 1998. "Taking Time Seriously: Time-Series–Cross-Section Analysis with a Binary Dependent Variable." *American Journal of Political Science* 42 (October): 1260–88.

Beck, Nathaniel, Gary King, and Langche Zeng. 2000. "Improving Quantitative Studies of International Conflict: A Conjecture." *American Political Science Review* 94 (March): 21–35.

Bennett, D. Scott. 1996. "Security, Bargaining, and the End of Interstate Rivalry." *International Studies Quarterly* 40 (June): 157–84.

Bennett, D. Scott. 1997. "Testing Alternative Models of Alliance Duration." *American Journal of Political Science* 41 (July): 846–78.

Bennett, D. Scott. 2002. "Towards a Continuous Specification of the Democracy-Autocracy Connection." Manuscript.

Bennett, D. Scott, and Matthew Rupert. 2003. "Comparing Measures of Political Similarity." *Journal of Conflict Resolution* 47 (June): 367–93.

Bennett, D. Scott, and Allan Stam. 1996. "The Duration of Interstate Wars, 1816–1985." *American Political Science Review* 90 (June): 239–57.

Bennett, D. Scott, and Allan Stam. 1998. "The Declining Advantages of Democracy: A Combined Model of War Outcomes and Duration." *Journal of Conflict Resolution* 42 (June): 344–66.

Bennett, D. Scott, and Allan Stam. 2000a. "Research Design and Estimator Choices in the Analysis of Interstate Dyads: When Decisions Matter." *Journal of Conflict Resolution* 44 (October): 653–85.

Bennett, D. Scott, and Allan Stam. 2000b. "A Cross-Validation of Bueno de Mesquita and Lalman's International Interaction Game." *British Journal of Political Science* 30 (October): 541–61.

Bennett, D. Scott, and Allan Stam. 2000c. "A Universal Test of an Expected Utility Theory of War." *International Studies Quarterly* 44:451–80.

Bennett, D. Scott, and Allan Stam. 2000d. "EUGene: A Conceptual Manual." *International Interactions* 26:179–204. <http://www.eugenesoftware.org>.

Betts, Richard. 1987. *Nuclear Blackmail and Nuclear Balance*. Washington, DC: Brookings.

Biddle, Stephen. 1998. "The Gulf War Debate Redux: Why Skill and Technology Are the Right Answer." *International Security* 22 (fall): 163–74.

Blainey, Geoffrey. 1988. *The Causes of War*. 3d ed. New York: Free Press.

Brams, Steven J. 1995. "Old and New Moving-Knife Schemes." *Mathematical Intelligencer* 17, no. 4 (fall): 30–47.

Bremer, Stuart A. 1992. "Dangerous Dyads: Conditions Affecting the Likelihood of Interstate War, 1816–1965." *Journal of Conflict Resolution* 36: 309–41.

Bremer, Stuart A. 1995. "Advancing the Scientific Study of War." In Stuart A.

Bremer and Thomas R. Cusack, eds., *The Process of War*. Amsterdam: Gordon and Breach.

Brooks, Stephen. 1997. "Dueling Realisms." *International Organization* 51 (summer): 445–77.

Brooks, Stephen. 2001. "The Globalization of Production and the Changing Benefits of Conquest." Ph.D. diss. Yale University, New Haven, CT.

Brooks, Stephen, and William C. Wohlforth. 2002. "American Primacy in Perspective. *Foreign Affairs* 81 (July/Aug): 20–33.

Bueno de Mesquita, Bruce. 1978. "Systemic Polarization and the Occurrence and Duration of War." *Journal of Conflict Resolution* 22:241–67.

Bueno de Mesquita, Bruce. 1980. "Theories of International Conflict: An Analysis and an Appraisal." In Ted R. Gurr, ed., *Handbook of Political Conflict*. New York: Free Press.

Bueno de Mesquita, Bruce. 1981. *The War Trap*. New Haven: Yale University Press.

Bueno de Mesquita, Bruce. 1985a. "The War Trap Revisited." *American Political Science Review* 79:156–77.

Bueno de Mesquita, Bruce. 1985b. "Toward a Scientific Understanding of International Conflict." *International Studies Quarterly* 29:121–36.

Bueno de Mesquita, Bruce. 1990. "Pride of Place: The Origins of German Hegemony." *World Politics* 43:28–52.

Bueno de Mesquita, Bruce, and David Lalman. 1988. "Empirical Support for Systemic and Dyadic Explanations of International Conflict." *World Politics* 41:1–20.

Bueno de Mesquita, Bruce, and David Lalman. 1992. *War and Reason*. New Haven: Yale University Press.

Bueno de Mesquita, Bruce, James Morrow, Randolph Siverson, and Alastair Smith. 1999. "Policy Failure and Political Survival: The Contribution of Political Institutions." *Journal of Conflict Resolution* 43 (April): 147–61.

Bueno de Mesquita, Bruce, James D. Morrow, Randolph Siverson, and Alastair Smith. 2001. "Political Competition and Economic Growth." *Journal of Democracy* 12 (January): 58–72.

Bueno de Mesquita, Bruce, David Newman, and Alvin Rabushka. 1985. *Forecasting Political Events*. New Haven: Yale University Press.

Bueno de Mesquita, Bruce, and William H. Riker. 1982. "An Assessment of the Merits of Selective Nuclear Proliferation." *Journal of Conflict Resolution* 26:283–306.

Bueno de Mesquita, Bruce, and Randolph M. Siverson. 1995. "War and the Survival of Political Leaders: A Comparative Study of Regime Types and Political Accountability." *American Political Science Review* 89 (December): 841–55.

Busch, M. L., and E. Reinhardt. 2000. "Geography, International Trade, and Political Mobilization in U.S. Industries." *American Journal of Political Science* 44, no. 4 (October): 703–19.

Butterfield, Herbert. 1951. *History and Human Relations*. London: Collins Press.

Carr, Edward Hallett. 1946. *The Twenty Years' Crisis, 1919–1939*. New York: MacMillan.

Cederman, Lars-Erik. 1997. *Emergent Actors in World Politics: How States and Nations Develop and Dissolve*. Princeton: Princeton University Press.

Cederman, Lars-Erik. 2001. *Constructing Europe's Identity: The External Dimension*. Lynne Rienner.

Clarke, Kevin. 2001. "Testing Non-Nested Models of International Relations." *American Journal of Political Science* 45 (July): 3–33.

Conte, Rosaria, and Cristiano Castelfranchi. 1995. *Cognitive and Social Action*. London: UCL Press Limited.

Converse, Philip. 1964. "The Nature of Belief Systems in Mass Publics." In David Apter, ed., *Ideology and Discontent*. New York: Basic Books.

Crescenzi, Mark J. C. 2000. "Exit Stage Market: Market Structure, Interstate Economic Interdependence, and Conflict." Ph.D. diss., University of Illinois at Urbana-Champaign.

De Soysa, Indra, John R. Oneal, and Yong-Hee Park. 1997. "Testing Power-Transition Theory Using Alternative Measures of National Capabilities." *Journal of Conflict Resolution* 41 (August): 509–28.

Denk, Charles E., and Steven E. Finkel. 1992. "The Aggregate Impact of Explanatory Variables in Logit and Linear Probability Models." *American Journal of Political Science* 36:785–804.

Deutsch, Karl. 1957. *Political Community and the North Atlantic Area: International Organization in the Light of Historical Experience*. Princeton: Princeton University Press.

Deutsch, Karl W., and J. David Singer. 1964. "Multipower Systems and International Stability." *World Politics* 16:390–406.

Diamond, Jared. 1997. *Guns, Germs, and Steel: The Fates of Human Societies*. New York: W. W. Norton.

Diehl, Paul F. 1983. "Arms Races and Escalation: A Closer Look." *Journal of Peace Research* 20:205–12.

Diehl, Paul F. 1985. "Contiguity and Military Escalation in Major Power Rivalries." *Journal of Politics* 47:1203–11.

Diehl, Paul F. 1991. "Geography and War: A Review and Assessment of the Empirical Literature." *International Interactions* 17:11–27.

Diehl, Paul F., and Gary Goertz. 1988. "Territorial Changes and Militarized Conflict." *Journal of Conflict Resolution* 32:103–22.

Diehl, Paul F., and Gary Goertz. 2000. *War and Peace in International Rivalry*. Ann Arbor: University of Michigan Press.

Dixon, William J. 1993. "Democracy and the Management of International Conflict." *Journal of Conflict Resolution* 37:42–68.

Dixon, William J. 1994. "Democracy and the Peaceful Settlement of International Conflict." *American Political Science Review* 88:14–32.

Doran, Charles F., and Wes Parsons. 1980. "War and the Cycle of Relative Power." *American Political Science Review* 74:947–65.

Dougherty, James E., and Robert L. Pfaltzgraff Jr. 1990. *Contending Theories of International Relations.* New York: Harper and Row.

Doyle, Michael. 1983. "Kant, Liberal Legacies, and Foreign Affairs." Pts. 1 and 2. *Philosophy and Public Affairs* 12:205–34, 323–53.

Doyle, Michael. 1986. "Liberalism and World Politics." *American Political Science Review* 80 (December): 1151–70.

Elster, Jon. 1989. *Nuts and Bolts for the Social Sciences.* New York: Cambridge University Press.

Enterline, Andrew. 1996. "Driving While Democratizing (DWD)." *International Security* 20:183–96.

Enterline, Andrew. 1998. "Regime Changes and Interstate Conflict, 1816–1992." *Political Research Quarterly* 51:385–410.

Evangelista, Matthew. 1988. *Innovation and the Arms Race: How the United States and the Soviet Union Develop New Military Technologies.* Ithaca: Cornell University Press.

Fearon, James D. 1994a. "Domestic Political Audiences and the Escalation of International Disputes." *American Political Science Review* 88 (September): 577–92.

Fearon, James D. 1994b. "Signaling versus the Balance of Power and Interests: An Empirical Test of a Crisis Bargaining Model." *Journal of Conflict Resolution* 38 (June): 236–69.

Fearon, James D. 1995. "Rationalist Explanations for War." *International Organization* 49, no. 3 (summer): 379–414.

Fearon, James D. 1997. "Signaling Foreign Policy Interests: Tying Hands versus Sinking Costs." *Journal of Conflict Resolution* 41 (February): 68–90.

Fearon, James. 2000. "Selection Effects and Deterrence." *International Interactions* 28:5–29.

Filson, Darren, and Suzanne Werner. 2001. "Bargaining and Fighting: The Impact of Regime Type on War Onset, Duration, and Outcomes." Paper presented at the Political Economy of Conflict Conference, Yale University, March 23–24.

Filson, Darren, and Suzanne Werner. 2002. "A Bargaining Model of War and Peace: Anticipating the Onset, Duration, and Outcome of War." *American Journal of Political Science* 46 (October): 819–37.

Fiorina, Morris P. 1990. "Information and Rationality in Elections." In John A. Ferejohn and James H. Kuklinski, eds., *Information and Democratic Processes.* Urbana: University of Illinois Press.

Fitzpatrick, Gary L., and Marilyn J. Modlin. 1996. *Direct-Line Distances.* U.S. ed. Metuchen, NJ: Scarecrow Press.

Fortna, Virginia Page. 2003. "Scraps of Paper? Agreements and the Durability of Peace." *International Organizations* 57 (2): 337–72.

Friedman, Jeffrey. 1996. *The Rational Choice Controversy.* New Haven: Yale University Press.

Garrett, Geoffrey. 1998. "Global Markets and National Politics: Collision Course or Virtuous Circle?" *International Organization* 52 (4): 787–824.

Gartner, Scott S. 1997. *Strategic Assessment in War*. New Haven: Yale University Press.

Gartner, Scott Sigmund, and Randolph M. Siverson. 1996. "War Expansion and War Outcome." *Journal of Conflict Resolution* 40 (March): 4–15.

Gartzke, Erik. 1998. "Kant We All Just Get Along? Opportunity, Willingness, and the Origins of the Democratic Peace." *American Journal of Political Science* 42 (January): 1–27.

Gartzke, Erik. 1999. "War Is in the Error Term." *International Organization* 53 (summer): 567–87.

Gartzke, Erik. 2001. "War, Bargaining, and the Military Commitment Problem: War or Peace?" Paper presented at the Political Economy of Conflict Conference, Yale University, March 23–24.

Gellner, Ernest. 1983. *Nations and Nationalism*. Ithaca: Cornell University Press.

Gellner, E. 1984. "The Scientific Status of the Social Sciences." *International Social Science Journal* 36, no. 4 (winter): 567–86.

Gelpi, Christopher. 1997. "Crime and Punishment: The Role of Norms in Crisis Bargaining." *American Political Science Review* 91 (2): 339–60.

Gerber, Elisabeth R., and John E. Jackson. 1993. "Endogenous Preferences and the Study of Institutions." *American Political Science Review* 87, no. 3 (September): 639–57.

Gilpin, Robert. 1981. *War and Change in World Politics*. New York: Cambridge University Press.

Glaser, Charles L. 1992. "Nuclear Policy without an Adversary." *International Security* 16 (4): 34–78.

Gleditsch, Kristian S. 2002. *All International Politics Is Local: The Diffusion of Conflict, Integration, and Democratization*. Ann Arbor: University of Michigan Press.

Gleditsch, Kristian S., and Michael D. Ward. 1997. "Double Take: A Reexamination of Democracy and Autocracy in Modern Polities." *Journal of Conflict Resolution* 41:361–83.

Gleditsch, Nils Petter, and Håvard Hegre. 1997. "Peace and Democracy: Three Levels of Analysis." *Journal of Conflict Resolution* 41 (April): 283–310.

Gochman, Charles S., and Zeev Maoz. 1984. "Militarized Interstate Disputes, 1816–1976." *Journal of Conflict Resolution* 28:585–615.

Goemans, H. E. 2000. *War and Punishment: The Causes of War Termination and the First World War*. Princeton: Princeton University Press.

Goemans, Henk, and Scott de Marchi. 2001. "Is Jerusalem Divisible? Preference Landscapes and Issue Indivisibility." Paper presented at the Political Economy of Conflict Conference, Yale University, March 23–24.

Goldberg, David E. 1989. "Genetic Algorithms in Search, Optimization, and Machine Learning." New York: Addison-Wesley.

Goldstein, Joshua S. 1988. *Long Cycles: Prosperity and War in the Modern Age*. New Haven: Yale University Press.

Goldstein, Joshua S. 1991. "The Possibility of Cycles in International Relations." *International Studies Quarterly* 35:477–80.

Gowa, Joanne. 1999. *Ballots and Bullets: The Elusive Democratic Peace*. Princeton: Princeton University Press.

Gowa, Joanne, and Henry S. Farber. 1995. "Common Interests or Common Polities? Reinterpreting the Democratic Peace." National Bureau of Economic Research Working Paper Series. Cambridge, MA.

Granato, Jim, Ronald Inglehart, and David Leblang. 1996. "The Effect of Cultural Values on Economic Development: Theory, Hypotheses, and Some Empirical Tests." *American Journal of Political Science* 40, no. 3 (August): 607–32.

Green, Donald, Soo-Young Kim, and David Yoon. 2001. "Dirty Pool." *International Organization* 55 (2): 441–68.

Green, Donald P., and Ian Shapiro. 1994. *Pathologies of Rational Choice Theory: A Critique of Applications in Political Science*. New Haven: Yale University Press.

Greene, William H. 1993. *Econometric Analysis*. 2d ed. New York: MacMillan.

Gurr, Ted Robert, ed. 1980. *Handbook of Political Conflict*. New York: Free Press.

Gurr, Ted Robert, Keith Jaggers, and Will H. Moore. 1989. *Polity II Codebook and Data Set*. Ann Arbor: Interuniversity Consortium for Political and Social Research.

Hanushek, Eric A., and John E. Jackson. 1977. *Statistical Methods for Social Scientists*. San Diego: Academic Press.

Henderson, Errol. 1997. "Culture or Contiguity? Ethnic Conflict, the Similarity of States, and the Onset of Interstate War, 1820–1989." *Journal of Conflict Resolution* 41 (5): 649–68.

Henderson, Errol A. 2002. *Democracies and War*. Boulder: Lynn Reiner.

Herz, John H. 1959. *International Politics in the Atomic Age*. New York: Columbia University Press.

Holland, John H. 1975. *Adaptation in Natural and Artificial Systems*. Ann Arbor: University of Michigan Press.

Holsti, Kalevi J. 1985. *The Dividing Discipline: Hegemony and Diversity in International Theory*. Boston: Allen and Unwin.

Holsti, Kalevi J. 1991. *Peace and War: Armed Conflicts and International Order, 1648–1989*. Cambridge: Cambridge University Press.

Holsti, Ole R., P. Terrence Hopmann, and John D. Sullivan. 1973. *Unity and Disintegration in International Alliances: Comparative Studies*. New York: John Wiley & Sons.

Holsti, Ole R., and James N. Rosenau. 1988. "The Domestic and Foreign Policy Beliefs of American Leaders." *Journal of Conflict Resolution* 32 (2): 248–96.

Hopf, Ted. 1991. "Polarity, the Offense-Defense Balance, and War." *American Political Science Review* 85 (2): 475–93.

Horn, Michael. 1990. Tolstoy. Computer program. Software available through Bruce Bueno de Mesquita, Hoover Institution, Stanford University.

Huber, P. J. 1967. "The Behavior of Maximum Likelihood Estimates under Non-Standard Conditions." In *Proceedings of the Fifth Berkeley Symposium in Mathematical Statistics and Probability*. Berkeley: University of California Press.

Huntington, Samuel P. 1958. "Arms Races: Prerequisites and Results." *Public Policy* 8:41–86.

Huntington, Samuel P. 1993. "Why International Primacy Matters." *International Security* 17 (4): 68–83.

Huntington, Samuel P. 1996. *The Clash of Civilizations and the Remaking of World Order*. New York: Touchstone.

Huth, Paul K. 1988. *Extended Deterrence and the Prevention of War*. New Haven: Yale University Press.

Huth, Paul K. 1990. "The Extended Deterrent Value of Nuclear Weapons." *Journal of Conflict Resolution* 34 (2): 270–90.

Huth, Paul, D. Scott Bennett, and Christopher Gelpi. 1992. "System Uncertainty, Risk Propensity, and International Conflict among the Great Powers." *Journal of Conflict Resolution* 36 (September): 478–517.

Huth, Paul, Christopher Gelpi, and D. Scott Bennett. 1993. "The Escalation of Great Power Militarized Disputes: Testing Rational Deterrence Theory and Structural Realism." *American Political Science Review* 87 (September): 609–23.

Huth, Paul K., and Bruce M. Russett. 1984. "What Makes Deterrence Work? Cases from 1900–1980." *World Politics* 36:496–526.

Huth, Paul, and Bruce Russett. 1993. "General Deterrence between Enduring Rivals: Testing Three Competing Models." *American Political Science Review* 87:61–73.

Intriligator, Michael, and Dagobert Brito. 1984. "Can Arms Races Lead to the Outbreak of War?" *Journal of Conflict Resolution* 28:63–84.

Jackman, Simon. 1998. "In and Out of War and Peace: The Statistical Analysis of Discrete Serial Data on International Conflict." Paper presented at the annual meeting of the Political Methodology Society, San Diego.

Jackman, Simon. 2000. "Estimation and Inference via Bayesian Simulation: An Introduction to Markov Chain Monte Carlo." *American Journal of Political Science* 44, no. 2 (April): 375–404.

Jaggers, Keith, and Ted Robert Gurr. 1995. "Tracking Democracy's Third Wave with the Polity III Data." *Journal of Peace Research* 32:469–82.

Janis, Irving, and Leon Mann. 1977. *Decision Making*. New York: Free Press.

Jervis, Robert. 1976. *Perception and Misperception in International Politics*. Princeton: Princeton University Press.

Jervis, Robert, Richard Ned Lebow, and Janice Gross Stein, eds. 1985. *Psychology and Deterrence*. Baltimore: Johns Hopkins University Press.

Jones, Daniel M., Stuart A. Bremer, and J. David Singer. 1996. "Militarized Interstate Disputes, 1816–1992: Rationale, Coding Rules, and Empirical Patterns." *Conflict Management and Peace Science* 15:162–213.

Kaplan, Morton A. 1957. *System and Process in International Politics*. New York: Wiley.

Kennedy, Paul M. 1987. *The Rise and Fall of the Great Powers: Economic Change and Military Conflict from 1500 to 2000*. New York: Random House.

Keohane, Robert O. 1984. *After Hegemony: Cooperation and Discord in the World Political Economy*. Princeton: Princeton University Press.

Keohane, Robert O., and Joseph S. Nye. 1989. *Power and Interdependence*. 2d ed. Boston: Scott, Foresman.

Key, V. O., Jr. 1961. *Public Opinion and American Democracy*. New York: Knopf.

Kilgore, D. M., and Frank C. Zagare. 1991. "Credibility, Uncertainty, and Deterrence." *American Journal of Political Science* 35:305–34.

Kim, Jacchun. 2001. "Democracies and Covert War." Ph.D. diss., Yale University, New Haven.

Kim, Woosang. 1989. "Power, Alliance, and Major Wars, 1816–1975." *Journal of Conflict Resolution* 33:255–73.

Kim, Woosang. 1992. "Power Transitions and Great Power War from Westphalia to Waterloo." *World Politics* 45:153–72.

Kim, Woosang, and James D. Morrow. 1992. "When Do Power Shifts Lead to War?" *American Journal of Political Science* 36:896–922.

Kinder, Donald R., and Lynn M. Sanders. 1994. *Divided by Color: Racial Politics and Democratic Ideals in the American Public*. Manuscript.

Kinder, Donald R., and D. O. Sears. 1985. "White's Opposition to Busing—On Conceptualizing and Operationalizing Group Conflict." *Journal of Personality and Social Psychology* 48, no. 5 (October): 1141–47.

Kindleberger, Charles P. 1981. *Power and Money: The Politics of International Economics and the Economics of International Politics*. New York: Basic Books.

King, Gary. 1989. *Unifying Political Methodology: The Likelihood Theory of Statistical Inference*. Cambridge: Cambridge University Press. Reprint, Ann Arbor: University of Michigan Press, 1998.

King, Gary, Robert Keohane, and Sidney Verba. 1999. *Designing Social Inquiry*. Princeton: Princeton University Press.

King, Gary, and Langche Zeng. 1999. "Logistic Regression in Rare Events Data." Manuscript. http://gking.harvard.edu/files/os.ps

King, Gary, and Langche Zeng. 2001. "Explaining Rare Events in International Relations." *International Organization* 55 (summer): 693–715.

King, Gary, and Langche Zeng. 2002. "Estimating Risk and Rate Levels, Ratios, and Differences in Case-Control Studies." *Statistics in Medicine* 21: 1409–27.

Kocs, Stephen A. 1995. "Territorial Dispute and Interstate War, 1945–1987." *Journal of Politics* 57:159–75.

Kondratieff, Nikolai D. [1935] 1978. "The Long Waves in Economic Life." *Lloyd's Bank Annual Review* 129:41–60.

Krasner, Stephen D. 1976. "State Power and the Structure of International Trade." *World Politics* 28 (fall): 317–47.

Krasner, Stephen D. 1983. *International Regimes*. Ithaca: Cornell University Press.

Kuhn, Thomas S. 1986. *The Structure of Scientific Revolutions*. New York: New America Library.

Kydd, Andrew. 1997. "Game Theory and the Spiral Model." *World Politics* 49 (3): 371–400.

Lakatos, Imre. 1978. *The Methodology of Scientific Research Programmes*. New York: Cambridge University Press.

Lake, David A. 1992. "Powerful Pacifists: Democratic States and War." *American Political Science Review* 86 (March): 24–37.

Lebow, Richard Ned. 1981. *Between Peace and War: The Nature of International Crisis*. Baltimore: Johns Hopkins University Press.

Lebow, Richard Ned. 1985. "Miscalculation in the South Atlantic: The Origins of the Falklands War." In Robert Jervis, Richard Ned Lebow, and Janice Gross Stein, eds., *Psychology and Deterrence*, 89–124. Baltimore: Johns Hopkins University Press.

Lebow, Richard Ned, and Janice Stein. 1989. "I Think, Therefore I Deter." *World Politics* 41:208–24.

Lemke, Douglas. 1993. "Multiple Hierarchies in World Politics." Ph.D. diss., Vanderbilt University, Nashville.

Lemke, Douglas. 1996. "Small States and War: An Expansion of Power Transition Theory." In Jacek Kugler and Douglas Lemke, eds., *Parity and War*. Ann Arbor: University of Michigan Press.

Lemke, Douglas. 1998. "Regions of War and Peace." Paper presented at the annual meeting of the Peace Science Society, Rutgers University, October 16–18.

Lemke, Douglas. 2002. *Regions of War and Peace*. Cambridge: Cambridge University Press.

Lemke, Douglas, and Jacek Kugler. 1996. *Parity and War: Evaluations and Extensions of the War Ledger*. Ann Arbor: University of Michigan Press.

Lemke, Douglas, and William Reed. 1996. "Regime Types and Status Quo Evaluations: Power Transition Theory and the Democratic Peace." *International Interactions* 22 (2): 143–64.

Lemke, Douglas, and William Reed. 1998. "Power Is Not Satisfaction: A Comment on de Soysa, Oneal, and Park." *Journal of Conflict Resolution* 42 (August): 511–16.

Lemke, Douglas, and William Reed. 2000. "The Relevance of Politically Relevant Dyads." Paper presented at the annual meeting of the American Political Science Association, Washington, DC, August 31–September 3.

Lemke, Douglas, and William Reed. 2001. "The Relevance of Politically Relevant Dyads." *Journal of Conflict Resolution* 45 (1):126–44.

Lemke, Douglas, and Suzanne Werner. 1996. "Power Parity, Commitment to Change, and War." *International Studies Quarterly* 40:235–60.

Levi, Margaret. 1997. *Consent, Dissent, and Patriotism*. Cambridge: Cambridge University Press.

Levy, Jack S. 1988. "Domestic Politics and War." *Journal of Interdisciplinary History* 18:653–73.

Levy, Jack S. 1989. "The Diversionary Theory of War: A Critique." In Manus I. Midlarsky, ed., *Handbook of War Studies*, 259–88. Boston: Unwin Hyman.

Levy, Jack S. 2002. "Regions of War and Peace." *Political Science Quarterly* 117 (4): 697–98.

Lewis, Jeffrey B., and Kenneth A. Schultz. 2002. "Limitations to the Direct Testing of Extensive Form Crisis Bargaining Games." Manuscript, UCLA Dept. of Political Science.

Liang, K. Y., and S. L. Zeger. 1986. "Longitudinal Data Analysis Using Generalized Linear Models." *Biometrika* 73:13–22.

Liberman, Peter. 1996. *Does Conquest Pay? The Exploitation of Occupied Industrial Societies*. Princeton: Princeton University Press.

Locke, John. 1980. *Second Treatise of Government*. Ed. C. B. Macpherson. Indianapolis: Hackett.

Londregan, John B., and Keith T. Poole. 1996. "Does High Income Promote Democracy?" *World Politics* 49 (October): 1–30.

Luttwak, Edward N. 1996. "A Post-Heroic Military Policy." *Foreign Affairs* 75 (July–August): 33–44.

Maddala, G. S. 1983. *Limited-Dependent and Qualitative Variables in Econometrics*. New York: Cambridge University Press.

Mansfield, Edward. 1994. *Power Trade and War*. Princeton: Princeton University Press.

Mansfield, Edward D., and Rachel Bronson. 1997. "The Political Economy of Major-Power Trade Flows." In Edward D. Mansfield and Helen V. Milner, eds., *The Political Economy of Regionalism*, 189–208. New York: Columbia University Press.

Mansfield, Edward D., and Jack Snyder. 1995. "Democratization and the Danger of War." *International Security* 20:5–38.

Maoz, Zeev. 1999. Dyadic MID data set, version 1.0. http://spirit.tau.ac.il/~zeevmaoz/.

Maoz, Zeev, and Bruce Russett. 1992. "Alliance, Contiguity, Wealth, and Political Stability: Is the Lack of Conflict among Democracies a Statistical Artifact?" *International Interactions* 17:245–67.

Maoz, Zeev, and Bruce M. Russett. 1993. "Normative and Structural Causes of Democratic Peace, 1946–1986." *American Political Science Review* 87 (September): 624–38.

Marshall, M. G., and Keith Jaggers. 2000. "Polity IV Project Handbook." Manuscript, University of Maryland, College Park.

Mastanduno, Michael, David Lake, and G. John Ikenberry. 1989. "Toward a Realistic Theory of State Action." *International Studies Quarterly* 33: 457–74.

McDermott, Rose. 1998. *Risk-Taking in International Politics: Prospect Theory in American Foreign Policy.* Ann Arbor: University of Michigan Press.

McDermott, Rose. 1999. "In the Stream of History." *Political Psychology* 20 (3): 659–61.

McDermott, Rose. 2002. "Experimental Methods in Political Science." In *Annual Review of Political Science.* Washington, DC: American Political Science Association.

McFadden, D. 1973. "Conditional Logit Analysis of Qualitative Choice Behavior." In P. Zarembka, ed., *Frontiers in Econometrics,* 105–22. New York: Academic Press.

McGillivray, Fiona. 1997. "Party Discipline as a Determinant of the Endogenous Formation of Tariffs." *American Journal of Political Science* 41 (2): 584–607.

McKelvey, Richard, and W. Zavoina. 1975. "A Statistical Model for the Analysis of Ordinal Level Dependent Variables." *Journal of Mathematical Sociology* 4:103–20.

Mearsheimer, John. 1983. *Conventional Deterrence.* Ithaca: Cornell University Press.

Mearsheimer, John. 2001. *The Tragedy of Great Power Politics.* New York: Norton.

Meernik, James. 2000. "Modeling International Crises and the Political Use of Military Force by the USA." *Journal of Peace Research* 37 (November): 547–62.

Mercer, Jonathan. 1996. *Reputation and International Politics.* Ithaca: Cornell University Press.

MID Version 2.1 Data Set. 1999. Correlates of War. Ann Arbor: Interuniversity Consortium for Political and Social Research.

Midlarsky, Manus I., ed. 1989. *Handbook of War Studies.* Boston: Unwin Hyman. Reprint, Ann Arbor: University of Michigan Press, 1993.

Midlarsky, Manus I., ed. 2000. *Handbook of War Studies II.* Ann Arbor: University of Michigan Press.

Mill, John Stuart. 1947. *On Liberty.* Ed. Alburey Castell. New York: Appleton Century Crofts.

Modelski, George. 1987. *Long Cycles in World Politics.* London: Macmillan.

Morgenthau, Hans J. 1956. *Politics among Nations.* 2d ed. New York: Alfred A. Knopf.

Morrow, James D. 1989. "A Twist of Truth: A Reexamination of the Effects of Arms Races on the Occurrence of War." *Journal of Conflict Resolution* 33:500–529.

Morrow, James D. 1992. "Signaling Difficulties with Linkage in Crisis Bargaining." *International Studies Quarterly* 36:153–72.

Morrow, James D. 1993. "Arms versus Allies: Trade-offs in the Search for Security." *International Organization* 47 (spring): 207–33.

Morrow, James D. 1999. "The Institutional Features of the Prisoners of War Treaties." Manuscript.

Morton, Rebecca B. 1999. *Methods and Models: A Guide to the Empirical Analysis of Formal Models in Political Science*. New York: Cambridge University Press.

Mousseau, Michael. 1998. "Peace in Anarchy: Democratic Governance and International Conflict." Ph.D. diss., SUNY Binghamton.

Mueller, John. 1994. *Policy and Opinion in the Gulf War*. Chicago: University of Chicago Press.

Murray, Shoon Kathleen. 1996. *Anchors against Change: American Opinion Leaders' Beliefs after the Cold War*. Ann Arbor: University of Michigan Press.

Neuhaus, J. M., J. D. Kalbfleisch, and W. W. Hauck. 1991. "A Comparison of Cluster-Specific and Population Averaged Approaches for Analyzing Correlated Binary Data." *International Statistical Review* 59 (1): 25–35.

Niou, Emerson M. S., Peter Ordeshook, and Gregory Rose. 1989. *The Balance of Power: Stability in International Systems*. New York: Cambridge University Press.

Nordstrom, Timothy. 2000. "Anarchy, Self-Interest, and the Duration of Interstate Peace." Ph.D. diss., Pennsylvania State University.

North, R. C. 1977. "Toward a Framework for Analysis of Scarcity and Conflict." *International Studies Quarterly* 21 (4): 569–91.

Olson, Mancur, and Richard Zeckhauser. 1966. "An Economic Theory of Alliances." *Review of Economics and Statistics* 48:266–79.

Oneal, John R., and Bruce M. Russett. 1997. "The Classical Liberals Were Right: Democracy, Interdependence, and Conflict, 1950–1985." *International Studies Quarterly* 41 (June): 267–94.

Oneal, John R., and Bruce Russett. 1999a. "Assessing the Liberal Peace Debate with Alternative Specifications: Trade Still Reduces Conflict." *Journal of Peace Research* 36 (4): 423–42.

Oneal, John R., and Bruce Russett. 1999b. "The Kantian Peace: The Pacific Benefits of Democracy, Interdependence, and International Organizations." *World Politics* 52 (1): 1–37.

Oneal, John R., and Bruce Russett. 2001. "Clear and Clean: The Fixed Effects of the Liberal Peace." *International Organization* 55 (2): 469–99.

Oneal, John R., Indra De Soysa, and Yong-Hee Park. 1998. "But Power and Wealth Are Satisfying: A Reply to Lemke and Reed." *Journal of Conflict Resolution* 42 (August): 517–20.

Oren, Ido. 1990. "The War Proneness of Alliances." *Journal of Conflict Resolution* 34:208–33.

Organski, A. F. K. 1958. *World Politics*. New York: Alfred Knopf.

Organski, A. F. K., and Jacek Kugler. 1980. *The War Ledger*. Chicago: University of Chicago Press.

Ostrom, C. W., and F. W. Hoole. 1978. "Alliances and Wars Revisited." *International Studies Quarterly* 22 (2): 215–36.

Parsons, Talcott. 1937. *The Structure of Social Action*. New York: Free Press.

Pollack, Kenneth M. 1996. "The Influence of Arab Culture on Arab Military Effectiveness." Ph.D. diss., Massachusetts Institute of Technology.

Pollins, Brian M. 1996. "Global Political Order, Economic Change, and Armed Conflict." *American Political Science Review* 90 (1): 103–17.

Popper, Karl R. 1968. *The Logic of Scientific Discovery*. New York: Harper and Row.

Powell, Robert. 1989. "Crisis Stability in the Nuclear Age." *American Political Science Review* 83 (1): 61–76.

Powell, Robert. 1990. *Nuclear Deterrence Theory*. New York: Cambridge University Press.

Powell, Robert. 1991. "Absolute and Relative Gains in International Relations Theory." *American Political Science Review* 85:1303–20.

Powell, Robert. 1996. "Stability and the Distribution of Power." *World Politics* 48:239–67.

Powell, Robert. 1999. *Bargaining in the Shadow of Power*. Princeton: Princeton University Press.

Powell, Robert. 2001. "Bargaining while Fighting." Paper presented at the Political Economy of Conflict Conference, Yale University, March 23–24.

Powell, Robert. 2002. "Bargaining Theory and International Conflict." *Annual Review of Political Science* 5:1–30.

Przeworski, Adam, Michael Alverez, José Antonio Cheibib, and Fernando Limongi. 2000. *Democracy and Development*. Cambridge: Cambridge University Press.

Raknerud, Arvid, and Håvard Hegre. 1997. "The Hazard of War: Reassessing the Evidence for the Democratic Peace." *Journal of Peace Research* 34 (4): 385–404.

Rasler, Karen, and William R. Thompson. 1999. "Predatory Initiators and Changing Landscapes for Warfare." *Journal of Conflict Resolution* 43 (August): 411–33.

Ray, James Lee. 1995. *Democracy and International Conflict: An Evaluation of the Democratic Peace Proposition*. Columbia: University of South Carolina Press.

Ray, James Lee. 1998. "Does Democracy Cause Peace?" *Annual Review of Political Science* 1:27–46.

Ray, James Lee, and Yijia Wang. 1998. "Integrating Levels of Analysis in World Politics: Increased Utility or Exercises in Futility?" Paper presented at the international annual meeting of the Peace Science Society, Rutgers University, October 16–18.

Reed, William. 2000. "A Unified Statistical Model of Conflict Onset and Escalation." *American Journal of Political Science* 44:84–93.

Reed, William, and David H. Clark. 2000. "War Initiators and War Winners: The Consequences of Linking Theories of Democratic War Success." *Journal of Conflict Resolution* 44:378–95.

Regan, Patrick, and Allan Stam. 2000. "In the Nick of Time: Conflict Management, Mediation Timing, and the Duration of Interstate Disputes." *International Studies Quarterly* 44 (June).

Reiter, Dan. 1995. "Exploding the Powder Keg Myth: Preemptive Wars Almost Never Happen." *International Security* 20 (fall): 5–34.

Reiter, Dan. 2000. "Democracy, Political Similarity, and International Alliance." *Journal of Conflict Resolution* 44 (2): 203–27.

Reiter, Dan. 2001. "Does Peace Nurture Democracy?" *Journal of Politics*. 63 (August): 935–40.

Reiter, Dan. 2003. "Exploring the Bargaining Model of War." *Perspectives on Politics* 1 (1): 25–50.

Reiter, Dan, and Allan C. Stam. 1998. "Democracy, War Initiation, and Victory." *American Political Science Review* 92 (June): 377–89.

Reiter, Dan, and Allan C. Stam. 2002. *Democracies at War*. Princeton: Princeton University Press.

Reiter, Dan, and Allan C. Stam. 2003. "Identifying the Culprit: Democracy, Dictatorship, and Dispute Initiation." *American Political Science Review* 97, no. 2 (May): 333–37.

Richardson, Lewis Frye. 1951. "Could an Arms Race End without Fighting?" *Nature* 42 (74): 567–69.

Richardson, Lewis Frye. 1960a. *Statistics of Deadly Quarrels*. Chicago and Pittsburgh: Quadrangle & Boxwood.

Richardson, Lewis Frye. 1960b. *Arms and Insecurity*. Pittsburgh: Boxwood Press.

Riker, W. H. 1980. "Implications from the Disequilibrium of Majority Rule for the Study of Institutions." *American Political Science Review* 74: 1235–47.

Risse-Kappen, Thomas. 1995a. "Democratic Peace—Warlike Democracies? A Social-Constructivist Interpretation of the Liberal Argument." *European Journal of International Relations* 1 (4): 491–518.

Risse-Kappen, Thomas. 1995b. *Cooperation among Democracies: The European Influence on U.S. Foreign Policy*. Princeton: Princeton University Press.

Ritter, Jeffrey M. 2001. "Silent Partners: International Cooperation in Secret Alliances." Ph.D. diss., Harvard University.

Robins, James M., and Sander Greenland. 1999. "Estimation of the Causal Effect of a Time-Varying Exposure on the Marginal Mean of a Repeated Binary Outcome." *Journal of the American Statistical Association* 94: 687–703.

Rosen, Stephen Peter. 1996. *Societies and Military Power: India and Its Armies*. Ithaca: Cornell University Press.

Rosen, Stephen Peter. 2002. "The Biological Logic of International Conflict." Manuscript, Olin Center for Strategic Studies, Harvard University.

Rummel, R. 1972. *The Dimensions of Nations*. Beverly Hills: Sage.

Russett, Bruce. 1990. *Controlling the Sword*. Cambridge: Harvard University Press.

Russett, Bruce, and John R. Oneal. 2001. *Triangulating Peace: Democracy, Interdependence, and International Organizations*. New York: Norton.

Russett, Bruce M., and Allan C. Stam. 1998. "Courting Disaster: An Expanded NATO vs. Russia and China." *Political Science Quarterly* 113 (fall): 361–82.

Sagan, Scott D. 1985. "Nuclear Alerts and Crisis Management." *International Security* 9 (4): 99–139.

Sagan, Scott D. 1986. "1914 Revisited: Allies, Offense, and Instability." *International Security* 11 (2): 151–75.

Sample, Susan G. 1997. "Arms Races and Dispute Escalation: Resolving the Debate." *Journal of Peace Research* 34:7–22.

Sartori, Anne E. 2002. "The Might of the Pen: A Reputational Theory of Communication in International Disputes." *International Organization* 56 (1): 121–46.

Savage, Leonard James. 1954. *The Foundations of Statistics*. New York: Wiley.

Schultz, Kenneth A. 1998. "Domestic Opposition and Signaling in International Crises." *American Political Science Review* 92 (December): 829–44.

Schultz, Kenneth A. 1999. "Do Democratic Institutions Constrain or Inform? Contrasting Two Institutional Perspectives on Democracy and War." *International Organization* 53 (spring): 233–66.

Schultz, Kenneth. 2000. "Looking in Black Boxes. Democracy and Bargaining in International Crises." Manuscript.

Schweller, Randall L. 1997. "New Realist Research on Alliances: Refining, Not Refuting, Waltz's Balancing Proposition." *American Political Science Review* 91 (4): 927–30.

Schweller, Randall L. 1998. *Deadly Imbalances: Tripolarity and Hitler's Strategy of World Conquest*. New York: Columbia University Press.

Scott, James C. 1976. *The Moral Economy of the Peasant: Rebellion and Subsistence in Southeast Asia*. New Haven: Yale University Press.

Sears, David O., and Carolyn L. Funk. 1990. "Self Interest in Americans' Political Opinions." In Jane Mansbridge, ed., *Beyond Self-Interest*. Chicago: University of Chicago Press.

Sears, David O., and Carolyn L. Funk. 1991. "The Role of Self-Interest in Social and Political Attitudes." *Advances in Experimental Social Psychology* 23:1–91.

Senese, Paul D. 1997. "Between Peace and War: The Effect of Joint Democracy on Interstate Conflict Escalation." *Journal of Politics* 59:1–27.

Shepsle, Kenneth A. 1995. "Statistical Political Philosophy and Positive Political Theory." *Critical Review* 9 (1–2): 213–23.

Signorino, Curtis S. 1999. "Strategic Interaction and the Statistical Analysis of International Conflict." *American Political Science Review* 93 (2): 279–98.

Signorino, Curtis S. 2002. "Strategy and Selection in International Relations." *International Interactions* 28 (1): 93–115.

Signorino, Curtis S., and Jeffrey M. Ritter. 1999. "Tau-b or Not Tau-b: Measuring the Similarity of Foreign Policy Positions." *International Studies Quarterly* 43 (March): 115–44.

Simon, Michael W., and Erik Gartzke. 1996. "Political System Similarity and the Choice of Allies." *Journal of Conflict Resolution* 40 (4): 617–35.

Simowitz, Roslyn, and Barry L. Price. 1990. "The Expected Utility Theory of Conflict: Measuring Theoretical Progress." *American Political Science Review* 84:439–60.

Singer, J. David. 1961. "The Level-of-Analysis Problem in International Relations." In Klaus Knorr and Sidney Verba, eds., *The International System: Theoretical Essays*. Princeton: Princeton University Press.

Singer, J. David, Stuart Bremer, and John Stuckey. 1972. "Capability Distribution, Uncertainty, and Major Power War, 1820–1965." In Bruce Russett, ed., *Peace, War and Numbers*. Beverly Hills: Sage.

Singer, J. David, and Melvin Small. 1966. "Formal Alliances, 1815–1939." *Journal of Peace Research* 3:1–31.

Singer, J. David, and Melvin Small. 1967. "Alliance Aggregation and the Onset of War, 1815–1945." In J. David Singer, ed., *Quantitative International Politics: Insights and Evidence*, 247–86. New York: Free Press.

Singer, J. David, and Melvin Small. 1972. *The Wages of War, 1816–1965: A Statistical Handbook*. New York: John Wiley.

Singer, J. David, and Melvin Small. 1982. *Resort to Arms: International and Civil Wars, 1816–1980*. Beverly Hills: Sage.

Siverson, Randolph, and Juliann Emmons. 1991. "Birds of a Feather: Democratic Political Systems and Alliance Choices." *Journal of Conflict Resolution* 35 (2): 285–306.

Siverson, Randolph M., and Joel King. 1980. "Attributes of National Alliance Membership and War Participation, 1815–1965." *American Journal of Political Science* 24:1–15.

Siverson, Randolph M., and Harvey Starr. 1990. "Opportunity, Willingness and the Diffusion of War: 1815–1965." *American Political Science Review* 84:67–87.

Siverson, Randolph M., and Michael P. Sullivan. 1984. "The Spread of War: Why So Much? Why So Little?" *Mathematical Social Sciences* 7 (April): 207–8.

Siverson, Randolph M., and Michael R. Tennefoss. 1984. "Power, Alliance, and the Escalation of International Conflict, 1815–1965." *American Political Science Review* 78:1057–69.

Slantchev, Branislav L. 2003. "The Power to Hurt: Costly Conflict with Completely Informed States." *American Political Science Review* 97:123–33.

Small, Melvin, and J. David Singer. 1969. "Formal Alliances, 1815–1965: An Extension of the Basic Data." *Journal of Peace Research* 6:257–82.

Small, Melvin, and J. David Singer. 1976. "The War-Proneness of Democratic Regimes, 1816–1965." *Jerusalem Journal of International Relations* 1: 50–69.

Small, Melvin, and J. David Singer. 1982. *Resort to Arms: International and Civil Wars, 1816–1980.* Beverly Hills: Sage.

Smith, Alastair. 1996a. "To Intervene or Not to Intervene: A Biased Decision." *Journal of Conflict Resolution* 40 (1): 16–40.

Smith, Alastair. 1996b. "Diversionary Foreign Policy in Democratic Systems." *International Studies Quarterly* 40:133–53.

Smith, Alastair. 1998. "International Crises and Domestic Politics." *American Political Science Review* 92 (September): 623–38.

Smith, Alastair. 1999. "Testing Theories of Strategic Choice." *American Journal of Political Science* 43 (4): 1254–83.

Smith, Alastair, and Allan Stam. 2001. "Bargaining through Conflict." Paper presented at the Political Economy of Conflict Conference, Yale University, March 23–24.

Smith, Alastair, and Allan Stam. 2002. "Bargaining and the Nature of War." Unpublished ms., New York University.

Snyder, Glenn H. 1984. "The Security Dilemma in Alliance Politics." *World Politics* 36:461–95.

Snyder, Glenn H. 1990. "Alliance Theory: A Neorealist First Cut." *Journal of International Affairs* 44:103–23.

Snyder, Jack. 2000. *From Voting to Violence.* New York: Norton.

Social Science Citation Index. 1990–99. Philadelphia: Institute for Scientific Information.

Stam, Allan C. III. 1996. *Win, Lose, or Draw: Domestic Politics and the Crucible of War.* Ann Arbor: University of Michigan Press.

Steinbrunner, John D. 1974. *The Cybernetic Theory of Decision.* Princeton: Princeton University Press.

Stigler, George J., and G. S. Becker. 1977. "De Gustibus Non Est Disputandum." *American Economic Review* 67, no. 2 (spring): 76–90.

Tannenwald, Nina. 2001. "U.S. Arms Control Policy in a Time Warp." *Ethic and International Affairs* 15 (1): 51–70.

Tannenwald, Nina. 2003. *The Nuclear Taboo.* Cambridge: Cambridge University Press.

Taylor, Michael. 1988. "Rationality and Revolutionary Collective Action." In Michael Taylor, ed., *Rationality and Revolution.* Cambridge: Cambridge University Press.

Taylor, Michael. 1989. "Structure, Culture, and Action in the Explanation of Social Change." *Politics and Society* 17, no. 1 (winter): 115–62.

Taylor, Michael. 1995. "Battering Rams." *Critical Review* 9 (winter–spring): 1–24.

Thompson, William R., and Richard Tucker. 1997. "A Tale of Two Democratic Peace Critiques." *Journal of Conflict Resolution* 41 (June): 428–54.

Van Evera, Stephen. 1998. "Offense, Defense, and the Causes of War." *International Security* 22 (spring): 5–43.

Van Evera, Stephen. 1999. *Causes of War: Power and the Roots of Conflict.* Ithaca: Cornell University Press.

Vasquez, John A. 1994. *The War Puzzle.* Cambridge: Cambridge University Press.

Vasquez, John A. 1996. "Distinguishing Rivals That Go to War from Those That Do Not." *International Studies Quarterly* 40 (December): 531–58.

Veall, Michael R., and Klaus F. Zimmerman. 1996. "Pseudo-R2 Measures for Some Common Limited Dependent Variable Models." *Journal of Economic Surveys* 10:241–59.

Wagner, R. Harrison. 2000. "Bargaining and War." *American Journal of Political Science* 44 (July): 469–84.

Wagner, R. Harrison. 2001. "Bargaining, Alliances, and War." Paper presented at the Political Economy of Conflict Conference, Yale University, March 23–24.

Wallace, Michael D. 1973. "Alliance Polarization, Cross Cutting, and International War." *Journal of Conflict Resolution* 17:575–604.

Wallace, Michael D. 1982. "Armaments and Escalation: Two Competing Hypotheses." *International Studies Quarterly* 26:37–56.

Walt, Stephen M. 1987. *The Origins of Alliances.* Ithaca: Cornell University Press.

Walt, Stephen M. 1999. "Rigor or Rigor Mortis? Rational Choice and Security Studies." *International Security* 25 (4): 5–48.

Walt, Stephen M. 2000. "Fads, Fever, and Firestorms." *Foreign Policy* 12 (November): 34–42.

Waltz, Kenneth. 1959. *Man, the State and War.* New York: Columbia University Press.

Waltz, Kenneth. 1979. *The Theory of International Politics.* New York: Addison-Wesley.

Waltz, Kenneth. 1981. "The Spread of Nuclear Weapons: More May Be Better." Adelphi Paper No. 171. London: International Institute of Strategic Studies.

Waltz, Kenneth. 1990. "Nuclear Myths and Political Realities." *American Political Science Review* 84:731–46.

Waltz, Kenneth. 1996. "International Politics Is Not Foreign Policy." *Security Studies* 6 (1): 54–57.

Ward, Michael D., and Kristian S. Gleditsch. 1998. "Democratizing for Peace." *American Political Science Review* 92 (March): 51–62.

Wayman, Frank. 1984. "Bipolarity and War." *Journal of Peace Research* 21:61–78.

Weede, Erich. 1984. "Democracy and War Involvement." *Journal of Conflict Resolution* 28:649–64.

Wendt, Alexander. 1992. "Anarchy Is What States Make of It: The Social Construction of Power Politics." *International Organization* 46 (2):391–425.

Wendt, Alexander. 1994. "Collective Identity Formation and the International State." *American Political Science Review* 88 (2): 384–97

Wendt, Alexander. 1999. *Social Theory of International Politics.* Cambridge: Cambridge University Press.

Werner, Suzanne. 1998. "Negotiating the Terms of Settlement: War Aims and Bargaining Leverage." *Journal of Conflict Resolution* 42 (June): 321–43.

Werner, Suzanne. 1999. "The Precarious Nature of Peace: Resolving the Issues, Enforcing the Settlement, and Renegotiating." *American Journal of Political Science* 43:912–33.

Werner, Suzanne. 2000. "The Effects of Political Similarity on the Onset of Militarized Disputes, 1816–1985." *Political Research Quarterly* 53 (June): 343–74.

Windmeijer, Fago. 2000. "Moment Effects for Fixed Effects Count Data Models with Endogenous Regressors. *Economic Letters* 68 (1): 21–24.

Wittman, Donald. 2001. "War or Peace?" Paper presented at the Political Economy of Conflict Conference, Yale University, March 23–24.

Wohlforth, William C. 2000. "Brother, Can You Spare a Paradigm? (Or Was Anybody Ever a Realist?) *International Security* 25 (1): 182–84.

Wright, Quincy. 1935. *The Causes of War and the Conditions of Peace.* London: Longmans, Green.

Wright, Quincy. 1942. *A Study of War.* Chicago: University of Chicago Press.

Zaller, John. 1992. *The Nature and Origins of Mass Opinion.* New York: Cambridge University Press.

Zinnes, D. A. 1967. "An Analytic Study of the Balance of Power Theories." *Journal of Peace Research* 4:270–88.

INDEX

Note: Page numbers in italics refer to figures.

Decision makers and decision making; International relations and politics; Politics and political issues

Learning. *See* Cognitive, learning, and psychological theories

Leblang, David, 175, 196

Lebow, Richard Ned, 7, 86, 89, 166, 183, 250n. 4

Lemke, Douglas, 27, 62, 74, 79, 82, 91, 92, 93, 94, 114, 138, 140, 251n. 6

Levi, Margaret, 27

Levy, Jack S., 72, 77

Lewis, Jeffrey B., 18, 85, 86, 172, 196, 215, 216, 249n. 1, 251n. 8, 253n. 4

Liang, K. Y., 57

Liberman, Peter, 74

Lippman, Walter, 9

Locke, John, and Lockian system, 177, 179

MAD. *See* Mutually Assured Destruction

Maddala, G. S., 250n. 7

Mann, Leon, 171

Mansfield, Edward D., 9, 29, 71, 103, 104, 117, 148, 150, 205

Maoz, Zeev, 6, 13, 61, 82, 88, 226, 228, 251n. 10

Marshall, M. G., 83

Mastanduno, Michael, 251n. 11

McDermott, Rose, 171, 250n. 4, 251n. 6

McFadden, D., 252n. 6

McGillivray, Fiona, 217, 218

McKelvey, Richard, 252n. 6

Mearsheimer, John, 26, 80

Medical research, 133–34, 154, 209

Mercer, Jonathan, 72

Methods and methodologies: analysis of international relations and politics, 2, 5–14, 18, 27; analysis of risk of conflict or war, 9–12, 13–14, 15–17, 19–21, 27–31, 105–6,

183–99, 200–221; artificial intelligence, 172; assessing explanatory power, 67–68; assessing strength of associations, 65–66; assessing substantive explanatory power, 66–67; case selection and exclusion, 53–56, 62–63; coefficients and coefficient variation, 22; conditionality, 29–30; hypothesis testing, 35, 107–8, 115, 151, 173–74, 208–12; limitations of, 195–99; predictions and predictability, 4–5, 8, 9, 11, 16–19, 25, 67; quantitative and qualitative analysis, 35–36, 44, 203, 204, 220–21; relative importance, 33–34; unit of analysis, 46, 59–61, 62–63; variables, 16, 18–20, 22, 26–27, 28, 29–33, 46–49, 52–53, 56–58, 60, 63–64, 65–68, 123, 163, 167, 184–88, 209. *See also* Data and data sets; Definitions; Equations; Summary information; Theories and theoretical issues

Methods and methodologies (specific): additive statistical models, 27–28; assessment of model reliability, 165–99; autocorrelation, 57–59, 69; block likelihood ratio tests, 66, 69; building of theories, 30–31; case exclusion, 53–56; coding, 50, 53–54, 55, 72, 73, 77, 83–84, 89, 90, 93, 95, 99, 100, 103, 104, 184–86; conditional probability, 60; country-year analysis, 45–46; data development and cumulation, 223–31; directed versus nondirected analysis, 46–56, 62; dualistic elimination, 3, 4; dyadic analysis, 44–61, 62, 69, 74–97, 103, 105, 107–9, 112–18, 119, 120–44; estimators and estimation, 20–21, 56–61, 64–65, 117, 252n. 6; event history models, 56; general estimating equations (GEE) panel estimation, 44, 57–59; Hausman test, 59, 60;